HUMAN RIGHTS CASES

HUMAN RIGHTS CASES

Alastair N. Brown

Solicitor

T&T CLARK
EDINBURGH
2000

T&T CLARK LTD
59 GEORGE STREET
EDINBURGH EH2 2LQ
SCOTLAND

First published 2000

ISBN 0 567 00539 9

British Library Cataloguing-in-Publication Data.
A catalogue record for this book is available from the British Library.

Typeset by Waverley Typesetters, Galashiels
Printed and bound in Great Britain by Bell & Bain Ltd, Glasgow

For Susan

PREFACE

One of the intentions of the Human Rights Act 1998 is to integrate the case law of the European Convention on Human Rights into the deliberations of courts and tribunals of all kinds. It is therefore necessary for lawyers studying and practising in all legal disciplines to have access to that case law. But sets of reports are expensive and not at all portable. This book is a collection of summaries of the cases most commonly cited in the textbooks and some of the more recent cases which have not yet appeared in textbooks but which will, I expect, do so in the near future. My intention has been to provide a way into the case law of the European Court of Human Rights applicable to the Convention rights and (for those who are already familiar with that case law) a portable aide-memoire. I have not included Article 14 as a separate heading because that Article, in its terms and in the case law of the Court, is not free-standing. It operates only in conjunction with other rights.

I make no larger claim for the book than that I hope it will prove useful to students and to practitioners trying to get to grips, in a short time, with an unfamiliar body of jurisprudence; and I recognise, of course, that such a book has distinct limitations. I offer the following by way of explanation but not apology.

For a start, I emphasise that the book is a collection of summaries and not of extended quotations of the judgments of the Court. Those judgments tend to be long and do not lend themselves to excerpting in the way that is more usual in collections of cases and materials. I have tried to use the words of the Court wherever possible, rendering them into reported speech; but it should not be assumed without checking that I have been able to use the words of the Court in any given case. What I have provided is roughly equivalent to a series of extended rubrics. I have not included dissenting judgments. The full text of each case (including proceedings before the Commission and dissent) is available at the web site of the Court at http://www.echr.coe.int.

I have also had to be selective. I have omitted the case law of the European Commission of Human Rights altogether and have, no doubt, left out several cases which others would have regarded as essential for inclusion. I have probably included cases which others would have omitted. My selection has been informed largely by the cases I have found useful in delivering seminars on human rights law for Central Law Training (Scotland) Ltd.

Finally, there is no straightforward and fully satisfactory way to arrange the material. I have chosen to publish each case under the Article of the Convention with which it is chiefly concerned. This is done on the basis that, although applications to Strasbourg typically invoke multiple Articles, most cases resolve themselves in the Court under a single Article, with the answers to the issues raised under other Articles following on from the answer to the question regarded by the Court as the main one in the case. Exceptions to this can, of course, be found without difficulty and at times the scheme adopted seems to approach the arbitrary; but other possible approaches seemed less satisfactory when I tried them out. The Table of Cases which appears below should assist anyone looking for a particular case.

I should like to take this opportunity of thanking David Fletcher and Dr Carole Dalgleish of T&T Clark for their encouragement and enthusiasm in connection with the preparation of this book. It is, of course, common for authors to use the Preface to say something of this sort but that does not mean that it is said as a mere formality. David and Carole have been a pleasure to work with, on this as on other projects.

The book is prepared according to material available on 1 January 2000.

Alastair Brown
February 2000

CONTENTS

TABLE OF CASES

ARTICLE 2

THE RIGHT TO LIFE

1. Everyone's right to life shall be protected by law. No one shall be deprived of his life intentionally save in the execution of a sentence of a court following his conviction of a crime for which this penalty is provided by law.
2. Deprivation of life shall not be regarded as inflicted in contravention of this article when it results from the use of force which is no more than absolutely necessary:
    a. in defence of any person from unlawful violence;
    b. in order to effect a lawful arrest or to prevent the escape of a person lawfully detained;
    c. in action lawfully taken for the purpose of quelling a riot or insurrection.

"Absolutely Necessary"

McCann and Others v United Kingdom (1995) 21 EHRR 97

The UK, Spanish and Gibraltar authorities were aware from intelligence that the Provisional IRA were planning a terrorist attack on Gibraltar. The participants (McCann, Farrell and Savage) were identified as persons who had used explosives in the past and it was considered that a remotely detonated car bomb was likely to be the means employed. It was also considered that it was likely if the terrorists were cornered they would try to explode the bomb and/or use weapons. An SAS unit was deployed to deal with the threat and the plan was for an arrest to be carried out once all the members of the IRA unit were present and identified and they had parked a car which they intended to leave. Any earlier action was considered premature as likely to raise suspicion in any unapprehended members of the IRA unit with possible risk resulting and as leaving no evidence for the police to use in court. In the event, they were all shot dead. The car which they had in Gibraltar contained no explosive but another vehicle which they had in Spain was found to contain explosives.

Held that as a provision which not only safeguards the right to life but sets out the circumstances when the deprivation of life may be justified, Article 2 ranks as one of the most fundamental provisions in the Convention. Its

1

provisions must be strictly construed. The exceptions delineated in paragraph 2 indicate that this provision extends to, but is not concerned exclusively with, intentional killing. The text of Article 2, read as a whole, demonstrates that paragraph 2 does not primarily define instances where it is permitted intentionally to kill an individual, but describes the situations where it is permitted to "use force" which may result, as an unintended outcome, in the deprivation of life. The use of force, however, must be no more than "absolutely necessary" for the achievement of one of the purposes set out in subparagraphs (a), (b) or (c). In this respect the use of the term "absolutely necessary" indicates that a stricter and more compelling test of necessity must be employed from that normally applicable when determining whether State action is "necessary in a democratic society" under paragraph 2 of Articles 8 to 11 of the Convention. In particular, the force used must be strictly proportionate to the achievement of the aims set out in subparagraphs 2(a), (b) and (c) of Article 2. In keeping with the importance of this provision in a democratic society, the Court must, in making its assessment, subject deprivations of life to the most careful scrutiny, particularly where deliberate lethal force is used, taking into consideration not only the actions of the agents of the State who actually administer the force but also all the surrounding circumstances including such matters as the planning and control of the actions under examination. The obligation to protect the right to life under this provision, read in conjunction with the State's general duty under Article 1 of the Convention to "secure to everyone within their jurisdiction the rights and freedoms defined in [the] Convention", requires by implication that there should be some form of effective official investigation when individuals have been killed as a result of the use of force by, *inter alios*, agents of the State. Although the applicants had criticised the inquest, the fact was that public inquest proceedings, at which the applicants were legally represented and which involved the hearing of 79 witnesses, did in fact take place. Moreover, the proceedings lasted 19 days and, as was evident from the inquest's voluminous transcript, involved a detailed review of the events surrounding the killings. Furthermore, it appeared from the transcript, including the Coroner's summing-up to the jury, that the lawyers acting on behalf of the applicants were able to examine and cross-examine key witnesses, including the military and police personnel involved in the planning and conduct of the anti-terrorist operation, and to make the submissions they wished to make in the course of the proceedings. In light of that, the Court did not consider that the alleged various short-comings in the inquest proceedings substantially hampered the carrying out of a thorough, impartial and careful examination of the circumstances surrounding the killings. It followed that there had been no breach of Article 2 on this ground.

The Court rejected as unsubstantiated the applicants' allegations that the killing of the three suspects was premeditated or the product of a tacit agreement amongst those involved in the operation. The Court had to bear in mind that the information that the United Kingdom authorities received that there would be a terrorist attack in Gibraltar presented them with a fundamental dilemma. On the one hand, they were required to have regard to their duty to protect the lives of the people in Gibraltar including their own military personnel and, on the other, to have minimum resort to the use of lethal force against those suspected of posing this threat in the light of the obligations flowing from both domestic and international law. Several other factors had also to be taken into consideration. First, the authorities were confronted by an active service unit of the IRA composed of persons who had been convicted of bombing offences and a known explosives expert. The IRA, judged by its actions in the past, had demonstrated a disregard for human life, including that of its own members. Second, the authorities had had prior warning of the impending terrorist action and thus had ample opportunity to plan their reaction and, in co-ordination with the local Gibraltar authorities, to take measures to foil the attack and arrest the suspects. Inevitably, however, the security authorities could not have been in possession of the full facts and were obliged to formulate their policies on the basis of incomplete hypotheses. Against this background, in determining whether the force used was compatible with Article 2, the Court had to scrutinise carefully not only whether the force used by the soldiers was strictly proportionate to the aim of protecting persons against unlawful violence but also whether the anti-terrorist operation was planned and controlled by the authorities so as to minimise, to the greatest extent possible, recourse to lethal force. The soldiers who carried out the shooting were informed by their superiors, in essence, that there was a car bomb in place which could be detonated by any of the three suspects by means of a radio-control device which might have been concealed on their persons; that the device could be activated by pressing a button; that they would be likely to detonate the bomb if challenged, thereby causing heavy loss of life and serious injuries, and were also likely to be armed and to resist arrest. McCann and Farrell were shot at close range after making what appeared to the soldiers to be threatening movements with their hands as if they were going to detonate the bomb. Savage was shot because he moved his right arm to the area of his jacket pocket, thereby giving rise to the fear that he was about to detonate the bomb. The Court accepted that the soldiers honestly believed, in the light of the information that they had been given, that it was necessary to shoot the suspects in order to prevent them from detonating a bomb and causing serious loss of life. The actions which they took, in obedience to superior orders, were thus perceived by them as absolutely necessary in order to safeguard innocent lives. The Court considered that the use of force by agents of the State in pursuit of one of the aims delineated in paragraph 2 of Article 2 of the Convention may be justified under this provision where it is based on an honest belief which is perceived, for good reasons, to be valid at the time but which subsequently turns out to be mistaken. To hold otherwise would be to impose an unrealistic burden on the State and its law-enforcement personnel in the execution of their duty, perhaps to the detriment of their lives and those of others. It followed that, having regard to the dilemma confronting the authorities in the circumstances of the case, the actions of the soldiers did not, in themselves, give rise to a violation of the provision.

The question arose, however, whether the anti-terrorist operation as a whole was controlled and organised in a manner which respected the requirements of Article 2 and whether the information and instructions given to the soldiers which, in effect, rendered inevitable the use of lethal force, took adequately into consideration the right to life of the three suspects. It had been the intention of the authorities to arrest the suspects at an appropriate stage. However, having had advance warning of the terrorists' intentions it would certainly have been possible for the authorities to have mounted an arrest operation on the arrival of the terrorists in Gibraltar. The danger to the population of Gibraltar in not preventing their entry had to be considered to outweigh the possible consequences of having insufficient evidence to warrant their detention and trial. There was a serious miscalculation by those responsible for controlling the operation. As a result, the scene was set in which the fatal shooting, given the intelligence assessments which had been made, was a foreseeable possibility if not a likelihood.

In the planning, a number of key assessments were made. In particular, it was thought that the terrorists would not use a blocking car; that the bomb would be detonated by a radio-control device; that the detonation could be effected by the pressing of a button; that it was likely that the suspects would detonate the bomb if challenged; that they would be armed and would be likely to use their arms if confronted. In the event, all of these crucial assumptions, apart from the terrorists' intentions to carry out an attack, turned out to be erroneous. Insufficient allowances appeared to have been made for other assumptions; for example, there was the possibility that the three terrorists were on a reconnaissance mission. It was disquieting in this context that an assessment made, after a cursory external examination of the car, that there was a "suspect car bomb" was conveyed to the soldiers as a definite identification that there was such a bomb. In the absence of sufficient allowances being made for alternative possibilities, and the definite reporting of the existence of a car bomb which, according to the assessments that had been made, could be detonated at the press of a button, a series of working hypotheses were conveyed to the soldiers as certainties, thereby making the use of lethal force almost unavoidable. The failure to make provision for a margin of error had also to be considered in combination with the training of the soldiers to continue shooting once they opened fire until the suspect was dead.

Against this background, the authorities were bound by their obligation to respect the right to life of the suspects to exercise the greatest of care in evaluating the information at their disposal before transmitting it to soldiers whose use of firearms automatically involved shooting to kill. It was not clear whether the soldiers had been trained or instructed to assess whether the use of firearms to wound their targets may have been warranted by the specific circumstances that confronted them at the moment of arrest. Their reflex action in this vital respect lacked the degree of caution in the use of firearms to be expected from law-enforcement personnel in a democratic society, even when dealing with dangerous terrorist suspects, and stood in marked contrast to the standard of care reflected in the instructions in the use of firearms by the police which emphasised the legal responsibilities of the individual officer in the light of conditions prevailing at the moment of engagement.

In sum, having regard to the decision not to prevent the suspects from travelling into Gibraltar, to the failure of the authorities to make sufficient allowances for the possibility that their intelligence assessments might, in some respects at least, be erroneous and to the automatic recourse to lethal force when the soldiers opened fire, the Court was not persuaded that the killing of the three terrorists constituted the use of force which was no more than absolutely necessary in defence of persons from unlawful violence within the meaning of Article 2. Accordingly, the Court found that there had been a breach of Article 2.

Andronicou and Constantinou v Cyprus (1997) 25 EHRR 491

Lefteris Andronicou and Elsie Constantinou were engaged and cohabited. Their neighbours called the police when it became clear that they were involved in a domestic disturbance in their flat. Andronicou was seen to be in possession of a gun. At various times he pointed it at Constantinou and threatened to shoot not only her but also other people. He threatened suicide. After a lengthy siege, and after a shot was heard, the decision was taken to storm the flat and specialist police officers, from a unit known as "MMAD" did so. Andronicou fired at the first officer into the flat and other officers opened fire on him, killing him. He had hold of Constantinou and she was struck by two bullets. She died in hospital later. Post-mortem examination found that Andronicou had been struck by at least 25 bullets. The injuries inflicted on Constantinou by Andronicou were not likely to have proved fatal; she had been killed by bullets fired by the police. There was a detailed Commission of Inquiry and its findings formed the basis of the approach of both the Commission and the Court.

Held that Article 2 ranks as one of the most fundamental provisions of the Convention and that its provisions must be strictly construed. This is particularly true of the exceptions delineated in paragraph 2 of that Article which apply not only to intentional deprivation of life but also to situations where it is permitted to use force which may result, as an unintended outcome, in the deprivation of life. The use of force must be no more than "absolutely necessary" for the achievement of one of the purposes defined in sub-paragraphs (a), (b) and (c). In this respect the use of the term "absolutely necessary" indicates that a stricter and more compelling test of necessity must be employed than that normally applicable when determining whether State action is "necessary in a democratic society" under paragraph 2 of

Articles 8 to 11 of the Convention. In particular, the force used must be strictly proportionate to the achievement of the aims set out in subparagraphs 2(a), (b) and (c) of Article 2. Furthermore, in keeping with the importance of this provision in a democratic society, the Court must, in making its assessment, subject deprivations of life to the most careful scrutiny, particularly where deliberate lethal force is used, taking into consideration not only the actions of the agents of the State who actually administer the force but also all the surrounding circumstances, including such matters as the planning and control of the actions under examination. The Court's sole concern must be to evaluate whether in the circumstances the planning and control of the rescue operation showed that the authorities had taken appropriate care to ensure that any risk to the lives of the couple had been minimised and that they were not negligent in their choice of action. It was not appropriate to discuss with the benefit of hindsight the merits of alternative tactics. The Court must have particular regard to the context in which the incident occurred as well as to the way in which the situation developed over the course of the day.

As to the context, the authorities clearly understood that they were dealing with a young couple and not with hardened criminals or terrorists. The negotiations and the resolve to negotiate up until the last possible moment clearly indicated that the authorities never lost sight of the fact that the incident had its origins in a "lovers' quarrel" and that this factor had to be taken into account if, in the final analysis, it transpired that force had to be used to free Elsie Constantinou. It was to be noted that the authorities tried to bring an end to the incident through persuasion and dialogue right up to the last possible moment. The police negotiator continued his attempts in the later phase of the incident to assure Andronicou that no harm would come to him if he were to release the young woman. This sustained effort by the authorities to resolve the situation through negotiations illustrated a deep concern on the part of the authorities to deploy the MMAD officers only as a last resort. While there may have been some shortcomings, the negotiations were in general conducted in a manner which could be said to be reasonable in the circumstances.

Irrespective of the domestic nature of the incident, however, the situation progressively developed in the eyes of the authorities present into a situation fraught with danger and in which critical decisions had to be taken. In these circumstances and in the knowledge that Andronicou was armed, the authorities could reasonably consider that, as the deadline set by him approached, the negotiations had failed and that an attempt had to be made to get into the flat, disarm and arrest him and free Constantinou. In the Court's view the authorities' decision to use the MMAD officers in the circumstances as they were known at the time was justified. Recourse to the skills of a highly professionally trained unit like the MMAD would appear to be quite natural given the nature of the operation which was contemplated. The decision to use the MMAD officers was a considered one of last resort. It was discussed both at the highest possible level in the police chain of command and at ministerial level and only implemented when the negotiations failed and in view of a reasonably held belief that the young woman's life was in imminent danger.

While it was true that the officers deployed were trained to shoot to kill if fired at, it was to be noted that they were issued with clear instructions as to when to use their weapons. They were told to use only proportionate force and to fire only if Constantinou's life or their own lives were in danger. The Court was of the view that it had not been shown that the rescue operation was not planned and organised in a way which minimised to the greatest extent possible any risk to the lives of the couple.

The officers' use of lethal force in the circumstances was the direct result of Andronicou's violent reaction to the storming of the flat. He sought to take the life of the first officer who entered the room. The second officer believed that Andronicou had shot dead one colleague and wounded another and that he still had not discharged the second cartridge in the shotgun. When he entered the room he saw Andronicou holding Elsie Constantinou and appearing to make a threatening move. He also believed (erroneously, as it turned out) that Andronicou might have other weapons. The officers honestly believed in the circumstances that it was necessary to kill him in order to save the life of Elsie Constantinou and their own lives and to fire at him repeatedly in order to remove any risk that he might reach for a weapon.

The use of force by agents of the State in pursuit of one of the aims delineated in paragraph 2 of Article 2 of the Convention may be justified under this provision where it is based on an honest belief which is perceived, for good reasons, to be valid at the time but subsequently turns out to be mistaken. To hold otherwise would be to impose an unrealistic burden on the State and its law-enforcement personnel in the execution of their duty, perhaps to the detriment of their lives and the lives of others. It was clearly regrettable that so much fire power was used in the circumstances to neutralise any risk presented by Lefteris Andronicou. However, the Court could not with detached reflection substitute its own assessment of the situation for that of the officers who were required to react in the heat of the moment in what was for them a unique and unprecedented operation to save life. The officers were entitled to open fire for this purpose and to take all measures which they honestly and reasonably believed were necessary to eliminate any risk either to the young woman's life or to their own lives. It transpired at the commission of inquiry that only two of the officers' bullets actually struck her. While tragically they proved to be fatal, it had to be acknowledged that the accuracy of the officers' fire was impaired through Andronicou's action in clinging on to her thereby exposing her to risk.

The Court considered, therefore, that the use of lethal force in the circumstances, however regrettable it may have been, did not exceed what was "absolutely necessary" for the purposes of defending the lives of Elsie Constantinou and of the officers and did not amount to a breach by the respondent State of their obligations under Article 2 of the Convention.

Effective Investigation

Yasa v Turkey (1999) 28 EHRR 408

While cycling to his newspaper kiosk, the applicant was shot at by two unknown assailants. He was hit by eight bullets and spent 11 days in hospital. Some months later, the applicant's uncle, who had been looking after the applicant's kiosk, was shot dead.

A preliminary investigation was opened immediately. The police prepared a sketch of the scene of the incident and interviewed three witnesses. No further progress was made. The applicant claimed that he and his uncle were shot due to their involvement in the sale of the newspaper, the *Özgür Gündem*, as part of a campaign of persecution and attacks against those involved in the publication and distribution of that and other pro-Kurdish newspapers. He noted that prosecutions had been brought against the newspaper and persons involved in its production and stated that other newsagents who sold it had been subject to threats and harassment. The Government denied any State involvement in the shooting of either the applicant or his uncle. The applicant complained of a breach of Article 2.

Held that the obligation to protect the right to life was not confined to cases where it had been established that the killing had been caused by an agent of the State. Nor was the issue of whether members of the deceased's family or others had lodged a formal complaint about the killing with the competent investigatory authorities decisive. The mere fact that the authorities had been informed of the murder of the applicant's uncle had given rise *ipso facto* to an obligation under Article 2 to carry out an effective investigation. A police investigation had been started into each of the incidents on the day they occurred. The Government had provided no concrete information on the state of progress of the investigations which, more than five years after the events, did not appear to have produced any tangible result or have made any credible headway. Although the prevailing climate at the time in south-east Turkey may have impeded the search for conclusive evidence in the domestic criminal proceedings, that could not relieve the authorities of their obligations under Article 2 to carry out an investigation, as otherwise it would exacerbate still further the climate of impunity and insecurity in the region. In addition, the investigatory authorities appeared to have excluded from the outset the possibility that State agents might have been implicated in the attacks. The Commission had not accepted that the authorities were or could have been unaware that those involved in the publication and distribution of the *Özgür Gündem* feared that they were falling victim to a concerted campaign tolerated, if not approved, by State officials. It had therefore been incumbent on the authorities to have regard, in their investigations, to that possibility. In that connection, whether or not the applicant had formally identified the security forces as being the assailants was of little relevance. In consequence there had been a violation of Article 2.

THE POSITIVE OBLIGATION TO PROTECT LIFE

Osman v United Kingdom (2000) 29 EHRR 245

The first applicant, Mrs Mulkiye Osman, was the widow of Mr Ali Osman who was shot dead by Mr Paul Paget-Lewis on 7 March 1988. The second applicant, Ahmet Osman, was her son. He was a former pupil of Paget-Lewis at Homerton House School. Ahmet Osman was wounded in the shooting incident which led to the death of his father. In 1986 the headmaster of the school noticed that Paget-Lewis had developed an attachment to Ahmet Osman. In January 1987 the mother of Leslie Green, another pupil at the school and the applicants' neighbour, telephoned another deputy head teacher to complain that Paget-Lewis had been following her son home after school and harassing him.

Paget-Lewis was interviewed and said that he had a special relationship with Ahmet Osman which had developed over a period of a year, which Leslie Green was trying to disrupt and that he was so upset on one occasion that he confronted Leslie and accused the boy of being a sexual deviant. He admitted that he had followed Leslie home on one occasion and had waited outside his parents' house for 45 minutes. He was in a highly irrational state during this interview and unwilling to admit that his behaviour displayed a serious lack of wisdom and professionalism. It was suggested to Paget-Lewis by the school that he should seek psychiatric help.

Between 3 March 1987 and 17 March 1987 the headmaster met with a police officer on four occasions and during these meetings information concerning Paget-Lewis' conduct towards Ahmet Osman was passed on to the police. The police officer did not keep any record of the meetings, nor did he make any report concerning the nature and extent of the information that was communicated to him. By 17 March 1987 graffiti had appeared at six locations around the school which asserted the existence of a sexual relationship between Leslie Green and Ahmet Osman. A deputy headmaster formed the view that Paget-Lewis had written the graffiti on the basis that he knew its precise wording and the exact locations of all the graffiti. It was then discovered that the files relating to Ahmet and Leslie Green had been stolen from the school office. The file relating to staff disciplinary matters was also found to be missing. Paget-Lewis denied any involvement in the theft.

On 14 April 1987, Paget-Lewis changed his name by deed poll to Paul Ahmet Yildirim Osman. On 1 May 1987, the headmaster wrote to the Inner London Education Authority (ILEA) informing them that Paget-Lewis had changed his name and that he was worried that some psychological imbalance might pose a threat to the safety of Ahmet Osman. He also stated that he was of the opinion that Paget-Lewis should be removed from the school as soon as possible. He continued to express concern to the police and to ILEA and on 19 May 1987 Paget-Lewis was seen by the ILEA psychiatrist, who reported that: "This teacher must indeed give cause for concern. He does not present as ill in formal terms, nor does he seem sexually deviant. He does have personality problems, and his judgment regarding his friendship with a pupil is reprehensibly suspect." He recommended that Paget-Lewis remain teaching at the school but that he should receive some form of counselling and psychotherapy.

In May and June 1987 there were incidents of vandalism to the applicants' house and car. Both incidents were reported to the police, but no police records relating to the offences could be found.

On 1 June 1987 the headmaster requested Paget-Lewis to take sick leave and he did so. The ILEA psychiatrist recommended that he should no longer teach at Homerton House and that transfer on medical grounds was strongly and urgently recommended. On 18 June 1987, Paget-Lewis was suspended pending an ILEA investigation for "unprofessional behaviour" towards Ahmet Osman. On 7 August 1987, ILEA sent a letter to Paget-Lewis officially reprimanding and severely warning him but lifting the suspension. The letter also stated that he was not to return to Homerton House. Shortly afterwards he began working as a supply teacher at two other local schools.

Between August and December 1987 there were further incidents of vandalism to the Osmans' property. Paget-Lewis was spoken to by the police but no detailed records were made by the police officer and entries in notebooks or registers could not later be traced.

On 9 December 1987 a Detective Sergeant took a detailed statement from Leslie Green and his mother concerning *inter alia* the fact that Paget-Lewis had followed Leslie home, the acts of harassment and the graffiti which had appeared at the school. In his statement Leslie claimed that Paget-Lewis had threatened to "get him" whether it took "30 days or 30 years". In a report dated 15 December 1987, the Detective Sergeant observed that ". . . there is no evidence to implicate Paget-Lewis in either of these offences [the graffiti at the school] or the acts of vandalism against Osman's address, although there is no doubt in everybody's mind that he was in fact responsible and this was just another example of his spite".

On 15 December 1987 Paget-Lewis was interviewed by officers of ILEA at his own request. An ILEA memorandum dated 15 December 1987 recorded that Paget-Lewis felt in a self-destructive mood, stating that it was all a symphony and the last chord had to be played. He admitted being deeply in debt and as a result was selling all his possessions. He blamed one of the deputy headmasters for all his troubles. He said that he would not "do a Hungerford" in a school but would see him at his home. The memorandum stated that the concerns of ILEA should be passed on to the police. ILEA informed the police and the school that it was considered that the head and deputy head were at risk of violence. The police decided to "pay casual attention" to the Osman's address.

Between January and March 1988 Paget-Lewis travelled around England hiring cars in his adopted name of Osman and was involved in a number of accidents. On 17 January 1988 Paget-Lewis broke into a car parked near a clay-pigeon shoot near Leeds in Yorkshire and stole a shotgun. He sawed off both barrels. While the theft was reported to the local police, because there was nothing to connect the incident to Paget-Lewis, the theft did not come to the attention of the Metropolitan police dealing with the case. On 1, 4 and 5 March 1988 Leslie Green saw Paget-Lewis wearing a black crash helmet near the applicants' home. According to the applicants, Mrs Green informed the police on each occasion, but her calls were not returned. On 7 March 1988 Paget-Lewis was seen near the applicants' home by a number of people. At about 11.00 pm Paget-Lewis shot and killed Ali Osman and seriously wounded Ahmet. He then drove to the home of the deputy headmaster where he shot and wounded him and killed his son. Early the next morning Paget-Lewis was arrested. On being arrested he stated: "Why didn't you stop me before I did it, I gave you all the warning signs?" On 28 October 1988 Paget-Lewis was convicted of two charges of manslaughter having pleaded guilty on grounds of diminished responsibility. He was sentenced to be detained in a secure mental hospital without limit of time pursuant to section 41 of the Mental Health Act 1983.

The applicants commenced proceedings against, *inter alios*, the Commissioner of Police of the Metropolis alleging negligence in that although the police were aware of Paget-Lewis' activities since May 1987 they failed to apprehend or interview him, search his home or charge him with an offence before March 1988. On 7 October 1992 the Court of Appeal held that in light of *Hill* v *Chief Constable of West Yorkshire* [1989] AC 53 no action could lie against the police in negligence in the investigation and suppression of crime on the grounds that public policy required an immunity from suit.

The applicants complained under *inter alia* Articles 2 and 6.1.

Held that the Court would approach the Article 2 issue in accordance with its usual practice in the light of all the material placed before it by the applicants and by the Government or, if necessary, material obtained of its own motion. This was a case in which the national courts had not considered the facts.

The first sentence of Article 2.1 enjoins the State not only to refrain from the intentional and unlawful taking of life, but also to take appropriate steps to safeguard the lives of those within its jurisdiction. It was common ground that the State's obligation in this respect extends beyond its primary duty to secure the right to life by putting in place effective criminal law provisions to deter the commission of offences against the person backed up by law-enforcement machinery for the prevention, suppression and sanctioning of breaches of such provisions. Article 2 of the Convention may also imply in certain well-defined circumstances a positive obligation on the authorities to take preventive operational measures to protect an individual whose life is at risk from the criminal acts of another individual.

The scope of this obligation was a matter of dispute between the parties. Bearing in mind the difficulties involved in policing modern societies, the unpredictability of human conduct and the operational choices which must be made in terms of priorities and resources, such an obligation must be interpreted in a way which does not impose an impossible or disproportionate burden on the authorities.

Accordingly, not every claimed risk to life can entail for the authorities a Convention requirement to take operational measures to prevent that risk from materialising. Another relevant consideration is the need to ensure that the police exercise their powers to control and prevent crime in a manner which fully respects the due process and other guarantees which legitimately place restraints on the scope of their action to investigate crime and bring offenders to justice, including the guarantees contained in Articles 5 and 8 of the Convention.

Where there is an allegation that the authorities have violated their positive obligation to protect the right to life in the context of their duty to prevent and suppress offences against the person, it must be established to the satisfaction of the Court that the authorities knew or ought to have known at the time of the existence of a real and immediate risk to the life of an identified individual or individuals from the criminal acts of a third party and that they failed to take measures within the scope of their powers which, judged reasonably, might have been expected to avoid that risk. The Court did not accept the Government's view that the failure to perceive the risk to life in the circumstances known at the time or to take preventive measures to avoid that risk must be tantamount to gross negligence or wilful disregard of the duty to protect life. Such a rigid standard must be considered to be incompatible with the requirements of Article 1 of the Convention and the obligations of Contracting States under that Article to secure the practical and effective protection of the rights and freedoms laid down therein, including Article 2. Having regard to the nature of the right protected by Article 2, a right fundamental in the scheme of the Convention, it is sufficient for an applicant to show that the authorities did not do all that could be reasonably expected of them to avoid a real and immediate risk to life of which they have or ought to have knowledge. This is a question which can only be answered in the light of all the circumstances of any particular case.

The concerns of the school about Paget-Lewis' disturbing attachment to Ahmet Osman had been communicated to the police and the police were informed of all relevant connected matters which had come to light by 4 May 1987 including the graffiti incident, the theft of the school files and Paget-Lewis' change of name. The applicants contended that by that stage the police should have been alert to the need to investigate further Paget-Lewis' alleged involvement in the graffiti incident and the theft of the school files or to keep a closer watch on him given their awareness of the obsessive nature of his behaviour towards Ahmet Osman and how that behaviour manifested itself. The Court was not persuaded that the police's failure to do so at this stage could be impugned from the standpoint of Article 2 having regard to the state of their knowledge at that time. While Paget-Lewis' attachment to Ahmet Osman could be judged by the police officers who visited the school to be most reprehensible from a professional point of view, there was never any suggestion that Ahmet Osman was at risk sexually from him or that his life was in danger. Only the deputy headmaster had reached the conclusion that Paget-Lewis had been responsible for the graffiti in the neighbourhood of the school and the theft of the files. Paget-Lewis had denied all involvement and there was nothing to link him with either incident. At that juncture, the police's appreciation of the situation and their decision to treat it as a matter internal to the school could not be considered unreasonable.

The applicants had attached particular weight to Paget-Lewis' mental condition and in particular to his potential to turn violent and to direct that violence at Ahmet Osman. However, it was to be noted that Paget-Lewis continued to teach at the school up until June 1987. A doctor examined him on three occasions and was satisfied that he was not mentally ill. On 7 August 1987 he was allowed to resume teaching. It was most improbable that the decision to lift his suspension from teaching duties would have been made if it had been believed at the time that there was the slightest risk that he constituted a danger to the safety of young people in his charge. If it appeared to a professional psychiatrist that he did not at the time display any signs of mental illness or a propensity to violence it would be unreasonable to have expected the police to have construed the actions of Paget-Lewis as they were reported to them by the school as those of a mentally disturbed and highly dangerous individual.

None of the acts of vandalism against the Osmans' home and property between May and November 1987 could be described as life-threatening and there was no evidence pointing to the involvement of Paget-Lewis.

The Court had examined carefully the strength of the applicants' arguments that Paget-Lewis on three occasions communicated to the police, either directly or indirectly, his murderous intentions. However, in its view these statements could not reasonably be considered to imply that the Osman family were the target of his threats and to put the police on notice of such. It would appear more likely that they were uttered with respect to Mr Perkins whom Paget-Lewis regarded as principally to blame for being forced to leave his teaching post at Homerton House.

The applicants had failed to point to any decisive stage in the sequence of the events leading up to the tragic shooting when it could be said that the police knew or ought to have known that the lives of the Osman family were at real and immediate risk from Paget-Lewis. While the applicants had pointed to a series of missed opportunities which would have enabled the police to neutralise the threat posed by Paget-Lewis, for example, by searching his home for evidence to link him with the graffiti incident or by having him detained under the Mental Health Act 1983 or by taking more active investigative steps following his disappearance, it could not be said that these measures, judged reasonably, would in fact have produced that result or that a domestic court would have convicted him or ordered his detention in a psychiatric hospital on the basis of the evidence adduced before it.

The police must discharge their duties in a manner which is compatible with the rights and freedoms of individuals. In the circumstances of the present case, they could not be criticised for attaching weight to the presumption of innocence or failing to use powers of arrest, search and seizure having regard to their reasonably held view that they lacked at relevant times the required standard of suspicion to use those powers or that any action taken would in fact have produced concrete results.

The Court therefore concluded that there had been no violation of Article 2.

As regards Article 6.1, the Government maintained that the applicants could not rely on any substantive right in domestic law to sue the police for their alleged failure to prevent Paget-Lewis from shooting dead Ali Osman and seriously wounding the second applicant. They explained that whether or not the police can be considered to owe a plaintiff a duty of care in a particular context depended not only on proof of proximity between the parties and the foreseeability of harm but also on the answer to the question whether it was fair, just and reasonable to impose a duty of care on the police. The Court of Appeal had answered the latter question in the negative, being satisfied that there were no other public policy considerations which would have led it to reach a different conclusion. Accordingly, since the applicants had failed to establish an essential ingredient of the duty of care under domestic law they did not have any substantive right for the purposes of the applicability of Article 6.1. Any other conclusion would result in the impermissible creation by the Convention institutions of a substantive right where none in fact existed in the domestic law of the respondent State. The applicants replied that the Court of Appeal had accepted their proposition that there was a special relationship of proximity between them and the police since the police knew that Paget-Lewis was conducting a campaign of victimisation against the Osman family and that the second applicant was especially at risk from the threat posed by Paget-Lewis to his life. The applicants maintained that although they had established all the constituent elements of the duty of care, the Court of Appeal was constrained by precedent to apply the doctrine of police immunity developed by the House of Lords to strike out their statement of claim. In their view, the doctrine of police immunity was not one of the essential elements of the duty of care as was claimed by the Government, but a separate and distinct ground for defeating a negligence action in order to ensure, *inter alia*, that police manpower was not diverted from their ordinary functions or to avoid overly cautious or defensive policing.

The Court recalled that Article 6.1 secures to everyone the right to have any claim relating to his civil rights and obligations brought before a court or tribunal. In this way the Article embodies the "right to a court", of which the right of access, that is the right to institute proceedings before courts in civil matters, constitutes one aspect only. Although the applicants had argued in terms which suggested that the exclusionary rule operated as an absolute immunity to negligence actions against the police in the context at issue, the Court accepted the Government's contention that the rule did not auto-matically doom to failure such a civil action from the outset but in principle allowed a domestic court to make a considered assessment on the basis of the arguments before it as to whether a particular case was or was not suitable for the application of the rule. On that understanding the Court considered that the applicants must be taken to have had a right, derived from the law of negligence, to seek an adjudication on the admissibility and merits of an arguable claim that they were in a relationship of proximity to the police, that the harm caused was foreseeable and that in the circumstances it was fair, just and reasonable not to apply the exclusionary rule outlined in the *Hill* case. In the view of the Court the assertion of that right by the applicants was in itself sufficient to ensure the applicability of Article 6.1 of the Convention.

It remained to be determined whether the restriction which was imposed on the exercise of the applicants' right under that provision was lawful. The right to a court is not absolute, but may be subject to limitations; these are permitted by implication since the right of access by its very nature calls for regulation by the State. In this respect, the Contracting States enjoy a certain margin of appreciation, although the final decision as to the observance of the Convention's requirements rests with the Court. It must be satisfied that the limitations applied do not restrict or reduce the access left to the individual in such a way or to such an extent that the very essence of the right is impaired. Furthermore, a limitation will not be compatible with Article 6.1 if it does not pursue a legitimate aim and if there is not a reasonable relationship of proportionality between the means employed and the aim sought to be achieved.

The applicants' claim never fully proceeded to trial in that there was never any determination on its merits nor on the facts on which it was based. The decision of the Court of Appeal striking out their statement of claim was given in the context of interlocutory proceedings initiated by the Metropolitian Police Commissioner and that court assumed for the purposes of those proceedings that the facts as pleaded in the applicants' statement of claim were true. The applicants' claim was rejected since it was found to fall squarely within the scope of the exclusionary rule formulated by the House of Lords in the *Hill* case. The reasons which led the House of Lords in the *Hill* case to lay down an exclusionary rule to protect the police from negligence actions in the context at issue were based on the view that the interests of the community as a whole are best served by a police service whose efficiency and effectiveness in the battle against crime were not jeopardised by the constant risk of exposure to tortious liability for policy and operational decisions. Although the aim of such a rule might be accepted as legitimate in terms of the Convention, as being directed to the maintenance of the effectiveness of the police service and hence to the prevention of disorder or crime, the Court must nevertheless, in turning to the issue of proportionality, have particular regard to its scope and especially its application in the case at issue. While the Government had contended that the exclusionary rule of liability is not of an absolute nature and that its application might yield to other public policy considerations, it appeared to the Court that in the instant case the Court of Appeal proceeded on the basis that the rule provided a watertight defence to the police and that it was impossible to prise open an immunity which the police enjoy from civil suit in respect of their acts and omissions in the investigation and suppression of crime. The application of the rule in this manner without further inquiry into the existence of competing public interest considerations only served to confer a blanket immunity on the police for their acts and omissions during the investigation and suppression of crime and amounted to an unjustifiable restriction on an applicant's right to have a determination on the merits of his or her claim against the police in deserving cases. It must be open to a domestic court to have regard to the presence of other public interest considerations which pull in the opposite direction to the application of the rule. The Court therefore concluded that the application of the exclusionary rule in the instant case constituted a disproportionate restriction on the applicants' right of access to a court. There had, accordingly, been a violation of Article 6.1 of the Convention.

ARTICLE 3

THE PROHIBITION OF TORTURE, etc.

No one shall be subjected to torture or to inhuman or degrading treatment or punishment.

TORTURE AND INHUMAN TREATMENT

Ireland v United Kingdom (1979–80) 2 EHRR 25

In order to combat a prolonged terrorist campaign the authorities exercised a series of extrajudicial powers of arrest, detention and internment. Persons who had been detained in the exercise of these powers were interrogated in order to determine whether they should be interned and to compile information about the IRA. Some were beaten. Some were subjected to a technique called "interrogation in depth". They were forced to stand, for hours at a time, spread-eagled against walls. Bags were placed over their heads. They were held in a room where there was a continuous, loud hissing noise. They were deprived of sleep. They were subjected to a reduced diet. Interrogations conducted under these conditions produced a substantial amount of intelligence information.

Complaints of ill-treatment were made at an early stage and, following two committees of inquiry, the use of these techniques was forbidden. Certain members of the security forces were prosecuted for assault and convicted. Compensation was paid to some of those who had been mistreated. Ireland referred the case to Court in relation, *inter alia*, to Article 3.

Held that the Court's judgments serve not only to decide the cases before it but also to elucidate, safeguard and develop the rules instituted by the Convention, thereby contributing to their observance by States. In relation to Article 3, the Convention prohibits in absolute terms torture and inhuman or degrading treatment or punishment, irrespective of the victim's conduct. Article 3 contains no provision for exceptions and is not amenable to derogation, even in the event of a public emergency threatening the life of the nation.

The five techniques were applied in combination, with premeditation and for hours at a stretch. They caused at least intense physical and mental suffering and led to acute psychiatric disturbances during interrogation. They accordingly fell into the category of inhuman treatment. They were also degrading since they were such as to arouse in their victims feelings of fear, anguish and inferiority capable of humiliating and debasing them and possibly breaking their physical and moral resistance. Recourse to the five techniques amounted to a practice of inhuman and degrading treatment in breach of Article 3. Some of the beatings which took place were also severe enough to constitute inhuman treatment.

The distinction between that and torture derives principally from the difference in the intensity of the suffering inflicted. The term "torture" attaches a special stigma to deliberate inhuman treatment causing very serious and cruel suffering. The five techniques did not occasion suffering of the particular intensity and cruelty implied by the word torture as so understood.

Ribitsch v Austria (1996) 21 EHRR 573

The applicant and his wife were detained in connection with drug-trafficking and in particular in connection with the deaths of two people from drug overdoses. During that detention, the applicant sustained injuries. He described a sustained course of ill-treatment whilst in custody. Police officers gave a different (though not very satisfactory) account of how he came by his injuries. In due course, a police officer by the name of Markl was convicted of assaulting the applicant but that conviction was quashed on appeal. It was not disputed by the Government that the applicant's injuries were sustained during his detention in police custody while he was entirely under the control of police officers.

Held that Police Officer Markl's acquittal in the criminal proceedings by a court bound by the presumption of innocence did not absolve Austria from its responsibility under the Convention. The Government were accordingly under an obligation to provide a plausible explanation of how the applicant's injuries were caused. But the Government did no more than refer to the outcome of the domestic criminal proceedings, where the high standard of proof necessary to secure a criminal conviction was not found to have been satisfied. On the basis of all the material placed before it, the Court concluded that the Government had not satisfactorily established that the applicant's injuries were caused otherwise than by the treatment he underwent while in police custody. The Government did not dispute that the applicant's injuries, assuming that it had been proved that they were deliberately inflicted on him while he was in police custody, reached a level of severity sufficient to bring them within the scope of Article 3. The Court emphasised that, in respect of a person deprived of his liberty, any recourse to physical force which has not been made strictly necessary by his own conduct diminishes human dignity and is in principle an infringement of the right set forth in Article 3 of the Convention. The requirements of an investigation and the undeniable difficulties inherent in the fight against crime cannot justify placing limits on the protection to be afforded in respect of the physical integrity of individuals. In the instant case, the injuries suffered by Mr Ribitsch showed that he had undergone ill-treatment which amounted to both inhuman and degrading treatment. There was a breach of Article 3.

Aydin v Turkey (1998) 25 EHRR 251

The applicant was a 17-year-old Turkish girl of Kurdish origin whose home was in a village about 10 kilometres from the town where the district gendarmerie headquarters were located. She had never travelled outside her village before the events which led to her application.

Since about 1985, serious disturbances had raged in the south-east of Turkey between the security forces and the members of the PKK (Workers' Party of Kurdistan). Since 1987, 10 of the 11 provinces of south-eastern Turkey had been subjected to emergency rule. According to the facts found by the Commission, the applicant had been detained and taken to the local police headquarters. There she was blindfolded, beaten, stripped, placed inside a tyre and sprayed with high-pressure water, and raped. It appeared probable that the applicant was subjected to such treatment on the basis of suspicion of collaboration by herself or members of her family with members of the PKK, the purpose being to gain information and/or to deter her family and other villagers from becoming implicated in terrorist activities. The Government asked the Court to depart from the Commission's findings.

Held that the establishment and verification of the facts were primarily a matter for the Commission and that it was only in exceptional circumstances that the Court would exercise its own powers in this area. In this case, the Court was satisfied that the Commission could properly reach the conclusion that the applicant's allegations were proved beyond reasonable doubt.

Article 3 of the Convention enshrines one of the fundamental values of democratic societies and as such it prohibits in absolute terms torture or inhuman or degrading treatment or punishment. Article 3 admits of no exceptions to this fundamental value and no derogation from it is permissible under Article 15 even having regard to the imperatives of a public emergency threatening the life of the nation or to any suspicion, however well-founded, that a person may be involved in terrorist or other criminal activities.

In order to determine whether any particular form of ill-treatment should be qualified as torture, regard must be had to the distinction drawn in Article 3 between this notion and that of inhuman treatment or degrading treatment. This distinction would appear to have been embodied in the Convention to allow the special stigma of "torture" to attach only to deliberate inhuman treatment causing very serious and cruel suffering. Rape of a detainee by an official of the State must be considered to be an especially grave and abhorrent form of ill-treatment given the ease with which the offender can exploit the vulnerability and weakened resistance of his victim. Furthermore, rape leaves deep psychological scars on the victim which do not respond to the passage of time as quickly as other forms of physical and mental violence. The applicant also experienced the acute physical pain of forced penetration, which must have left her feeling debased and violated both physically and emotionally.

The applicant was also subjected to a series of particularly terrifying and humiliating experiences while in custody at the hands of the security forces having regard to her sex and youth and the circumstances under which she was held. She was detained over a period of three days during which she must have been bewildered and disoriented by being kept blindfolded, and in a constant state of physical pain and mental anguish brought on by the beatings administered to her during questioning and by the apprehension of what would happen to her next. She was also paraded naked in humiliating circumstances thus adding to her overall sense of vulnerability and on one occasion she was pummelled with high-pressure water while being spun around in a tyre.

The applicant and her family must have been taken from their village and brought to the police headquarters for a purpose which could only be explained on account of the security situation in the region and the need of the security forces to elicit information. The suffering inflicted on the applicant during the period of her detention must also be seen as calculated to serve the same or related purposes. Against this background the Court was satisfied that the accumulation of acts of physical and mental violence inflicted on the applicant and the especially cruel act of rape to which she was subjected amounted to torture in breach of Article 3 of the Convention. Indeed, the Court would have reached this conclusion on either of these grounds taken separately. There had been a violation of Article 3 of the Convention.

Article 13 guarantees the availability at the national level of a remedy to enforce the substance of the Convention rights and freedoms in whatever form they might happen to be secured in the domestic legal order. The effect of this Article is thus to require the provision of a domestic remedy allowing the competent national authority both to deal with the substance of the relevant Convention complaint and to grant appropriate relief, although Contracting States are afforded some discretion as to the manner in which they conform to their obligations under this provision. The scope of the obligation under Article 13 varies depending on the nature of the applicant's complaint under the Convention. Nevertheless, the remedy required by Article 13 must be "effective" in practice as well as in law, in particular in the sense that its exercise must not be unjustifiably hindered by the acts or omissions of the authorities of the respondent State. The nature of the right safeguarded under Article 3 of the Convention has implications for Article 13. Given the fundamental importance of the prohibition of torture and the especially vulnerable position of torture victims, Article 13 imposes, without prejudice to any other remedy available under the domestic system, an obligation on States to carry out a thorough and effective investigation of incidents of torture.

The applicant was entirely reliant on the public prosecutor and the police acting on his instructions to assemble the evidence necessary for corroborating her complaint. The public prosecutor had the legal powers to interview members of the security forces, summon witnesses, visit the scene of the incident, collect forensic evidence and take all other crucial steps for establishing the truth of her account. His role was critical not only to the pursuit of criminal proceedings against the perpetrators of the offences but also to the pursuit by the applicant of other remedies to redress the harm she suffered. The ultimate effectiveness of those remedies depended on the proper discharge by the public prosecutor of his functions. The public prosecutor had only carried out an incomplete inquiry to determine the veracity of the applicant's statement and to secure the prosecution and conviction of the culprits. He was content to conduct much of the inquiry by correspondence and accepted too readily the denial of security forces that the Aydin family had been detained. His failure to look for corroborating evidence at the headquarters and his deferential attitude to the members of the security forces had to be considered to be a particularly serious shortcoming in the investigation. The requirement of a thorough and effective investigation into an allegation of rape in custody at the hands of a State official implies that the victim be examined, with all appropriate sensitivity, by medical professionals with particular competence in this area and whose independence is not circumscribed by instructions given by the prosecuting authority as to the scope of the examination. It could not be concluded that the medical examinations ordered by the public prosecutor fulfilled this requirement. They were directed to whether the applicant had lost her virginity rather than whether she had been raped and were made by doctors without expertise in the examination of rape victims. No thorough and effective investigation was conducted into the applicant's allegations and that this failure undermined the effectiveness of any other remedies which may have existed given the centrality of the public prosecutor's role to the system of remedies as a whole, including the pursuit of compensation. There had been a violation of Article 13 of the Convention.

Selmouni v France (25803/94)

The applicant was arrested and questioned in connection with alleged drug-trafficking. Having been questioned and taken back to the court cells, he had a dizzy spell. The court cell officers took him to hospital, where he was found to have several superficial bruises and injuries on both arms. There was bruising on his face and head. Thereafter, he was questioned again and after that questioning was again seen by a doctor, who noted injuries. He was seen by several doctors over the next few days and the burden of their findings may be summed up in the words of one of them, who said that: "He presents lesions of traumatic origin on his skin that were sustained at a time which corresponds to the period of police custody."

The applicant made a complaint against the police and alleged that, during his first interrogation, he had been struck repeatedly by police officers, one of whom used a baseball bat. He said that he had been assaulted again on the following day during a further interrogation. He said that he had been taken into the corridor, where one of the police officers took out his penis and told the applicant to suck it. When he refused, that officer urinated over him. He was threatened with blowlamps and with a syringe if he did not talk. One of the officers inserted a small black truncheon into the applicant's anus. These allegations of sexual abuse could neither be confirmed nor invalidated by medical evidence, partly because some of them were not such as to leave injuries and partly because of lapse of time between the alleged acts and their disclosure by the applicant.

Police officers were subsequently convicted of assault (but not indecent assault) on the applicant and prison sentences were imposed. At the time the case was heard by the Human Rights Court, the procedure in relation to the prosecution of the officers was not complete and the French Government maintained that the police officers in question should have the benefit of the presumption of innocence, in accordance with Article 6.2 of the Convention.

Held that where an individual is taken into police custody in good health but is found to be injured at the time of release, it is incumbent on the State to provide a plausible explanation of how those injuries were caused, failing which a clear issue arises under Article 3 of the Convention. Whatever the outcome of the domestic proceedings, the police officers' conviction or acquittal does not absolve the respondent State from its responsibility under the Convention. The Court reiterated that Article 3 enshrines one of the most fundamental values of democratic societies. Even in the most difficult circumstances, such as the fight against terrorism and organised crime, the Convention prohibits in absolute terms torture or inhuman or degrading treatment or punishment. Unlike most of the substantive clauses of the Convention and of Protocols Nos 1 and 4, Article 3 makes no provision for exceptions and no derogation from it is permissible even in the event of a public emergency threatening the life of the nation.

In order to determine whether a particular form of ill-treatment should be qualified as torture, the Court must have regard to the distinction, embodied in Article 3, between this notion and that of inhuman or degrading treatment. It was the intention that the Convention should, by means of this distinction, attach a special stigma to deliberate inhuman treatment causing very serious and cruel suffering. The injuries recorded in the various medical certificates and the applicant's statements regarding the ill-treatment to which he had been subjected while in police custody established the existence of physical and mental pain and suffering. The course of the events also showed that pain and suffering were inflicted on the applicant intentionally for the purpose of, *inter alia*, making him confess to the offence which he was suspected of having committed. The medical certificates annexed to the case file showed clearly that the numerous acts of violence were directly inflicted by police officers in the performance of their duties.

The acts complained of were such as to arouse in the applicant feelings of fear, anguish and inferiority capable of humiliating and debasing him and possibly breaking his physical and moral resistance. The Court therefore found elements which were sufficiently serious to render such treatment inhuman and degrading. It remained to establish in the instant case whether the "pain or suffering" inflicted on Mr Selmouni could be defined as "severe" within the meaning of Article 1 of the United Nations Convention against Torture and Other Cruel, Inhuman or Degrading Treatment or Punishment. The Court considered that this "severity" is, like the "minimum severity" required for the application of Article 3, in the nature of things, relative; it depends on all the circumstances of the case, such as the duration of the treatment, its physical or mental effects and, in some cases, the sex, age and state of health of the victim.

Having regard to the fact that the Convention is a "living instrument which must be interpreted in the light of present-day conditions" the Court considered that certain acts which were classified in the past as "inhuman and degrading treatment" as opposed to "torture" could be classified differently in future. It took the view that the increasingly high standard being required in the area of the protection of human rights and fundamental liberties correspondingly and inevitably requires greater firmness in assessing breaches of the fundamental values of democratic societies. A large number of blows were inflicted on Mr Selmouni. Whatever a person's state of health, it could be presumed that such intensity of blows will cause substantial pain. The conduct described by the applicant would be heinous and humiliating for anyone, irrespective of their condition. Moreover, the applicant endured repeated and sustained assaults over a number of days of questioning. Under these circumstances, the Court was satisfied that the physical and mental violence, considered as a whole, committed against the applicant's person caused "severe" pain and suffering and was particularly serious and cruel. Such conduct must be regarded as acts of torture for the purposes of Article 3 of the Convention. There had therefore been a violation of Article 3.

DEGRADING TREATMENT

Tyrer v United Kingdom (1979–80) 2 EHRR 1

The applicant and three other boys, having been caned at school for taking beer into school, assaulted the senior pupil who had reported them, occasioning actual bodily harm. Charged with assault, he pled guilty and was sentenced to three strokes of the birch. He was medically examined and found fit to be punished. The birching was carried out in a police station in the presence of his father and a doctor. He had to wait a considerable time for the doctor to arrive. He was made to take down his trousers and underpants and bend over a table; two policemen held him while the third administered the punishment. Pieces of the birch broke on the first stroke. Afterwards, his skin was raised but not cut and he was sore for about a week and a half afterwards.

He applied to the Commission whilst still under age, arguing on the basis of Article 3 that there had been torture or inhuman or degrading treatment or punishment or a combination of these. Once he attained majority, he declared that he wished to withdraw his application. Meanwhile, the Manx Government had begun the legislative procedure necessary to remove the offence of which the applicant had been convicted from the list of offences for which corporal punishment was available. The Government argued that the applicant's wish to withdraw the application and the legislative steps which were being taken should lead to the striking out of the case. The Commission declined to strike the case out since the case raised questions of a general character affecting the observance of the Convention. The Government further argued that such punishment did not outrage public opinion on the island.

Held that the declaration of an individual, who is not entitled to refer a case to the Court, could not entail the effects of a discontinuance and that legislation which is envisaged cannot be regarded as fact. In any event, the substance of the issue was whether judicial corporal punishment (for any offence) is consistent with the Convention. As to the merits, the applicant had not undergone suffering of the level inherent in the notion of torture as interpreted in *Ireland* v *United Kingdom*. Nor did his treatment reach such a level that it could be said to be "inhuman". For a punishment to be "degrading" and in breach of Article 3, the humiliation or debasement involved must attain a particular level and must in any event be other than the usual element of humiliation involved in judicial punishment. The assessment is relative and depends on all the circumstances and, in particular, on the nature and context of the punishment itself and the manner and method of its execution. The fact that public opinion was not outraged did not mean that the punishment was not degrading; indeed it might well be that it was the very element of degradation which caused the public to regard birching as an effective deterrent. The fact that it might be an effective deterrent did not mean that there was no breach of Article 3. Nor did the fact that it was an alternative to detention. The very nature of judicial corporal punishment is institutionalised violence, constituting an assault on precisely that which it is one of the main purposes of Article 3 to protect, namely a person's dignity and physical integrity and compounded by the whole aura of official procedure attending the punishment and the fact that those inflicting it were strangers. The applicant had been subjected to a punishment in which the element of humiliation attained the level inherent in the notion of "degrading punishment" and there was a breach of Article 3.

Campbell and Cosans v United Kingdom (1982) 4 EHRR 293

The case originated in two applications against the UK lodged by the mothers of children at state schools in Scotland. Mrs Campbell had sought from the education authority a guarantee that her son would not be subjected to corporal punishment. That guarantee was refused, although he was never in fact so punished. Mrs Cosan's 15-year-old son had refused to accept corporal punishment for a particular piece of misbehaviour and had been suspended from school as a result. After the suspension had lasted for some time, the corporal punishment was waived on the basis that the suspension had been punishment enough but it was made a condition of the boy's return to school that he would obey the rules, regulations and disciplinary requirements of the school. However, Mr and Mrs Cosans stipulated that if their son were to be readmitted to the school, he should not receive corporal punishment for any incident while he was a pupil. The education authority replied that this constituted a refusal to accept the aforesaid condition. Accordingly, the suspension was not lifted and his parents were warned that they might be prosecuted for failure to ensure his attendance at school. In the event, the boy never returned to school.

Mrs Campbell and Mrs Cosans claimed that, on account of the use of corporal punishment as a disciplinary measure in school, their sons were victims of a violation of Article 3.

Held that, provided it is sufficiently real and immediate, a mere threat of conduct prohibited by Article 3 may itself be in conflict with that provision. Thus, to threaten an individual with torture might in some circumstances constitute at least "inhuman treatment". Although the system of corporal punishment can cause a certain degree of apprehension in those who may be subject to it, the Court did not consider that the situation in which the applicants' sons found themselves amounted to "torture" or "inhuman treatment", within the meaning of Article 3: there was no evidence that they underwent suffering of the level inherent in these notions as they were interpreted in *Ireland* v *United Kingdom*. The *Tyrer* case indicated certain criteria concerning the notion of "degrading punishment". It followed from that judgment that "treatment" itself will not be "degrading" unless the person concerned has undergone—either in the eyes of others or in his own eyes—humiliation or debasement attaining a minimum level of severity. Corporal chastisement was traditional in Scottish schools and, indeed, appeared to be favoured by a large majority of parents.

Of itself, this was not conclusive of the issue before the Court for the threat of a particular measure is not excluded from the category of "degrading", within the meaning of Article 3, simply because the measure has been in use for a long time or even meets with general approval. However, particularly in view of the circumstances obtaining in Scotland, it was not established that pupils at a school where such punishment was used were, solely by reason of the risk of being subjected thereto, humiliated or debased in the eyes of others to the requisite degree or at all. As to whether the applicants' sons were humiliated or debased in their own eyes, the Court observed first that a threat directed to an exceptionally insensitive person may have no significant effect on him but nevertheless be incontrovertibly degrading; and conversely, an exceptionally sensitive person might be deeply affected by a threat that could be described as degrading only by a distortion of the ordinary and usual meaning of the word. In any event, in the case of these two children, the Court noted that it had not been shown by any means that they suffered any adverse psychological or other effects. The boy Cosans may well have experienced feelings of apprehension or disquiet when he came close to an infliction of punishment but such feelings are not sufficient to amount to degrading treatment, within the meaning of Article 3. No violation of Article 3 was established.

Costello-Roberts v United Kingdom (1995) 19 EHRR 112

The applicant was a seven-year-old pupil at an independent boarding preparatory school. The school operated a system whereby corporal punishment was administered upon acquisition of five demerit marks. The applicant received his fifth demerit mark for talking in the corridor. The other demerit marks were for similar conduct and for being a little late for bed on one occasion. Having discussed the matter with his colleagues, the headmaster decided that the only answer to the applicant's lack of discipline, about which he had received three warnings from the headmaster, was to give him three "whacks" on the bottom through his shorts with a rubber-soled gym shoe. He so informed the applicant. The punishment was administered by the headmaster three days later, eight days after the boy had received his fifth demerit mark. No other persons were present. In a letter to his mother postmarked 21 October, the boy wrote "come and picke me up I have had the wacke". He continued to write to her in some distress about the "slippering". The applicant's mother complained to the police but was told that there was no action they could take without any visible bruising on the child's buttocks.

The applicant alleged that the treatment to which he had been subjected had given rise to violations of Articles 3 and 8 of the Convention. Whilst conceding that the State exercised a limited degree of control and supervision over independent schools, such as the applicant's, the Government denied that they were directly responsible for every aspect of the way in which they were run; in particular, they assumed no function in matters of discipline.

Held that the responsibility of a State is engaged if a violation of one of the rights and freedoms defined in the Convention is the result of non-observance by that State of its obligation under Article 1 to secure those rights and freedoms in its domestic law to everyone within its jurisdiction. Functions relating to the internal administration of a school, such as discipline, cannot be said to be merely ancillary to the educational process. That a school's disciplinary system falls within the ambit of the right to education had been recognised in Article 28 of the United Nations Convention on the Rights of the Child 1989. Moreover, the State cannot absolve itself from responsibility by delegating its obligations to private bodies or individuals (such as independent schools). Accordingly, the treatment complained of, although it was the act of a headmaster of an independent school, was none the less such as might engage the responsibility of the UK under the Convention.

As was pointed out in *Tyrer*, in order for punishment to be "degrading" and in breach of Article 3, the humiliation or debasement involved must attain a particular level of severity and must in any event be other than that usual element of humiliation inherent in any punishment. Article 3, by expressly prohibiting "inhuman" and "degrading" punishment, implies that there is a distinction between such punishment and punishment more generally. The assessment of this minimum level of severity depends on all the circumstances of the case. Factors such as the nature and context of the punishment, the manner and method of its execution, its duration, its physical and mental effects and, in some instances, the sex, age and state of health of the victim must all be taken into account. Beyond the consequences to be expected from measures taken on a purely disciplinary plane, the applicant had adduced no evidence of any severe or long-lasting effects as a result of the treatment complained of. A punishment which does not occasion such effects may fall within the ambit of Article 3 provided that in the particular circumstances of the case it may be said to have reached the minimum threshold of severity required. While the Court had certain misgivings about the automatic nature of the punishment and the three-day wait before its imposition, it considered that minimum level of severity not to have been attained in this case. Accordingly, no violation of Article 3 had been established.

Article 3 provides the first point of reference in a case of punishment of this sort. Whilst the Court did not exclude the possibility that there might be circumstances in which Article 8 could be regarded as affording in relation to disciplinary measures a protection which goes beyond that given by Article 3, having regard to the purpose and aim of the Convention taken as a whole, and bearing in mind that the sending of a child to school necessarily involves some degree of interference with his or her private life, the Court considered that the treatment complained of by the applicant did not entail adverse effects for his physical or moral integrity sufficient to bring it within the scope of the prohibition contained in Article 8. While not wishing to be taken to approve in any way the retention of corporal punishment as part of the disciplinary regime of a school, the Court concluded that in the circumstances of this case there had been no violation of Article 8.

A v United Kingdom (1999) 27 EHRR 611

The applicant had, as a nine-year-old boy, been beaten repeatedly by his stepfather with a garden cane. The stepfather was prosecuted but was acquitted by the jury after a direction that reasonable chastisement was a defence. The Government conceded that there had been a breach of Article 3.

Held that the treatment of the applicant by his stepfather had been sufficiently severe to reach the level prohibited by Article 3. The State should be held responsible under the Convention, since children and other vulnerable individuals in particular were entitled to protection, in the form of effective deterrence, from such forms of ill-treatment. English law, which provided that the prosecution had to prove that an assault on a child went beyond the limits of reasonable punishment, had not provided adequate protection to the applicant. There was a breach of Article 3.

EXTRADITION AND DEPORTATION

Soering v United Kingdom (1989) 11 EHRR 439

The parents of the applicant's girlfriend were murdered in Virginia in March 1985. The applicant and his girlfriend disappeared together in October 1985 but were arrested in England in April 1986 in connection with a cheque fraud. Whilst in custody in England, the applicant made a statement in which he admitted the murders. The USA requested his extradition on charges, *inter alia*, of capital murder. After serving a prison sentence for the cheque fraud, the applicant was arrested pursuant to the extradition request. The UK sought an assurance that the death penalty, if imposed, would not be carried out. However, the only assurance which was forthcoming was that the prosecutor would inform the sentencing court that it was the wish of the UK that the death penalty should not be imposed. It emerged later that he himself intended to seek the death penalty. The applicant applied to the Commission on the basis that, notwithstanding the assurance given to the UK Government, there was a serious likelihood that he would be sentenced to death if extradited to the USA and that, having regard to the death row phenomenon, he would thereby be subjected to inhuman and degrading treatment and punishment contrary to Article 3.

Held that since Article 5.1(f) permits the lawful detention of a person against whom action is being taken with a view to extradition, no right not to be extradited as such is protected by the Convention. Nevertheless, in so far as a measure of extradition has consequences adversely affecting the enjoyment of a Convention right, it may, assuming the consequences are not too remote, attract the obligations of a contracting State under the relevant Convention guarantee. The issue was whether Article 3 could be applicable when the adverse consequences would be suffered outside the jurisdiction of the extraditing State as a result of treatment or punishment administered in the receiving State.

Article 1 sets a limit, notably territorial, on the reach of the Convention. The engagement undertaken by the Contracting State is confined to securing the listed rights and freedoms to persons within its own jurisdiction. The Convention does not govern the actions of States not party to it, nor does it purport to be a means of requiring the Convention States to impose Convention standards on other States. Article 1 cannot be read as justifying a general principle to the effect that, notwithstanding its extradition obligations, a contracting State cannot surrender an individual unless the conditions awaiting him in the country of destination are in full accord with each of the safeguards of the Convention. Nor can the beneficial purpose of extradition in preventing fugitive offenders from evading justice be ignored in determining the scope of application of the Convention and of Article 3 in particular.

The UK had no power over the arrangements in Virginia. Other international instruments, such as the 1984 UN Convention against Torture and other Cruel, Inhuman and Degrading Treatment or Punishment, specifically address the problem of removing a person to another jurisdiction where unwanted consequences may follow. However, these considerations cannot absolve the contracting parties from responsibility for all and any foreseeable consequences of extradition suffered outside their jurisdiction. In interpreting the Convention, regard must be had to its special character as a treaty for the collective enforcement of human rights and fundamental freedoms. Thus, the object and purpose of the Convention require that its provisions be interpreted and applied so as to make its safeguards practical and effective. Article 3 makes no provision for exceptions and derogation is not possible. This absolute prohibition on torture and on inhuman or degrading treatment or punishment shows that Article 3 enshrines one of the fundamental values of the democratic societies making up the Council of Europe. Article 3 of the UN Convention against Torture provides that no State shall extradite a person where there are substantial grounds for believing that he would be subjected to torture. But this does not mean that an essentially similar obligation is not already inherent in the general terms of Article 3 ECHR. It would not be compatible with the underlying values of the Convention if a Contracting State were knowingly to surrender a fugitive to another State where there were substantial grounds for believing that he would be in danger of being subjected to torture, however heinous the crime allegedly committed. In the Court's view, this inherent obligation not to extradite also extends to cases in which the fugitive would be faced in the receiving State by a real risk of exposure to inhuman or degrading treatment or punishment proscribed by Article 3.

What amounts to such treatment depends on all the circumstances of the case. Inherent in the whole of the Convention is a search for a fair balance between the demands of the general interest of the community and the requirements of the protection of the individual's fundamental rights. It is increasingly in the interest of all nations that suspected offenders who flee abroad should be brought to justice. The establishment of safe havens for fugitives would not only result in danger for the State obliged to harbour the fugitive but also tend to undermine the foundations of extradition. These considerations must be taken into account in the interpretation and application of the notions of inhuman and degrading treatment or punishment in extradition cases. In sum, the decision by a Contracting State to extradite a fugitive may give rise to an issue under Article 3, and hence engage the responsibility of that State under the Convention, where substantial grounds have been shown for believing that the person concerned, if extradited, faces a real risk of being subjected to torture or to inhuman or degrading treatment in the requesting country.

This involves an assessment of conditions in the requesting country against the standards of Article 3 of the Convention but there is no question of adjudicating on or establishing the responsibility of the receiving country, whether under general international law, under the Convention or otherwise. Any liability incurred is incurred by the Contracting State by reason of having taken action which has as a direct consequence the exposure of an individual to proscribed ill-treatment. Since it could not be said that the undertaking to inform the sentencing judge of the UK's position as regards the death penalty would eliminate the risk of that penalty being imposed, especially since the prosecutor proposed to seek that penalty, the likelihood of the feared exposure of the applicant to the death row phenomenon was such as to bring Article 3 into play.

Capital punishment is permitted under certain conditions by Article 2 of the Convention and it is only by Protocol 6, to which the UK was not then a party, that it is required to be abolished. That being so, and notwithstanding the virtual consensus in Western European legal systems that the death penalty is not consistent with regional standards of justice and the need to interpret the Convention as a living instrument, Article 3 cannot be read as prohibiting the death penalty as such. It can, however, have relevance to the manner in which it is imposed and carried out, the personal circumstances of the condemned person, disproportionality to the crime committed and the conditions of detention whilst awaiting execution.

A condemned prisoner in Virginia could expect to spend six to eight years on death row and the fact that most of that time would be a result of his taking advantage of all avenues of appeal did not alter the fact that he had to endure those conditions for many years and the anguish and mounting tension of living in the ever-present shadow of death. The applicant would be (necessarily) subject to a severe regime. He was young and suffering from disturbed mental health. The Secretary of State's decision to extradite the applicant to Virginia would, if implemented, give rise to a breach of Article 3.

Vilvarajah and Others v United Kingdom (1991) 14 EHRR 248

The five applicants were all Tamils who had sought asylum in the UK. Each of them had first hand experience of ill-treatment at the hands of the Sri Lankan security forces, though the UK Immigration Service noted that in each case this had been ill-treatment of an indiscriminate kind, not directed at them in particular. The Immigration Service therefore took the view that none of them had a well-founded fear of persecution in Sri Lanka and deported them to that country, though an Adjudicator under the Immigration Act 1971 concluded, in their appeals, that they did indeed have such a fear and that they were entitled to asylum. All had, however, been deported before their appeals were heard but after their applications for judicial review had ended in failure in the House of Lords. Some of them had experienced further ill-treatment on their return to Sri Lanka. Once the Adjudicator had found in their favour, all were allowed to return to the UK and their further applications for asylum were still under consideration when the Court considered their applications under ECHR. They applied to the Commission on the basis that their return to Sri Lanka constituted a breach of Article 3 and that there was also a breach of Article 13 in that they had no effective remedy in national law.

Held that the Court would apply three principles in assessing the risk of ill-treatment. First, it would assess the issue in the light of all the material placed before it or obtained *ex proprio motu*. Second, since the nature of the Contracting State's responsibility in such cases lies in the act of exposing an individual to the risk of ill-treatment, the existence of the risk must be assessed primarily with reference to the facts which were known or ought to have been known to the Contracting State at the time of the expulsion; though the Court was not precluded from having regard to information which came to light after the expulsion which might help in confirming or refuting the State's appreciation or the applicant's fears. Third, ill-treatment must reach a minimum level of severity before it falls within the scope of Article 3.

The Court's examination of the existence of a breach of Article 3 must be a rigorous one in view of the absolute character of the provision and the fact that it enshrines one of the fundamental values of democratic societies making up the Council of Europe. The evidence did not establish that the position of the applicants had been any worse than that of other young male Tamils. There was a possibility of ill-treatment but a mere possibility is not in itself sufficient to give rise to a breach of Article 3.

The Court attached importance to the knowledge and experience of the UK authorities in dealing with large numbers of asylum seekers from Sri Lanka, many of whom were granted leave to stay, and to the fact that the circumstances of the applicants had been considered in the light of a substantial body of material about the situation in Sri Lanka. Following the *Soering* case, the Court considered judicial review to be an effective remedy in such cases. The reasonableness of the decision could be reviewed and the UK court could rule the exercise of executive discretion unlawful. The UK court would have jurisdiction to quash a decision to send a fugitive to a country where there was a serious risk of inhuman or degrading treatment on the basis that in all the circumstances the decision was one which no reasonable Secretary of State could take. There was no breach of Article 3.

Chahal v United Kingdom (1996) 23 EHRR 413

The four applicants were members of the same family and were Sikhs. The first applicant had entered the UK illegally in 1971 in search of employment. In 1974 he applied to the Home Office to regularise his stay and on 10 December 1974 was granted indefinite leave to remain under the terms of an amnesty for illegal entrants who arrived before 1 January 1973. The second, third and fourth applicants were his wife and children. In March 1984, the first applicant was arrested by the Punjab police during a visit to India. He was taken into detention and held for 21 days, during which time he was, he contended, kept handcuffed in insanitary conditions, beaten to unconsciousness, electrocuted on various parts of his body and subjected to a mock execution. He was subsequently released without charge. He was able to return to the UK in May 1984, and had not visited India since.

In October 1985 Mr Chahal was detained under the Prevention of Terrorism (Temporary Provisions) Act 1984 on suspicion of involvement in a conspiracy to assassinate the Indian Prime Minister during an official visit to the UK. He was released for lack of evidence. In 1986 he was arrested and questioned twice because he was believed to be involved in a conspiracy to murder moderate Sikhs in the UK. On both occasions he was released without charge. Mr Chahal denied involvement in any of these conspiracies. In March 1986 he was charged with assault and affray following disturbances in London. He was convicted and imprisoned but the Court of Appeal quashed the two convictions on the grounds that Mr Chahal's appearance in court in handcuffs had been seriously prejudicial to him.

In August 1990 the Home Secretary decided that Mr Chahal ought to be deported because his continued presence in the UK was unconducive to the public good for reasons of national security and other reasons of a political nature, namely the international fight against terrorism. A notice of intention to deport was served and he was then detained for deportation purposes. He applied for asylum, claiming that if returned to India he had a well-founded fear of persecution.

The Home Secretary refused the request for asylum. In a letter to the applicant, he expressed the view that the latter's known support of Sikh separatism would be unlikely to attract the interest of the Indian authorities unless that support were to include acts of violence against India. He continued that he was

"not aware of any outstanding charges either in India or elsewhere against
[Mr Chahal] and on the account [Mr Chahal] has given of his political
activities, the Secretary of State does not accept that there is a reasonable
likelihood that he would be persecuted if he were to return to India. The
media interest in his case may be known by the Indian authorities and,
given his admitted involvement in an extremist faction of the ISYF, it is
accepted that the Indian Government may have some current and legitimate interest in his activities".

The Home Secretary did not consider that Mr Chahal's experiences in India
in 1984 had any continued relevance, since that had been a time of particularly
high tension in Punjab. In July 1991 the Home Secretary signed an order for
Mr Chahal's deportation.

In December 1991, the High Court quashed the refusal of asylum, finding
that the reasoning behind it was inadequate. The Court did not decide on the
validity of the deportation order. After further consideration, on 1 June 1992
the Home Secretary took a fresh decision to refuse asylum. He considered
that the breakdown of law and order in Punjab was due to the activities of
Sikh terrorists and was not evidence of persecution. Furthermore, he expressed
the view that, even if Mr Chahal were at risk of persecution, he posed a threat
to national security. The Home Secretary had sought and received an assurance from the Indian Government that, if the applicant were to be deported
to India, he would enjoy the same legal protection as any other Indian
citizen, and that he would have no reason to expect to suffer mistreatment of
any kind at the hands of the Indian authorities. The applicant complained
that his deportation to India would constitute a violation of Article 3 of the
Convention.

Held that Contracting States have the right, as a matter of well-established
international law and subject to their treaty obligations including the Convention, to control the entry, residence and expulsion of aliens. Moreover, it
had to be noted that the right to political asylum is not contained in either the
Convention or its Protocols. However, it is well established in the case law of
the Court that expulsion by a Contracting State may give rise to an issue
under Article 3, and hence engage the responsibility of that State under the
Convention, where substantial grounds have been shown for believing that
the person in question, if expelled, would face a real risk of being subjected to
treatment contrary to Article 3 in the receiving country. In these circumstances,
Article 3 implies the obligation not to expel the person in question to that
country. The crucial question was whether it had been substantiated that there
was a real risk that Mr Chahal, if expelled, would be subjected to treatment
prohibited by Article 3. Since he had not yet been deported, the material point
in time must be that of the Court's consideration of the case.

The Court was persuaded that, until mid-1994 at least, elements in the
Punjab police were accustomed to act without regard to the human rights of
suspected Sikh militants and were fully capable of pursuing their targets into
areas of India far away from Punjab. The evidence demonstrated that problems

still persisted in connection with the observance of human rights by the security forces in Punjab. The Court also attached significance to the fact that attested allegations of serious human rights violations have been levelled at the police elsewhere in India. The Court was not persuaded that the assurances obtained would provide Mr Chahal with an adequate guarantee of safety. The Court therefore found it substantiated that there was a real risk of Mr Chahal being subjected to treatment contrary to Article 3 if he was returned to India, so that deportation would breach Article 3. Having no reason to doubt that the respondent Government would comply with the judgment, the Court considered that it was not necessary to decide the hypothetical question whether, in the event of expulsion to India, there would also be a violation of the rights of all four applicants under Article 8 of the Convention.

Ahmed v Austria (1997) 24 EHRR 278

The applicant was a Somali citizen born in 1963, who obtained refugee status in Austria in November 1990 on the basis that he stated that his uncle had been an active member of the United Somali Congress ("the USC") and that his father and his brother, though not members of the USC, had assisted his uncle and been executed on that account in May 1990. Since then he and his family had been suspected of belonging to the USC and taking part in acts of rebellion. His car had been confiscated and he had been assaulted, as was evidenced by a still-visible scar on his arm. He had left Somalia through fear of being arrested and executed. However, in 1994, following his conviction for attempted robbery by striking a passer-by in the face and attempting to steal his wallet, his refugee status was revoked.

The revocation and consequent expulsion order went through several appeals but the final position of the Austrian authorities was that a refugee lost refugee status if he committed a "particularly serious crime" within the meaning of Article 33(2) of the Geneva Convention on the Status of Refugees 1951. The applicant had been found guilty of attempted robbery and, before that, had been convicted of criminal damage and of threatening behaviour. Although, taken separately, these offences did not represent any danger to society, taken together they nevertheless revealed a clear tendency to aggression. It could not be excluded, therefore, that the applicant might commit further offences in future, which made him a danger to society. He could not yet be regarded as integrated into Austrian society, as he had lived there for only four years and had been in prison since March 1993. Nor did he have family or other links with the country. As for his occupational activities, these did not require any particular qualification and could therefore also be carried on abroad. Moreover, the applicant had been unemployed at the time of his arrest.

In April 1995 the applicant asserted to the Austrian authorities that the situation in Somalia had deteriorated since his departure in 1990 and that he could not return to that country without risking his life. However, the

Federal Refugee Office declared the proposed expulsion of the applicant lawful. It took the view that, taken together, the offences he had committed revealed a tendency towards aggressive behaviour and even increasing aggressiveness, which did not stop short of violence against the person. It could not be excluded, therefore, that Mr Ahmed might commit other offences in future, so that he constituted a danger to the community. That being the case, even the fact that he risked persecution in the event of his return to Somalia could not make his deportation to that country unlawful.

He applied to the Commission on the basis that his expulsion to Somalia would expose him to a serious risk of being subjected to treatment contrary to Article 3 of the Convention there. The Commission declared the application admissible and expressed the opinion that there would be a violation of Article 3 if the applicant were to be deported to Somalia.

Held that Contracting States have the right, as a matter of well-established international law and subject to their treaty obligations including the Convention, to control the entry, residence and expulsion of aliens. The right to political asylum is not contained in either the Convention or its Protocols. However, the expulsion of an alien by a Contracting State may give rise to an issue under Article 3, and hence engage the responsibility of that State under the Convention, where substantial grounds have been shown for believing that the person in question, if expelled, would face a real risk of being subjected to treatment contrary to Article 3 in the receiving country. In these circumstances, Article 3 implies the obligation not to expel the person in question to that country.

Article 3, which enshrines one of the fundamental values of democratic societies, prohibits in absolute terms torture or inhuman or degrading treatment or punishment, irrespective of the victim's conduct. Unlike most of the substantive clauses of the Convention and of Protocols Nos 1 and 4, Article 3 makes no provision for exceptions and no derogation from it is permissible even in the event of a public emergency threatening the life of the nation. Accordingly, the activities of the individual in question, however undesirable or dangerous, cannot be a material consideration. The protection afforded by Article 3 is thus wider than that provided by Article 33 of the United Nations 1951 Convention on the Status of Refugees. In granting the applicant refugee status in the first place, the Austrian authorities had found credible his allegations that his activities in an opposition group and the general situation in Somalia gave grounds to fear that, if he returned there, he would be subjected to persecution.

Although the applicant lost his refugee status two years later, this was solely due to his criminal conviction; the consequences of expulsion for the applicant were not taken into account. In order to assess the risks in the case of an expulsion that has not yet taken place, the material point in time must be that of the Court's consideration of the case. Although the historical position is of interest in so far as it may shed light on the current situation and its likely evolution, it is the present conditions which are decisive. Somalia was still in a state of civil war and fighting was going on between a number of clans vying with each other for control of the country. There was no indication that the dangers to which the applicant would have been exposed in 1992 had ceased to exist or that any public authority would be able to protect him; indeed the Government did not contest the applicant's submission that there was no observable improvement of the situation in his country. On the contrary, they explained that the Austrian authorities had decided to stay execution of the expulsion in issue because they too considered that, as matters stood, Mr Ahmed could not return to Somalia without being exposed to the risk of treatment contrary to Article 3.46. That being the case, the Court reached the same conclusion, which was not invalidated by the applicant's criminal conviction. It followed that the applicant's deportation to Somalia would breach Article 3 of the Convention for as long as he faced a serious risk of being subjected there to torture or inhuman or degrading treatment.

ARTICLE 4

THE RIGHT NOT TO BE HELD IN SLAVERY OR REQUIRED TO PERFORM FORCED LABOUR

1. No one shall be held in slavery or servitude.
2. No one shall be required to perform forced or compulsory labour.
3. For the purpose of this Article the term "forced or compulsory labour" shall not include:
   a. any work required to be done in the ordinary course of detention imposed according to the provisions of Article 5 of this Convention or during conditional release from such detention;
   b. any service of a military character or, in case of conscientious objectors in countries where they are recognised, service exacted instead of compulsory military service;
   c. any service exacted in case of an emergency or calamity threatening the life or well-being of the community;
   d. any work or service which forms part of normal civic obligations.

Forced or Compulsory Labour

Van der Mussele v Belgium (1983) 6 EHRR 163

The applicant was a Belgian avocat (lawyer). During his time as a pupil avocat, the Legal Advice and Defence Office of the Antwerp Bar appointed him, pursuant to the Judicial Code, to defend one Njie Ebrima, a Gambian national, who had been arrested two days earlier on suspicion of theft and of dealing in, and possession of, narcotics. The applicant acted for Mr Ebrima throughout the proceedings and estimated that he devoted from 17 to 18 hours to the matter. The Legal Advice and Defence Office then notified the applicant that it was releasing him from the case and that because of Mr Ebrima's lack of resources no assessment of fees and disbursements could be made against him.

The applicant called in question his appointment by the Antwerp Legal Advice and Defence Office to assist Mr Ebrima; he complained, not of this appointment as such, but because a refusal to act would have made him liable to sanctions and because he had not been entitled to any remuneration or reimbursement of his expenses. In his submission, these circumstances gave rise both to "forced or compulsory labour" contrary to Article 4.2.

Held that Article 4 does not define what is meant by "forced or compulsory labour" and no guidance on this point was to be found in the various Council of Europe documents relating to the preparatory work of the European Convention. It was evident that the authors of the European Convention—following the example of the authors of Article 8 of the draft International Covenant on Civil and Political Rights—based themselves, to a large extent, on an earlier treaty of the International Labour Organisation, namely Convention No. 29 concerning Forced or Compulsory Labour. Under that Convention, States undertook "to suppress the use of forced or compulsory labour in all its forms within the shortest possible period". The main aim of the Convention was originally to prevent the exploitation of labour in colonies, which were still numerous at that time. The Court would take into account the ILO Conventions—which were binding on nearly all the Member States of the Council of Europe, including Belgium. Under the ILO Convention, the term "forced or compulsory labour" meant "all work or service which is exacted from any person under the menace of any penalty and for which the said person has not offered himself voluntarily". This definition could provide a starting point for interpretation of Article 4 of the European Convention. However, sight should not be lost of that Convention's special features or of the fact that it is a living instrument to be read "in the light of the notions currently prevailing in democratic States".

It was common ground between those appearing before the Court that the services rendered by Mr Van der Mussele to Mr Ebrima amounted to "labour" for the purposes of Article 4.2. It was true that the English word "labour" is often used in the narrow sense of manual work, but it also bears the broad meaning of the French word "travail" and it is the latter that should be adopted in the present context. It remained to be ascertained whether there was "forced or compulsory" labour. The first of these adjectives brought to mind the idea of physical or mental constraint, a factor that was certainly absent in the present case. As regards the second adjective, it could not refer just to any form of legal compulsion or obligation. For example, work to be carried out in pursuance of a freely negotiated contract could not be regarded as falling within the scope of Article 4 on the sole ground that one of the parties had undertaken with the other to do that work and would be subject to sanctions if he did not honour his promise. What there has to be is work exacted under the menace of a penalty and also performed against the will of the person concerned, that is work for which he had not offered himself voluntarily.

Had Mr Van der Mussele refused without good reason to defend Mr Ebrima, his refusal would not have been punishable with any sanction of a criminal character. On the other hand, he would have run the risk of having his name struck off the roll of pupils or his application for entry on the register of avocats being rejected. These prospects were sufficiently daunting to be capable of constituting "the menace of [a] penalty", having regard both to the use of the adjective "any" in the definition and to the standards adopted by the ILO on this point.

It had next to be determined whether the applicant "offered himself voluntarily" for the work in question. Mr Van der Mussele undoubtedly chose to enter the profession of avocat appreciating that under its rules he would, in accordance with a long-standing tradition, be bound on occasions to render his services free of charge and without reimbursement of his expenses. However, he had to accept this requirement, whether he wanted to or not, in order to become an avocat and his consent was determined by the normal conditions of exercise of the profession at the relevant time. Nor should it be overlooked that what he gave was an acceptance of a legal regime of a general character. The applicant's prior consent, without more, did not, therefore, warrant the conclusion that the obligations incumbent on him in regard to legal aid did not constitute compulsory labour for the purposes of Article 4.2 of the Convention. Account must necessarily also be taken of other factors.

The Commission had expressed the opinion that for there to be forced or compulsory labour, for the purposes of Article 4.2, two cumulative conditions have to be satisfied: not only must the labour be performed by the person against his or her will, but either the obligation to carry it out must be "unjust" or "oppressive" or its performance must constitute "an avoidable hardship", in other words be "needlessly distressing" or "somewhat harassing". The Court, however, preferred to adopt a different approach. Having held that there existed a risk comparable to "the menace of [a] penalty" and then that relative weight was to be attached to the argument regarding the applicant's "prior consent", the Court would have regard to all the circumstances of the case in the light of the underlying objectives of Article 4 of the European Convention in order to determine whether the service required of Mr Van der Mussele fell within the prohibition of compulsory labour. This could be so in the case of a service required in order to gain access to a given profession, if the service imposed a burden which was so excessive or disproportionate to the advantages attached to the future exercise of that profession, that the service could not be treated as having been voluntarily accepted beforehand; this could apply, for example, in the case of a service unconnected with the profession in question.

The structure of Article 4 was informative on this point. Paragraph 3 is not intended to "limit" the exercise of the right guaranteed by paragraph 2, but to "delimit" the very content of this right, for it forms a whole with paragraph 2 and indicates what "the term 'forced or compulsory labour' shall not include". The four subparagraphs of paragraph 3, notwithstanding their diversity, are grounded on the governing ideas of the general interest, social solidarity and what is in the normal or ordinary course of affairs. The final subparagraph which excludes "any work or service which forms part of normal civil obligations" from the scope of forced or compulsory labour, was of particular significance in the context of the present case.

The services to be rendered by Mr van der Mussele did not fall outside the ambit of the normal activities of an avocat; they differed from the usual work of members of the Bar neither by their nature nor by any restriction of freedom in the conduct of the case. A compensatory factor was to be found in the advantages attaching to the profession, including the exclusive right of audience and of representation enjoyed by avocats in Belgium as in several other countries. In addition, the services in question contributed to the applicant's professional training in the same manner as did the cases in which he had to act on the instructions of paying clients of his own or of his pupil-master. They gave him the opportunity to enlarge his experience and to increase his reputation. In this respect, a certain degree of personal benefit went hand in hand with the general interest which was foremost. Moreover, the obligation to which Mr Van der Mussele objected constituted a means of securing for Mr Ebrima the benefit of Article 6.3 of the Convention. To this extent, it was founded on a conception of social solidarity and could not be regarded as unreasonable. By the same token, it was an obligation of a similar order to the "normal civic obligations" referred to in Article 4.3(d).

Finally, the burden imposed on the applicant was not disproportionate. According to his own evidence, acting for Mr Ebrima accounted for only 17 or 18 hours of his working time. Even if one added to this the other cases in which he was appointed to act during his pupillage, it could be seen that there remained sufficient time for performance of his paid work.

While remunerated work may also qualify as forced or compulsory labour, the lack of remuneration and of reimbursement of expenses constitutes a relevant factor when considering what is proportionate or in the normal course of affairs. In this connection, it was noteworthy that the respective laws of numerous Contracting States have evolved or were evolving, albeit in varying degrees, towards the assumption by the public purse of the cost of paying lawyers or trainee lawyers appointed to act for indigent litigants. At the relevant time, the state of affairs complained of undoubtedly caused Mr Van der Mussele some prejudice by reason of the lack of remuneration and of reimbursement of expenses, but that prejudice went hand in hand with advantages and had not been shown to be excessive. The applicant did not have a disproportionate burden of work imposed on him and the amount of expenses directly occasioned by the cases in question was relatively small. The applicant had voluntarily entered the profession of avocat with knowledge of the practice complained of. This being so, a considerable and unreasonable imbalance between the aim pursued—to qualify as an avocat—and the obligations undertaken in order to achieve that aim would alone be capable of warranting the conclusion that the services exacted of Mr Van der Mussele in relation to legal aid were compulsory despite his consent. No such imbalance was disclosed by the evidence before the Court, notwithstanding the lack of remuneration and of reimbursement of expenses. There was thus no compulsory labour for the purposes of Article 4.2 of the Convention.

WORK BY PRISONERS

Van Droogenbroeck v Belgium (1982) 4 EHRR 443

The applicant was a recidivist who was sentenced to repeated terms of imprisonment following repeated offences and failures to co-operate with the terms on which he was, from time to time, released. Various attempts were made to rehabilitate him but he was reluctant to do the work which formed part of the rehabilitative process. The Recidivists Board, charged with considering whether he could be released, found that he had saved nothing during his detention and that he had no prospects of finding work outside prison. It, therefore, declined to recommend his release unless and until he had saved 12,000 BF through his prison work. The applicant complained, *inter alia*, that he had been held in servitude and forced to work, contrary to Article 4 of the Convention.

Held that Article 4 authorises, in paragraph 3(a), work required to be done in the ordinary course of detention which has been imposed, as was here the case, in a manner that does not infringe paragraph 1 of Article 5. Moreover, the work which the applicant was asked to do did not go beyond what was "ordinary" in this context since it was calculated to assist him in reintegrating himself into society and had as its legal basis provisions which found an equivalent in certain other Member States of the Council of Europe. Accordingly, the Belgian authorities did not fail to observe the requirements of Article 4.

ARTICLE 5

LIBERTY AND SECURITY OF PERSON

1. Everyone has the right to liberty and security of person. No one shall be deprived of his liberty save in the following cases and in accordance with a procedure prescribed by law:
    a. the lawful detention of a person after conviction by a competent court;
    b. the lawful arrest or detention of a person for non- compliance with the lawful order of a court or in order to secure the fulfilment of any obligation prescribed by law;
    c. the lawful arrest or detention of a person effected for the purpose of bringing him before the competent legal authority on reasonable suspicion of having committed an offence or when it is reasonably considered necessary to prevent his committing an offence or fleeing after having done so;
    d. the detention of a minor by lawful order for the purpose of educational supervision or his lawful detention for the purpose of bringing him before the competent legal authority;
    e. the lawful detention of persons for the prevention of the spreading of infectious diseases, of persons of unsound mind, alcoholics or drug addicts or vagrants;
    f. the lawful arrest or detention of a person to prevent his effecting an unauthorised entry into the country or of a person against whom action is being taken with a view to deportation or extradition.
2. Everyone who is arrested shall be informed promptly, in a language which he understands, of the reasons for his arrest and of any charge against him.
3. Everyone arrested or detained in accordance with the provisions of paragraph 1.c of this article shall be brought promptly before a judge or other officer authorised by law to exercise judicial power and shall be entitled to trial within a reasonable time or to release pending trial. Release may be conditioned by guarantees to appear for trial.
4. Everyone who is deprived of his liberty by arrest or detention shall be entitled to take proceedings by which the lawfulness of his detention shall be decided speedily by a court and his release ordered if the detention is not lawful.

5. Everyone who has been the victim of arrest or detention in contravention of the provisions of this article shall have an enforceable right to compensation.

DEPRIVATION OF LIBERTY

Engel and Others v The Netherlands (1979–80) 1 EHRR 647

All the applicants were, when submitting their applications to the Commission, conscript soldiers serving in different non-commissioned ranks in The Netherlands armed forces. On separate occasions, various penalties had been passed on them by their respective commanding officers for offences against military discipline. The applicants had appealed to the complaints officer and finally to the Supreme Military Court which in substance confirmed the decisions challenged but, in two cases, reduced the punishment imposed.

Dr Engel had been serving as a sergeant in The Netherlands Army. He was a candidate for the vice-presidency of the Conscripts' Association and on 12 March he submitted a request to his company commander for leave of absence on 17 March in order to attend a general meeting in Utrecht at which the elections were to be held. He did not, however, mention his candidature. Subsequently, he became ill and stayed home under the orders of his doctor who gave him sick leave until 18 March and authorised him to leave the house on 17 March. On 16 March, the company commander had a talk with the battalion commander and it was agreed that no decision should be taken regarding the above-mentioned request pending further information from the applicant who had given no notice of his absence or return. However, on the following day a check was made at the applicant's home and it was discovered that he was not there. In fact, he had gone to the meeting where he had been elected vice-president. On 18 March he returned to his unit and on the same day his company commander punished him with four days' light arrest for having been absent from his residence on the previous day.

The applicant considered this penalty a serious interference with his personal affairs in that it prevented him from properly preparing himself for his doctoral examination at the University of Utrecht which had been fixed for 24 March. According to the applicant, he had made several attempts on 18 March to speak to an officer on this point but without success. Believing that under the army regulations non-commissioned officers were allowed to serve their light arrest at home, he left the barracks in the evening and spent the night at home. However, the next day his company commander imposed a penalty of three days' aggravated arrest on him for having disregarded his first punishment.

He again left the barracks in the evening and went home. He was arrested on Saturday 20 March by the military police and provisionally detained in strict arrest for about two days. On Monday 22 March his company commander imposed a penalty of three days' strict arrest for having disregarded his two previous punishments. The execution of these punishments was suspended by ministerial decision in order to permit the applicant to take his doctoral examination, which he passed. Moreover, on 21, 22 and 25 March the applicant complained to the complaints officer about the penalties imposed on him by the company commander. On 5 April the complaints officer decided, after having heard the parties, that the first punishment of four days' light arrest should be reduced to a reprimand, the second punishment of three days' aggravated arrest to three days' light arrest, and the third punishment of three days' strict arrest to two days' strict arrest. The complaints officer further decided that the punishment of two days' strict arrest should be deemed to have been served from 20 to 22 March, during his provisional arrest. The Supreme Military Court in due course confirmed the contested decision.

Mr van der Wiel, at the time of his application to the Commission, was serving as a corporal in The Netherlands Army. One morning he was about four hours late for duty. His car had broken down during his weekend leave and he had had it repaired before returning to his unit instead of taking the first train. On these grounds, the acting company commander imposed a penalty of four days' light arrest on the applicant. The following day he revised the grounds to include a reference that the applicant had not previously requested the commander's leave of absence. The applicant complained about his punishment to the complaints officer and, following the rejection by the complaints officer of his complaint appealed to the Supreme Military Court, which quashed the complaints officer's decision but confirmed the punishment of four days' light arrest imposed on the applicant on the original grounds.

Mr de Wit, at the time of his application to the Commission, was serving as a private in The Netherlands Army. He was sentenced to committal to a disciplinary unit for a period of three months by his company commander on the grounds that he had driven a jeep in an irresponsible manner over uneven territory at a speed of about 40 to 50 km per hour; that he had not immediately carried out his mission, namely to pick up a lorry at a certain place, but that he had only done so after having been stopped, asked about his orders and summoned to execute them at once; that, in view of his repeatedly irregular behaviour and failure to observe discipline, he had previously been warned about the possibility of being committed to a disciplinary unit. The complaints officer confirmed the punishment while altering slightly the grounds stated. The applicant appealed to the Supreme Military Court which, without mentioning the applicant's previous behaviour, reduced the punishment to 12 days' aggravated arrest, which sentence was executed thereafter.

Mr Dona was serving as a private in The Netherlands Army at the time of his application to the Commission. As editor of a journal called "Alarm", published in stencilled form by the Conscripts' Association, he had collaborated in particular in the preparation of an issue of that journal which was considered to be inconsistent with military discipline. The applicant was sentenced by his superior to three months' committal to a disciplinary unit for having taken part in the publication and distribution of a writing tending to undermine discipline.

Mr Schul, a private in The Netherlands Army at the time of his application to the Commission, was also an editor of the journal "Alarm". The facts regarding his case were identical to those of Mr Dona's except that his punishment initially amounted to four months' committal to a disciplinary unit owing to the additional aggravating circumstance of his participation in the publication of an "Information Bulletin" for new recruits, the distribution of which had been prohibited by reason of its negative content. Mr Dona and Mr Schul appealed to the Supreme Military Court, which ordered release of the applicants after they had promised to accept the Court's judgment on the merits of the case, to comply therewith in the future and, while proceedings were pending against them, to refrain from any activity in connection with the compilation and distribution of written material the contents of which could be deemed to be at variance with military discipline. According to the applicants, this undertaking was given only *in extremis* as there was no legal remedy available to terminate their interim custody.

The Supreme Military Court subsequently confirmed Mr Dona's committal to a disciplinary unit for three months, reduced Mr Schul's committal from four to three months and modified slightly the grounds for punishment in both cases. A few days after the dismissal of their appeals, Mr Dona and Mr Schul were sent to the Disciplinary Barracks in order to serve their punishment. They were not allowed to leave this establishment during the first month; moreover, they were both locked up in a cell during the night.

Held that the Convention applies in principle to members of the armed forces and not only to civilians. It specifies in Articles 1 and 14 that "everyone within (the) jurisdiction" of the Contracting States is to enjoy "without discrimination" the rights and freedoms set out in Section I. Nevertheless, when interpreting and applying the rules of the Convention in the present case, the Court had to bear in mind the particular characteristics of military life and its effects on the situation of individual members of the armed forces. A system of military discipline that by its very nature implies the possibility of placing on certain of the rights and freedoms of the members of these forces limitations incapable of being imposed on civilians. The existence of such a system does not in itself run counter to the obligations of States under the Convention.

Military discipline, none the less, does not fall outside the scope of Article 5.1. The list of deprivations of liberty set out therein is exhaustive, as is shown by the words "save in the following cases". A disciplinary penalty or measure may in consequence constitute a breach of Article 5.1.

In proclaiming the "right to liberty", paragraph 1 of Article 5 is contemplating individual liberty in its classic sense, that is to say the physical liberty of the person. Its aim is to ensure that no one should be dispossessed of this liberty in an arbitrary fashion. It does not concern mere restrictions upon liberty of movement. In order to determine whether someone has been "deprived of his liberty" within the meaning of Article 5, the starting point must be his concrete situation. Military service, as encountered in the Contracting States, does not on its own in any way constitute a deprivation of liberty under the Convention, since it is expressly sanctioned in Article 4.3(b). In addition, rather wide limitations upon the freedom of movement of the members of the armed forces are entailed by reason of the specific demands of military service so that the normal restrictions accompanying it do not come within the ambit of Article 5 either.

Each State is competent to organise its own system of military discipline and enjoys in the matter a certain margin of appreciation. The bounds that Article 5 requires the State not to exceed are not identical for servicemen and civilians. A disciplinary penalty or measure which, on analysis, unquestionably would be deemed a deprivation of liberty were it to be applied to a civilian may not possess this characteristic when imposed upon a serviceman. Nevertheless, such penalty or measure does not escape the terms of Article 5 when it takes the form of restrictions that clearly deviate from the normal conditions of life within the armed forces of the Contracting States. In order to establish whether this is so, account should be taken of a whole range of factors such as the nature, duration, effects and manner of execution of the penalty or measure in question.

No deprivation of liberty resulted from the three and four days' light arrest awarded respectively against Mr Engel and Mr van der Wiel. Although confined during off-duty hours to their dwellings or to military buildings or premises, as the case may be, servicemen subjected to such a penalty were not locked up and continue to perform their duties. They remained, more or less, within the ordinary framework of their army life. Aggravated arrest differed from light arrest on one point alone: in off-duty hours, soldiers served the arrest in a specially designated place which they could not leave in order to visit the canteen, cinema or recreation rooms, but they were not kept under lock and key. Consequently, neither did the Court consider as a deprivation of liberty the 12 days' aggravated arrest complained of by Mr de Wit.

Strict arrest differed from light arrest and aggravated arrest in that non-commissioned officers and ordinary servicemen served it by day and by night were locked in a cell and were accordingly excluded from the performance of their normal duties. It thus involved deprivation of liberty. It followed that the provisional arrest inflicted on Mr Engel in the form of strict arrest had the same character despite its short duration.

Committal to a disciplinary unit represented the most severe penalty under military disciplinary law in The Netherlands. Privates condemned to this penalty following disciplinary proceedings were not separated from those so sentenced by way of supplementary punishment under the criminal law, and during a month or more they were not entitled to leave the establishment. The committal lasted for a period of three to six months; this was considerably longer than the duration of the other penalties, including strict arrest which could be imposed for one to 14 days. Furthermore, it appeared that Mr Dona and Mr Schul spent the night locked in a cell. For these various reasons, the Court considered that in the circumstances deprivation of liberty occurred.

Subparagraph (a) of Article 5.1 permits the "lawful detention of a person after conviction by a competent court". The Court noted that this provision makes no distinction based on the legal character of the offence of which a person has been found guilty. It applies to any "conviction" occasioning deprivation of liberty pronounced by a "court", whether the conviction be classified as criminal or disciplinary by the internal law of the State in question. The Supreme Military Court constituted a court from the organisational point of view. Doubtless its four military members are not irremovable in law, but like the two civilian members they enjoyed the independence inherent in the Convention's notion of a "court". It did not appear from the file in the case that Mr Dona and Mr Schul failed to receive before the Supreme Military Court the benefit of adequate judicial guarantees under Article 5.1(a), an autonomous provision whose requirements are not always co-extensive with those of Article 6. The penalty inflicted was imposed and then executed "lawfully" and "in accordance with a procedure prescribed by law". It did not contravene Article 5.

The provisional arrest of Mr Engel for its part clearly did not come within the ambit of subparagraph (a) of Article 5.1. The Government had derived argument from subparagraph (b) in so far as it permits "lawful arrest or detention" intended to "secure the fulfilment of any obligation prescribed by law". The Court considered that the words "secure the fulfilment of any obligation prescribed by law" concern only cases where the law permits the detention of a person to compel him to fulfil a specific and concrete obligation which he has until then failed to satisfy. A wide interpretation would entail consequences incompatible with the notion of the rule of law from which the whole Convention draws its inspiration. It would justify, for example, administrative internment meant to compel a citizen to discharge, in relation to any point whatever, his general duty of obedience to the law. In fact, Mr Engel's provisional arrest was in no way designed to secure the fulfilment in the future of such an obligation. The measure was a preparatory stage of military disciplinary proceedings and was thus situated in a punitive context. Perhaps this measure also had on occasions the incidental object or effect of inducing a member of the armed forces to comply henceforth with his obligations, but only with great contrivance could it be brought under subparagraph (b). The measure really more resembled that spoken of in subparagraph (c) of Article 5.1. However, in the present case it did not fulfil one of the requirements of that provision since the detention of Mr Engel had not been "effected for the purpose of bringing him before the competent legal authority". Neither was Mr Engel's provisional arrest "lawful" within the meaning of Article 5.1 in so far as it exceeded the maximum period of 24 hours laid down by domestic law. The backdating of the subsequently imposed sentence did not cure this breach.

As to Article 6, all the Contracting States make a distinction of long-standing, albeit in different forms and degrees, between disciplinary proceedings and criminal proceedings. For the individuals affected, the former usually offer substantial advantages in comparison with the latter, for example, as concerns the sentences passed. Disciplinary sentences, in general less severe, do not appear in the person's criminal record and entail more limited consequences. It might nevertheless be otherwise; moreover, criminal proceedings are ordinarily accompanied by fuller guarantees.

In order to determine whether there is a criminal charge, for the purposes of Article 6, it is first necessary to know whether the provision(s) defining the offence charged belong, according to the legal system of the respondent State, to criminal law, disciplinary law or both concurrently. This, however, provides no more than a starting point. The indications so afforded have only a formal and relative value and must be examined in the light of the common denominator of the respective legislation of the various Contracting States. The very nature of the offence is a factor of greater import. When a serviceman finds himself accused of an act or omission allegedly contravening a legal rule governing the operation of the armed forces, the State may in principle employ against him disciplinary law rather than criminal law. The "charges" against Mr de Wit, Mr Dona and Mr Schul did indeed come within the "criminal" sphere since their aim was the imposition of serious punishments involving deprivation of liberty. Article 6 was, therefore, applicable but the proceedings in the Supreme Military Court satisfied all its requirements.

Guzzardi v Italy (1980) 3 EHRR 333

The applicant was arrested in February 1973 and charged with being an accomplice in an abduction. Under the Italian Code of Criminal Procedure the applicant's detention on remand could not continue for more than two years: it thus had to terminate in February 1975 at the latest. He was taken under police escort to the island of Asinara, which is long, narrow and rugged. The island as a whole covers 50 sq km but the area reserved for persons in compulsory residence represented a fraction of not more than 2.5 sq km. This area was bordered by the sea, roads and a cemetery; there was no fence to mark out the perimeter. About nine-tenths of the island was occupied by a prison. The principal settlement on the island, Cala d'Oliva, housed nearly all of the island's permanent population—approximately 200 people; this population comprises the prison staff and their families, schoolteachers, a priest, the post office employees and a few tradesmen. In January 1975, the Milan Regional Court directed that the applicant should be placed under special supervision for three years and required to live on the island. The significant additional measures applied to the applicant are summarised below. The island was removed from the list of places authorised for such compulsory residence part way through the applicant's stay there. Ultimately, in December 1979, the applicant was convicted and sentenced to 18 years' imprisonment.

Held that in proclaiming the "right to liberty", paragraph 1 of Article 5 is contemplating the physical liberty of the person; its aim is to ensure that no one should be dispossessed of this liberty in an arbitrary fashion. The paragraph is not concerned with mere restrictions on liberty of movement. In order to determine whether someone has been "deprived of his liberty" within the meaning of Article 5 the starting point must be his concrete situation and account must be taken of a whole range of criteria such as the type, duration, effects and manner of implementation of the measure in question. The difference between deprivation of and restriction upon liberty is none the less merely one of degree or intensity, and not one of nature or substance. Whilst the area around which the applicant could move far exceeded the dimensions of a cell and was not bounded by any physical barrier, it covered no more than a tiny fraction of an island to which access was difficult and about nine-tenths of which was occupied by a prison. Mr Guzzardi was housed in part of the hamlet of Cala Reale which consisted mainly of the buildings of a former medical establishment which were in a state of disrepair or even dilapidation, a carabinieri station, a school and a chapel. He lived there principally in the company of other persons subjected to the same measure and of policemen. The permanent population of Asinara resided almost entirely at Cala d'Oliva, which Mr Guzzardi could not visit, and would appear to have made hardly any use of its right to go to Cala Reale. Consequently, there were few opportunities for social contacts available to the applicant other than with his near family, his fellow "residents" and the supervisory staff.

Supervision was carried out strictly and on an almost constant basis. Thus, Mr Guzzardi was not able to leave his dwelling between 10 pm and 7 am without giving prior notification to the authorities in due time. He had to report to the authorities twice a day and inform them of the name and number of his correspondent whenever he wished to use the telephone. He needed the consent of the authorities for each of his trips to Sardinia or the mainland. Such trips were rare and made under the strict supervision of the carabinieri. He was liable to punishment by "arrest" if he failed to comply with any of his obligations. More than 16 months elapsed between his arrival at Cala Reale and his departure.

It was not possible to speak of "deprivation of liberty" on the strength of any one of these factors taken individually, but cumulatively and in combination they certainly raised an issue of categorisation from the viewpoint of Article 5. On balance, the case was to be regarded as one involving deprivation of liberty. It remained to be determined whether the situation was one of those, exhaustively listed in Article 5.1, in which the Contracting States reserve the right to arrest or detain individuals. The Government relied on Article 5.1(e), maintaining that mafiosi like the applicant were "vagrants". However, the applicant's way of life at the time, as disclosed by the documentary evidence filed, was in no way consonant with the ordinary meaning of the word "vagrant", this being the meaning that has to be utilised for Convention purposes. In addition to vagrants, subparagraph (e), refers to persons of unsound mind, alcoholics and drug addicts. The reason why the Convention allows the latter individuals, all of whom are socially maladjusted, to be deprived of their liberty is not only that they have to be considered as occasionally dangerous for public safety but also that their own interests may necessitate their detention. One cannot, therefore, deduce from the fact that Article 5 authorises the detention of vagrants that the same or even stronger reasons apply to anyone who may be regarded as still more dangerous. Nor was the detention of the applicant within any of the other subparagraphs of Article 5.1. There was a breach of Article 5.

Amuur v France (1996) 22 EHRR 533

The applicants were Somali nationals who arrived at Paris-Orly Airport on board a Syrian Airlines flight from Damascus (Syria), where they had stayed for two months after travelling there via Kenya. They asserted that they had fled Somalia because, after the overthrow of the regime of President Siyad Barre, their lives were in danger and several members of their family had been murdered. However, the airport and border police refused to admit them to French territory, on the ground that their passports had been falsified, and held them in the international zone at the airport for 20 days. They were then returned to Syria without being able to make an effective application to the authority having jurisdiction to rule on their refugee status. They complained that holding them thus constituted deprivation of liberty contrary to Article 5.1(f) of the Convention.

Held that Contracting States have the undeniable sovereign right to control aliens' entry into and residence in their territory. However, this right must be exercised in accordance with the provisions of the Convention, including Article 5. In proclaiming the right to liberty, paragraph 1 of Article 5 contemplates the physical liberty of the person; its aim is to ensure that no one should be dispossessed of this liberty in an arbitrary fashion. On the other hand, it is not in principle concerned with mere restrictions on the liberty of movement; such restrictions are governed by Article 2 of Protocol No. 4. In order to determine whether someone has been "deprived of his liberty" within the meaning of Article 5, the starting point must be his concrete situation, and account must be taken of a whole range of criteria such as the type, duration, effects and manner of implementation of the measure in question.

The difference between deprivation of and restriction upon liberty is merely one of degree or intensity, and not one of nature or substance. Holding aliens in the international zone does indeed involve a restriction upon liberty, but one which is not in every respect comparable to that which obtains in centres for the detention of aliens pending deportation. Such confinement, accompanied by suitable safeguards for the persons concerned, is acceptable only in order to enable States to prevent unlawful immigration while complying with their international obligations, particularly under the 1951 Geneva Convention Relating to the Status of Refugees and the European Convention on Human Rights. States' legitimate concern to foil the increasingly frequent attempts to circumvent immigration restrictions must not deprive asylum-seekers of the protection afforded by these Conventions.

Such holding should not be prolonged excessively, otherwise there would be a risk of it turning a mere restriction on liberty—inevitable with a view to organising the practical details of the alien's repatriation or, where he has requested asylum, while his application for leave to enter the territory for that purpose is considered—into a deprivation of liberty. In that connection, account should be taken of the fact that the measure is applicable not to those who have committed criminal offences but to aliens who, often fearing for their lives, have fled from their own country. Although by the force of circumstances the decision to order holding must necessarily be taken by the administrative or police authorities, its prolongation requires speedy review by the courts, the traditional guardians of personal liberties. Above all, such confinement must not deprive the asylum-seeker of the right to gain effective access to the procedure for determining refugee status.

The Government had argued that the applicants had at all times the option of bringing their confinement to an end simply by leaving France but the mere fact that it is possible for asylum-seekers to leave voluntarily the country where they wish to take refuge cannot exclude a restriction on liberty, the right to leave any country, including one's own, being guaranteed, moreover, by Protocol No. 4 to the Convention. Furthermore, this possibility becomes theoretical if no other country offering protection comparable to the protection they expect to find in the country where they are seeking asylum is inclined or prepared to take them in. Sending the applicants back to Syria only became possible, apart from the practical problems of the journey, following negotiations between the French and Syrian authorities. The assurances of the latter were dependent on the vagaries of diplomatic relations, in view of the fact that Syria was not bound by the Geneva Convention relating to the Status of Refugees.

Holding the applicants in the transit zone of Paris-Orly Airport was equivalent in practice, in view of the restrictions suffered, to a deprivation of liberty. Article 5.1 was, therefore, applicable to the case. In laying down that any deprivation of liberty must be effected "in accordance with a procedure prescribed by law", Article 5.1 primarily requires any arrest or detention to have a legal basis in domestic law. However, these words do not merely refer back to domestic law; like the expressions "in accordance with the law" and "prescribed by law" in the second paragraphs of Articles 8 to 11, they also relate to the quality of the law, requiring it to be compatible with the rule of law, a concept inherent in all the Articles of the Convention. In order to ascertain whether a deprivation of liberty has complied with the principle of compatibility with domestic law, it falls to the Court to assess not only the legislation in force in the field under consideration, but also the quality of the other legal rules applicable to the persons concerned. Quality in this sense implies that where a national law authorises deprivation of liberty—especially in respect of a foreign asylum-seeker—it must be sufficiently accessible and precise, in order to avoid all risk of arbitrariness. These characteristics are of fundamental importance with regard to asylum-seekers at airports, particularly in view of the need to reconcile the protection of fundamental rights with the requirements of States' immigration policies.

From 9 to 29 March 1992 the applicants were in the situation of asylum-seekers whose application had not yet been considered. At the material time none of the French legal texts allowed the ordinary courts to review the conditions under which aliens were held or, if necessary, to impose a limit on the administrative authorities as regards the length of time for which they were held. They did not provide for legal, humanitarian and social assistance, nor did they lay down procedures and time-limits for access to such assistance so that asylum-seekers like the applicants could take the necessary steps. The French legal rules in force at the time, as applied in the present case, did not sufficiently guarantee the applicants' right to liberty. There had accordingly been a breach of Article 5.1.

PROCEDURE PRESCRIBED BY LAW

Bozano v France (1986) 9 EHRR 297

The applicant had been the subject of an extradition request to France from Italy following his conviction in absence in the Italian courts of abduction, attempted extortion, murder and various offences of indecency. The French Court refused extradition on the ground that trial in absence for serious offences without any requirement to hold a retrial in the presence of the accused was incompatible with French public policy. He was released from French custody. About a month later, in Limoges, where he lived, three plain clothes policemen forced him into an unmarked car. He was taken to police headquarters and served with a deportation order which required him to leave France. He was told that it was out of the question that he should be brought before the Appeals Board charged with dealing with such cases and was instead placed in a car and taken, not to the Spanish border (which was the closest) but to the Swiss border, 12 hours and several hundred kilometres away. From Switzerland he was extradited to Italy and there incarcerated to serve the life sentence which had been imposed on him in his absence. He applied to the Commission *inter alia* on the basis that he had been deprived of his liberty and security of person in the absence of any of the reasons contemplated by Article 5 ECHR, so that there had been a breach of Article 5.1.

Held that there was a distinction between the situation in which State agents conduct themselves unlawfully in good faith and that in which the State authorities act knowingly in contravention of domestic law and in such a way as to abuse their powers. In the former case, the unlawfulness of the act will not necessarily invalidate any further measures taken thereafter. In the instant case, although the lawfulness of what had been done had not been determined conclusively, the Court had the gravest doubts about whether

French legal requirements had been satisfied. "Lawfulness", in any event, also implies absence of arbitrariness and in this respect the Court attached great weight to the circumstances in which the applicant had been forcibly conveyed to the Swiss border. Viewing the circumstances as a whole, the Court concluded that the applicant's deprivation of liberty was neither lawful nor compatible with the right to security of person and there had been a breach of Article 5.1.

Erkalo v The Netherlands (89/1997/873/1085)

In June 1990 the Groningen Regional Court convicted the applicant of two counts of manslaughter. It sentenced him to five years' imprisonment, to be followed by placement at the disposal of the Government with committal to a psychiatric institution. Due to his disturbed mental state the authorities decided to place the applicant in a psychiatric institution for a two-year period commencing 3 July 1991. The time-limit within which it was open to the prosecuting authorities to apply for an extension of the applicant's placement at the Government's disposal following the initial period was due to expire on 3 June 1993. By letter of 17 May 1993 the Public Prosecutor informed the applicant that he had prepared a request for a one-year extension of the applicant's placement. Approximately three and a half months after receiving the Public Prosecutor's letter, the applicant told the staff of the psychiatric institution that he had received no further information concerning the extension of his placement. The Public Prosecutor's application was eventually found in the Regional Court's archives on 7 September 1993—where it had been filed by mistake—and was forwarded to the registry the following day. The Court examined the Public Prosecutor's application on 15 September 1993. Although it agreed with the applicant's submission that the application was out of time and, therefore, in principle no longer admissible, it none the less declined to order his release, considering that it was imperative in the public interest that he remain in detention. No appeal lay against this decision.

Held that the lawfulness of the extension of the applicant's placement under domestic law is not in itself decisive. It must also be established that his detention during the period under consideration was in conformity with the purpose of Article 5.1 of the Convention, namely to protect individuals from arbitrariness. Since the request of the public prosecutor was not received at the registry of the court until 8 September 1993, for 82 days the placement of the applicant was not based on any judicial decision. Although all the relevant authorities were aware that the applicant's placement was due to expire, none of them took any steps to verify whether the request had been received at the registry of the Groningen Regional Court and whether a date had been fixed for a hearing on the request. The detention of the applicant from 3 July to 23 September 1993 was not compatible with the purpose of Article 5 and was for that reason unlawful.

Steel and Others v United Kingdom (1999) 28 EHRR 603

The applicants were all arrested in the course of demonstrations—one against grouse shooting, one against road building and three against the sale of arms. The first two (whose protests had been disruptive) refused to be bound over and were sentenced to short periods of imprisonment. The proceedings against the other three (whose protest had been peaceful) were dropped. They all complained that their arrests and detention had not been "prescribed by law" as required by Article 5.1 of the Convention and had amounted to disproportionate interferences with their right to freedom of expression in breach of Article 10.

Held that the expression "lawful" requires *inter alia* full compliance with domestic law and also that the applicable domestic law be formulated with sufficient precision to allow the citizen—if need be with legal advice—to foresee to a reasonable degree the legal consequences of any given action. The concept of breach of the peace had been clarified by the English courts to the extent that it was sufficiently established that a breach of the peace was committed only when a person caused harm, or appeared likely to cause harm, to persons or property or acted in a manner the natural consequence of which was to provoke others to violence. It was clear that English law allowed a person to be arrested if he or she caused a breach of the peace or was reasonably feared to be likely to cause one.

Under the Convention system the interpretation and application of domestic law was principally a task for the national courts. However, since failure to comply with domestic law entails a breach of Article 5.1, the Court could and should exercise a power of review. Having examined the evidence before it, it found no cause to doubt that the police had been justified in fearing that the first and second applicants' behaviour, if persisted in, might provoke others to violence. However, it found that the protest of the third, fourth and fifth applicants had been entirely peaceful and did not involve any behaviour which could have justified the police in fearing that a breach of the peace was likely to be caused. For this reason, in the absence of any national decision on the question, it found that the arrest of these three applicants and their detention for seven hours had not been lawful, either in terms of English law or Article 5.1 of the Convention. There had, therefore, been no violation of Article 5.1 of the Convention in respect of the arrest and initial detention of the first and second applicants, but there had been a violation in respect of the arrest and detention of the third, fourth and fifth applicants.

The Court recalled that the first and second applicants were ordered to agree to be bound over to keep the peace and be of good behaviour. When they refused, they were committed to prison. This detention fell within the scope of Article 5.1(b) of the Convention: detention for non-compliance with the order of a court. The Court had to consider whether the detention was lawful, including whether the national law was formulated with sufficient precision. In this respect, it was satisfied that the applicants could reasonably have foreseen that, if they acted in a manner the natural consequence of which was to provoke others to violence, they might be ordered to be bound over to keep the peace, and that if they refused to be bound over, they might be committed to prison.

The Court also assessed whether the binding over orders applied to the applicants were specific enough for the purposes of Article 5.1(b). It noted that the orders were expressed in rather vague and general terms. However, it considered that, given the context, it must have been sufficiently clear to the applicants that they were being asked to agree to refrain from causing further, similar, breaches of the peace in the ensuing 12 months. Having found no evidence of any failure to comply with English law, the Court held that there had been no violation of Article 5.1 in respect of the detention of the first and second applicants for refusing to be bound over.

LAWFUL ARREST OR DETENTION FOR THE PURPOSE OF BRINGING BEFORE THE COMPETENT LEGAL AUTHORITY

Brogan and Others v United Kingdom (1988) 11 EHRR 117

All four applicants were arrested in September or October 1984 under section 12 of the Prevention of Terrorism (Temporary Provisions) Act 1984. All of the applicants were informed by the arresting officer that they were being arrested under section 12 of the 1984 Act and that there were reasonable grounds for suspecting them to have been involved in the commission, preparation or instigation of acts of terrorism connected with the affairs of Northern Ireland. They were cautioned that they need not say anything, but that anything they did say might be used in evidence. On the day following his arrest, each applicant was informed by police officers that the Secretary of State for Northern Ireland had agreed to extend his detention by a further five days under section 12(4) of the 1984 Act. They were detained for periods between four days and six hours and six days and sixteen and a half hours. Each was questioned about a particular terrorist offence and about his suspected membership of the IRA (or, in one case, the Irish National Liberation Army). All maintained silence. None of the applicants was brought before a judge or other officer authorised by law to exercise judicial power, nor were any of them charged after their release.

The applicants all claimed that their arrest and detention were not justified under Article 5.1 of the Convention and that there had also been breaches of, *inter alia*, paragraphs 2 and 3 of that Article. The complaint under Article 5.2 was subsequently withdrawn but the applicants attempted to reinstate it before the Court.

Held that the scope of the Court's jurisdiction was determined by the Commission's decision declaring the originating application admissible. As a result of the express withdrawal of the claim under paragraph 2, the Commission discontinued its examination of the admissibility of this complaint. To have permitted the applicants to resuscitate this complaint before the Court would have been to circumvent the machinery established for the examination of petitions under the Convention and so the allegation that there had been a breach of Article 5.2 could not be entertained.

The Court, having taken notice of the growth of terrorism in modern society, had already recognised the need, inherent in the Convention system, for a proper balance between the defence of the institutions of democracy in the common interest and the protection of individual rights.

There was no dispute that the applicants' arrest and detention were "lawful" under Northern Ireland law and, in particular, "in accordance with a procedure prescribed by law". The applicants argued that the deprivation of liberty they suffered by virtue of section 12 of the 1984 Act failed to comply with Article 5.1(c) on the ground that they were not arrested on suspicion of an "offence", nor was the purpose of their arrest to bring them before the competent legal authority. Under the first head of argument, the applicants maintained that their arrest and detention were grounded on suspicion, not of having committed a specific offence, but rather of involvement in unspecified acts of terrorism, something which did not constitute a breach of the criminal law in Northern Ireland and could not be regarded as an "offence" under Article 5.1(c). However, section 14 of the 1984 Act defined terrorism as "the use of violence for political ends", which includes "the use of violence for the purpose of putting the public or any section of the public in fear". The same definition of acts of terrorism had (in *Ireland* v *United Kingdom*) already been found by the Court to be "well in keeping with the idea of an offence". In addition, all of the applicants were questioned within a few hours of their arrest about their suspected involvement in specific offences and their suspected membership of proscribed organisations. Accordingly, the arrest and subsequent detention of the applicants were based on a reasonable suspicion of commission of an offence within the meaning of Article 5.1(c).

Article 5.1(c) also requires that the purpose of the arrest or detention should be to bring the person concerned before the competent legal authority. The Government and the Commission had argued that such an intention was present and that if sufficient and usable evidence had been obtained during the police investigation that followed the applicants' arrest, they would undoubtedly have been charged and brought to trial. The applicants contested these arguments and referred to the fact that they were neither charged nor brought before a court during their detention. No charge had necessarily to follow an arrest under section 12 of the 1984 Act and the requirement under the ordinary law to bring the person before a court had been made inapplicable to detention under this Act. In the applicants' contention, this was, therefore, a power of administrative detention exercised for the purpose of gathering information, as the use in practice of the special powers corroborated.

The Court considered that the fact that the applicants were neither charged nor brought before a court did not necessarily mean that the purpose of their detention was not in accordance with Article 5.1(c). The existence of such a purpose must be considered independently of its achievement and sub-paragraph (c) of Article 5.1 does not presuppose that the police should have obtained sufficient evidence to bring charges, either at the point of arrest or while the applicants were in custody. Such evidence may have been unobtainable or, in view of the nature of the suspected offences, impossible to produce in court without endangering the lives of others. There was no reason to believe that the police investigation in this case was not in good faith or that the detention of the applicants was not in-tended to further that investigation by way of confirming or dispelling the concrete suspicions which grounded their arrest. Had it been possible, the police would, it could be assumed, have laid charges and the applicants would have been brought before the competent legal authority. Their arrest and detention must, therefore, be taken to have been effected for the purpose specified in paragraph 1(c) and so there had been no violation of Article 5.1.

Under the 1984 Act, a person arrested under section 12 on reasonable suspicion of involvement in acts of terrorism might be detained by police for an initial period of 48 hours, and, on the authorisation of the Secretary of State for Northern Ireland, for a further period or periods of up to five days. The applicants noted that a person arrested under the ordinary law of Northern Ireland must be brought before a Magistrates' Court within 48 hours and that under the ordinary law in England and Wales the maximum period of detention permitted without charge was four days, judicial approval being required at the 36-hour stage. The Commission, in its report, cited its established case law to the effect that a period of four days in cases concerning ordinary criminal offences, and of five days in exceptional cases, could be considered compatible with the requirement of promptness in Article 5.3. The Commission concluded that the periods of four days and six hours (Mr McFadden) and four days and eleven hours (Mr Tracey) did satisfy the requirement of promptness, whereas the periods of five days and eleven hours (Mr Brogan) and six days and sixteen and a half hours (Mr Coyle) did not.

The fact that a detained person is not charged or brought before a court does not in itself amount to a violation of the first part of Article 5.3. No violation of Article 5.3 can arise if the arrested person is released "promptly" before any judicial control of his detention would have been feasible. If the arrested person is not released promptly, he is entitled to a prompt appearance before a judge or judicial officer. The assessment of "promptness" has to be made in the light of the object and purpose of Article 5, which enshrines a fundamental human right, namely the protection of the individual against arbitrary interferences by the State with his right to liberty. Judicial control of interferences by the executive with the individual's right to liberty is an essential feature of the guarantee embodied in Article 5.3, which is intended to minimise the risk of arbitrariness.

The obligation expressed in English by the word "promptly" and in French by the word "aussitôt" is clearly distinguishable from the less strict requirement in the second part of paragraph 3 ("reasonable time") and even from that in paragraph 4 of Article 5 ("speedily"). The term "promptly" also occurs in the English text of paragraph 2 where the French text uses the words "dans le plus court délai". "Promptly" in paragraph 3 may be understood as having a broader significance than "aussitôt", which literally means immediately. Thus, confronted with versions of a law-making treaty which are equally authentic but not exactly the same, the Court must interpret them in a way that reconciles them as far as possible and is most appropriate in order to realise the aim and achieve the object of the treaty. The use in the French text of the word "aussitôt", with its constraining connotation of immediacy, confirms that the degree of flexibility attaching to the notion of "promptness" is limited, even if the attendant circumstances can never be ignored for the purposes of the assessment under paragraph 3. Whereas promptness is to be assessed in each case according to its special features, the significance to be attached to those features can never be taken to the point of impairing the very essence of the right guaranteed by Article 5, paragraph 3, that is to the point of effectively negativing the State's obligation to ensure a prompt release or a prompt appearance before a judicial authority.

The investigation of terrorist offences undoubtedly presents the authorities with special problems. Subject to the existence of adequate safeguards, the context of terrorism in Northern Ireland had the effect of prolonging the period during which the authorities might, without violating Article 5.3, keep a person suspected of serious terrorist offences in custody before bringing him before a judge or other judicial officer. The difficulties of judicial control over decisions to arrest and detain suspected terrorists might affect the manner of implementation of Article 5.3, for example, in calling for appropriate procedural precautions in view of the nature of the suspected offences. However, they could not justify dispensing altogether with "prompt" judicial control. In the Court's view, even the shortest of the four periods of detention, namely the four days and six hours spent in police custody by Mr McFadden, fell outside the strict constraints as to time permitted by the first part of Article 5.3. To attach such importance to the special features of this case as to justify so lengthy a period of detention without appearance before a judge or other judicial officer would be an unacceptably wide interpretation of the plain meaning of the word "promptly". An interpretation to this effect would import into Article 5.3 a serious weakening of a procedural guarantee to the detriment of the individual and would entail consequences impairing the very essence of the right protected by this provision. The Court thus had to conclude that none of the applicants was either brought "promptly" before a judicial authority or released "promptly" following his arrest. The undoubted fact that the arrest and detention of the applicants were inspired by the legitimate aim of protecting the community as a whole from terrorism was not on its own sufficient to ensure compliance with the specific requirements of Article 5.3. There had thus been a breach of Article 5.3 in respect of all four applicants.

Fox, Campbell and Hartley v United Kingdom (1990) 13 EHRR 157

The first and second applicants had criminal records for terrorist offences. They were stopped by the police in Belfast and taken to a police station, where a full search of the vehicle in which they were travelling was carried out. Twenty-five minutes after their arrival at the police station, they were formally arrested under section 11(1) of the Northern Ireland (Emergency Provisions) Act 1978 on the basis that the arresting officer suspected them of being terrorists. They were also told that they could be detained for up to 72 hours. They were taken to another police station, where they were separately interviewed by the police on the same day between 8.15 pm and 10.00 pm. During their detention, they were asked about their suspected involvement that day in intelligence gathering and courier work for the Provisional IRA. According to the Government, the information underlying the suspicion against them was already known to the police when they stopped their car. No charges were brought against either applicant and they were released after being detained for around 44 hours.

The third applicant was arrested at his home. He was informed at the time of his arrest that he was being arrested under section 11(1) of the 1978 Act as he was suspected of being a terrorist. In particular, he was suspected of involvement in a kidnapping incident which had taken place earlier that month. He was taken to a police station and interviewed there by the police between 11.05 am and 12.15 pm. No charges were brought against him. He was released after 30 hours and 15 minutes in detention. All three applicants complained, *inter alia*, that their arrest and detention were not justified under Article 5.1 of the Convention and that there had also been a breach of Article 5.2. The applicants did not dispute that their arrest was "lawful" under Northern Ireland law for the purposes of this provision and, in particular, "in accordance with a procedure prescribed by law". They did, however, argue that they had not been arrested and detained on "reasonable" suspicion of having committed an offence and that section 11(1) of the 1978 Act, which provided that "any constable may arrest without warrant any person whom he suspects of being a terrorist" was itself in direct conflict with Article 5.1(c) in that it did not contain any requirement of reasonableness. They further agreed with the Commission's opinion that their arrests had not been shown on the facts to have been based on reasonable suspicion. Finally, they maintained that the purpose of their arrest was not to bring them before the "competent legal authority" but rather to gather information without necessarily intending to charge them with a criminal offence.

Held that the Court had already recognised, in the context of the campaign of terrorism waged in Northern Ireland, the need, inherent in the Convention system, for a proper balance between the defence of the institutions of democracy in the common interest and the protection of individual rights. It would, therefore, take into account the special nature of terrorist crime and the exigencies of dealing with it, as far as was compatible with the applicable provisions of the Convention in the light of their particular wording and its overall object and purpose. The "reasonableness" of the suspicion on which an arrest must be based forms an essential part of the safeguard against arbitrary arrest and detention which is laid down in Article 5.1(c). Having a "reasonable suspicion" presupposes the existence of facts or information which would satisfy an objective observer that the person concerned may have committed the offence. What may be regarded as "reasonable" will, however, depend upon all the circumstances. In this respect, terrorist crime falls into a special category. Because of the attendant risk of loss of life and human suffering, the police are obliged to act with utmost urgency in following up all information, including information from secret sources. Further, the police may frequently have to arrest a suspected terrorist on the basis of information which is reliable but which cannot, without putting in jeopardy the source of the information, be revealed to the suspect or produced in court to support a charge. In view of the difficulties inherent in the investigation and prosecution of terrorist-type offences in Northern Ireland, the "reasonableness" of the suspicion justifying such arrests could not always be judged according to the same standards as are applied in dealing with conventional crime. Nevertheless, the exigencies of dealing with terrorist crime could not justify stretching the notion of "reasonableness" to the point where the essence of the safeguard secured by Article 5.1(c) is impaired.

Article 5.1(c) should not be applied in such a manner as to put disproportionate difficulties in the way of the police authorities of the Contracting States in taking effective measures to counter organised terrorism. It followed that the Contracting States could not be asked to establish the reasonableness of the suspicion grounding the arrest of a suspected terrorist by disclosing the confidential sources of supporting information or even facts which would be susceptible of indicating such sources or their identity. Nevertheless, the Court must be enabled to ascertain whether the essence of the safeguard afforded by Article 5.1(c) has been secured. Consequently, the respondent Government had to furnish at least some facts or information capable of satisfying the Court that the arrested person was reasonably suspected of having committed the alleged offence. This was all the more necessary where, as in the present case, the domestic law did not require reasonable suspicion but set a lower threshold by merely requiring honest suspicion. The Court accepted that the arrest and detention of each of the applicants was based on a bona fide suspicion that he or she was a terrorist, and that each of them was questioned during his or her detention about specific terrorist acts of which he or she was suspected. The fact that Mr Fox and Ms Campbell both had previous convictions for acts of terrorism connected with the IRA, although it could reinforce a suspicion linking them to the commission of terrorist-type offences, could not form the sole basis of a suspicion justifying their arrest in 1986, some seven years later; and the fact that all the applicants, during their detention, were questioned about specific terrorist acts, did no more than confirm that the arresting officers had a genuine suspicion that they had been involved in those acts, but it could not satisfy an objective observer that the applicants may have committed these acts. These elements on their own were insufficient to support the conclusion that there was "reasonable suspicion".

The Government had not provided any further material on which the suspicion against the applicants was based. Their explanations, therefore, did not meet the minimum standard set by Article 5.1(c) for judging the reasonableness of a suspicion for the arrest of an individual. There had, then, been a breach of Article 5.1 and it was not necessary to go into the question of the purpose of the applicants' arrests.

As to Article 5.2, the purpose of the guarantee is to ensure that any person arrested must be told, in simple, non-technical language that he can understand the essential legal and factual grounds for his arrest, so as to be able, if he sees fit, to apply to a court to challenge its lawfulness in accordance with Article 5.4. Whilst this information must be conveyed "promptly" it need not be related in its entirety by the arresting officer at the very moment of the arrest. Whether the content and promptness of the information conveyed were sufficient is to be assessed in each case according to its special features.

Within a few hours of their arrests all of the applicants were interrogated by the police about their suspected involvement in specific criminal acts and their suspected membership of proscribed organisations. There was no ground to suppose that these interrogations were not such as to enable the applicants to understand why they had been arrested. The reasons why they were suspected of being terrorists were thereby brought to their attention during their interrogation. Intervals of a few hours could not be regarded as falling outside the constraints of time imposed by the notion of promptness in Article 5.2.

RELEASE PENDING TRIAL

Wemhoff v Federal Republic of Germany (1979–80) 1 EHRR 55

The applicant, a broker, was arrested in November 1961 for offences of breach of trust. His detention on remand was ordered because it was feared, for particular reasons, that, if left at liberty, he would abscond and attempt to suppress evidence. His trial on charges of extremely complex financial crime, opened in November 1964 and lasted until 7 April 1965, when he was convicted and sentenced to imprisonment. He sought provisional release unsuccessfully pending his appeal.

His appeal against conviction failed. He complained that his Article 5.3 right to be brought to trial within a reasonable time or released pending trial had been violated. The Court had also to consider his Article 6.1 right to a hearing of the charge against him within a reasonable time.

Held that comparison of the English and French versions of Article 5.3 in light of the object of the treaty indicated that the Article 5.3 protection against unduly long detention on remand continues up to delivery of judgment (and not merely the commencement of the trial) but not to the determination of any appeal because detention after conviction is separately authorised by Article 5.1.

The reasonableness of an accused person's detention must be assessed in each case according to its particular features. The national judicial authorities will have given reasoned judgments in ordering continued detention and the Court must judge whether those reasons show that detention was not unreasonably prolonged. Where the only reason for continued detention is the fear that the accused will abscond, release must be ordered if sufficient guarantees of attendance can be obtained. In this case the accused's conduct had indicated that he would not have been prepared to furnish such guarantees. The exceptional length of the investigation and trial were justified by the exceptional complexity of the case and the right of an accused person in detention to have his case conducted with particular expedition must not stand in the way of full clarification of the facts in issue, the giving to defence and prosecution all facilities for putting forward their evidence and the pronouncing of judgment only after careful reflection. There was no breach of Article 5.3. As to Article 6.1, since the period before trial relevant for that purpose coincided with that of detention, which had been held to be justified, there was, *a fortiori*, no breach of Article 6.1.

Neumeister v Austria (1979–80) 1 EHRR 91

The applicant was arrested in February 1961 in connection with a complex tax fraud. He was released in May 1961 but rearrested and detained on remand in July 1961 after statements made by a co-accused during a confrontation procedure worsened his position. The basis for continued detention was that there was a risk of flight: the fraud involved a large amount of money so heavy punishment was to be anticipated, another accused had already absconded, the confrontation had made continued denial untenable and the applicant intended to travel abroad on holiday. The Regional Appeal Court, which dealt with the applicant's requests for liberation after hearing the prosecutor but in the absence of the defence, considered that the deposit of security would not be sufficient to dispel the danger. The investigation continued with the applicant in detention. He filed his application with the Commission in July 1963. For three months in the summer of 1963 no investigative steps were taken. The applicant was provisionally released in September 1964. The trial opened in November 1964. In June 1965, after 102 days of hearing, the completion of the trial was postponed indefinitely to allow further investigation to take place.

The Commission Report was adopted in May 1966. The trial resumed in December 1967 and was expected to last for four to six months. The Court had to rule on the Government's argument that the period after the filing of the application with the Commission should be left out of account, as not being the subject of any application. It had also to consider whether the length of detention on remand breached Article 5.3, whether the length of the proceedings breached Article 6.1 and whether the determination of applications for release in the absence of the defence breached Articles 5.4 and 6.1.

Held that the period after filing the application was relevant because it was the situation of which the applicant complained and not isolated acts. The danger of flight could not be evaluated solely on the basis of the foregoing considerations. Other factors, especially those relating to the character of the person involved, his morals, home, occupation, assets, family ties and links with the country in which he is being prosecuted may either confirm the danger of flight or make it appear too small to justify detention pending trial. The danger of flight decreases with the passage of time because of the probability that time spent on remand will count towards the sentence. In the applicant's circumstances the taking of guarantees should not have been dismissed as ineffective. The amount of any guarantees is to be fixed by reference to the circumstances of the accused person, at a level which will act as a deterrent to any wish to abscond, and not by reference to the amount of the loss for which he is alleged to be responsible. There was a violation of Article 5.3.

As regards Article 6.1, that more than seven years had elapsed since the laying of charges without any determination of them having yet been made indicated an exceptionally long period which in most cases should be considered as exceeding a reasonable time. Moreover, the period of inaction in 1963 and general lack of progress with the investigation gave rise to serious disquiet. However, the case was of extraordinary complexity and the Austrian authorities could not be held responsible for difficulties in getting evidence from abroad. Severance of the applicant's case from those of his co-accused might have accelerated the procedure but would not have been compatible with the good administration of justice. Concern for speed cannot dispense the judges from taking every measure likely to throw truth or falsehood on the charges. There was no breach of Article 6.1.

Stogmüller v Austria (1979–80) 1 EHRR 155

The applicant was a money lender, arrested in 1958 for fraud and usury. He was released provisionally after one month and eighteen days on an undertaking to inform the court of any change of address. After his release, he took flying lessons and made international flights. He continued to manage his business. He was rearrested in August 1961, it being said that he had travelled abroad without the permission of the court and that he had committed further offences. He was remanded in custody until August 1963 when he was released on a large security. In 1968 he was convicted of several offences and sentenced to four and a half years' imprisonment, his time in detention on remand counting towards that total. The Court had to decide whether the detention on remand exceeded the reasonable time laid down in Article 5.3.

Held that Article 5.3 requires special diligence in the conduct of the prosecution of persons detained in custody but that it is not feasible to translate the concept of reasonable time into a fixed period. Following *Neumeister* and *Wemhoff*, the grounds on which the national judicial authorities acted are to be considered. In this case the danger of further offending was not made out. The danger of absconding does not arise just because it is possible or easy for a person to cross the frontier. Rather, there must be a whole set of circumstances, particularly, the heavy sentence to be expected or the accused's particular distaste of detention, or the lack of well-established ties in the country, which give reason to suppose that the consequences and hazards of flight will seem to him to be a lesser evil than continued imprisonment. Such circumstances were not made out in this case. There was a breach of Article 5.3.

Matznetter v Austria (1979–80) 1 EHRR 198

The applicant was a severely disabled man, arrested in May 1963 on charges of abetting bankruptcy and aggravated fraud. He made several applications for release but these were rejected on the grounds that he was likely to re-offend and likely to abscond. He was, however, released in June 1965, when a medical report stated that he was no longer fit to be detained. He had, whilst in custody, lodged his application under the Convention. The investigation continued after his release and he went on trial at the beginning of 1967. He was convicted of certain offences and sentenced to seven years' imprisonment, the period on remand counting towards that total. The Court had to decide whether the period on remand had exceeded the reasonable time permitted by Article 5.3.

Held that initial concerns about the danger of absconding were justified, the applicant having foreign connections, having transferred money out of the country and having been apprehended only after a chase and in company with another accused who was in possession of her passport and a large amount of money. As to the danger of repetition of offences, it was proper for the Austrian courts to have taken account of the "very prolonged continuation of reprehensible activities, the huge extent of the loss sustained by the victims and the wickedness of the person charged". As at the date of the application the detention had not exceeded a reasonable time. Whilst thereafter information was laid before the Austrian courts which would, together with a sufficient security, have been enough to dispel the danger of absconding, there remained the danger of repetition of offending. Granted the detention had been relatively prolonged but the unusual length of the investigation was justified by the exceptional complexity of the case.

Letellier v France (1991) 14 EHRR 83

The applicant was charged with securing the contract killing of her husband. She was remanded in custody. In support of her application for release, she asserted that she possessed all the necessary guarantees that she would appear for trial: her home, the business (which she ran single-handed) and her eight children, some of whom were still dependent on her. On 24 December 1985 the investigating judge ordered her release subject to court supervision. However, on appeal by the public prosecutor, the indictments division of the Paris Court of Appeal set aside the order on 22 January 1986, declaring that it would thereafter exercise sole jurisdiction on questions concerning the detention. As a result, the applicant, who had been released on 24 December 1985, returned to prison on 22 January 1986. Her repeated further applications for release and appeals were unsuccessful. She was eventually tried and convicted. She was sentenced to three years' imprisonment for being an accessory to murder. The applicant claimed that the length of her detention on remand had violated Article 5.3.

Held that the period to be taken into consideration began on the date on which the applicant was remanded in custody and ended with the judgment of the Assize Court, less the period during which the applicant was released subject to court supervision. It therefore lasted two years and nine months. It falls in the first place to the national judicial authorities to ensure that, in a given case, the pre-trial detention of an accused person does not exceed a reasonable time. To this end they must examine all the facts arguing for or against the existence of a genuine requirement of public interest justifying, with due regard to the principle of the presumption of innocence, a departure from the rule of respect for individual liberty and set them out in their decisions on the applications for release. It was essentially on the basis of the reasons given in these decisions and of the true facts mentioned by the applicant in his appeals, that the Court was called upon to decide whether or not there has been a violation of Article 5.3.

The persistence of reasonable suspicion that the person arrested has committed an offence is a condition *sine qua non* for the validity of the continued detention but after a certain lapse of time, it no longer suffices; the Court must then establish whether the other grounds cited by the judicial authorities continue to justify the deprivation of liberty. Where such grounds are relevant and sufficient, the Court must also ascertain whether the competent national authorities displayed special diligence in the conduct of the proceedings.

In order to justify their refusal to release Mrs Letellier, the indictments divisions of the Paris and Amiens Courts of Appeal had stressed in particular that it was necessary to prevent her from bringing pressure to bear on the witnesses, that there was a risk of her absconding which had to be countered, that court supervision was not sufficient to achieve these objectives and that her release would gravely disturb public order.

The Court accepted that a genuine risk of pressure being brought to bear on the witnesses may have existed initially, but took the view that it diminished and indeed disappeared with the passing of time. The danger of absconding cannot be gauged solely on the basis of the severity of the sentence risked but must be assessed with reference to a number of other relevant factors which may either confirm the existence of a danger of absconding or make it appear so slight that it cannot justify detention pending trial. In this case the decisions of the indictments divisions did not give the reasons why they considered the risk of absconding to be decisive.

When the only remaining reason for continued detention is the fear that the accused will abscond and thereby subsequently avoid appearing for trial, he must be released if he is in a position to provide adequate guarantees to ensure that he will so appear, for example by lodging a security. The indictments divisions did not establish that this was not the case in this instance.

The Court accepted that, by reason of their particular gravity and public reaction to them, certain offences may give rise to a social disturbance capable of justifying pre-trial detention, at least for a time. In exceptional circumstances this factor may, therefore, be taken into account for the purposes of the Convention. However, this ground can be regarded as relevant and sufficient only provided that it is based on facts capable of showing that the accused's release would actually disturb public order. In addition, detention will continue to be legitimate only if public order remained actually threatened; its continuation could not be used to anticipate a custodial sentence. In this case, these conditions were not satisfied. The indictments divisions assessed the need to continue the deprivation of liberty from a purely abstract point of view, taking into consideration only the gravity of the offence. There had consequently been a violation of Article 5.3.

Toth v Austria (1991) 14 EHRR 551

A warrant was issued for the arrest of the applicant. He was suspected of aggravated fraud; he had in particular made out a number of bad cheques drawn on bank accounts opened by an accessory and then cashed in different banks. The warrant stated that there was a risk of his absconding because his address was unknown, and of repetition of the offences as he had several previous convictions. He was arrested and placed in detention on remand because of the risk of his absconding and that of repetition of the offences. Previously he had tried to evade prosecution by changing his place of residence so that if released he was liable to evade trial or to go into hiding to forestall his future conviction. In addition, he was not socially integrated and was unemployed, which gave grounds for fearing new offences, likely to have serious consequences, of the type of those which had already brought him two convictions.

The maximum period of detention should have been eight months but that was judicially extended four times on the basis that the scope and complexity of the case made it necessary to leave the prosecuting authorities sufficient time to prepare. Repeated applications for liberation were unsuccessful until finally the relevant Court of Appeal took the view that nearly 25 months' detention had significantly reduced the risk of the applicant's absconding and of repetition of the offences and made it possible to impose more lenient measures. It attached several conditions to the release: an undertaking not to evade the trial and not to go into hiding before the conclusion of the trial or to impede the investigation; an obligation to choose a permanent place of residence in Austria and to communicate it to the court and to report every two days to the police; and his identity papers were provisionally confiscated. The applicant was released on the same day.

In due course, the applicant was convicted and sentenced to four and a half years' imprisonment (reduced to four years on appeal), the pre-trial detention being automatically deducted from the sentence.

The applicant complained, *inter alia*, of a breach of Article 5.3. The Commission acknowledged that the investigation raised some difficult questions of fact which contributed to lengthening the proceedings. It also considered that several of the applications and appeals by the applicant must have had the same effect, although it did not regard the number of such steps as excessive. On the other hand, it drew up a list of seven periods of inactivity totalling approximately 11 months.

Held that the Court fully appreciated that the right of an accused in detention to have his case examined with particular expedition must not unduly hinder the efforts of the judicial authorities to carry out their tasks with proper care. However, the evidence disclosed that the Austrian courts did not in this instance act with all the necessary dispatch. Although the offences of which Mr Toth was accused were numerous and concerned several countries, they were relatively commonplace and repetitive. The speed of the investigation suffered considerably from the transmission of the whole file to the relevant court not only on the occasion of each application for release and each appeal by Mr Toth, but also on that of each request from the investigating judge or public prosecutor for the extension of the detention. There were, therefore, numerous interruptions because the officers concerned relinquished the file, sometimes for quite long periods, to their colleagues. The use of copies, which was the practice in other Member States of the Council of Europe, would have avoided these repeated suspensions of the investigation during the examination of the question. These suspensions could hardly be reconciled with the importance attached to the right to liberty secured under Article 5.1. In conclusion, there had been a violation of Article 5.3.

Demir and Others v Turkey (71/1997/855/1062–1064)

The applicant Demir was arrested and taken into police custody on 22 January 1993 (26 January according to the Government) and the applicants Süsin and Kaplan on 28 January (26 and 30 January respectively according to the Government). All three were accused of being members of the PKK (the Kurdistan Workers' Party). The applicant Kaplan was not brought before a judge until 15 February 1993 and the applicants Demir and Süsin were not brought before a judge until 18 February 1993. When they were brought before a judge, he ordered that they should be kept in custody pending trial, though some months later they were released pending trial. In 1996 they were convicted and sentenced to imprisonment.

The Court observed that in the *Brogan and Others* v *United Kingdom* case it had held that a period of detention in police custody of four days and six hours without judicial scrutiny fell outside the strict constraints as to time permitted by Article 5.3. In the present case Mr Demir and Mr Süsin had been held in police custody for at least 23 days and Mr Kaplan for at least 16 days, during which time none of them had appeared before a judge or other judicial officer.

Held that the periods of detention concerned failed to satisfy the requirement of promptness laid down by Article 5.3. The requirements of an investigation, even into alleged terrorism, could not absolve the authorities from the obligation to bring any person arrested in accordance with Article 5.1(c) "promptly" before a judge, as required by Article 5.3.

PROCEEDINGS BY WHICH THE LAWFULNESS OF DETENTION SHALL BE DECIDED

Winterwerp v The Netherlands (1979–80) 2 EHRR 387

The applicant had sustained severe brain damage in an accident. He committed some "fairly serious acts" without appreciating their consequences and was committed to a psychiatric hospital under an emergency procedure. Six weeks later, during the currency of the emergency order, a court order committing him to that hospital was made on his wife's application and on the basis of a medical report which said that he suffered from schizophrenia. On her further application and subsequently at the request of the public prosecutor the order was renewed from year to year by a court on the basis of medical reports from a succession of doctors treating him. Those reports were all to the effect that he continued to suffer from schizophrenic and paranoid conditions. One of the effects of those orders was to deprive him of capacity to manage his property.

He was given leave of absence for various periods, all of which resulted in his readmission when he was found not to have followed prescribed treatment and to be living in filthy conditions. He made unsuccessful applications for release, generally on the ground that he was not mentally deranged. He complained to the Commission that he was never heard by the courts which dealt with his case or notified of the orders, that he did not receive legal assistance and that he had no opportunity of challenging the medical reports.

Held that the term "persons of unsound mind" in Article 5.3 of the Convention (where it forms one of the permitted exceptions to the guarantee against deprivation of liberty) cannot be given a definitive interpretation. It cannot refer simply to someone whose views or behaviour deviate from the norms prevailing in a particular society because that would not be reconcilable with Article 5.1, whose object and purpose is to ensure that no one is dispossessed of his liberty in an arbitrary fashion and which sets out an exhaustive list of exceptions calling for a narrow interpretation. The practice of The Netherlands courts whereby the confinement of a "mentally ill person" was authorised only if his mental disorder was of such a kind or such a gravity as to make him an actual danger to himself or others is in principle within Article 5.1(e). In deciding whether an individual is to be detained as being of unsound mind, the national authorities have a certain discretion, since it is for them to evaluate the evidence. The events which prompted the emergency order were of a nature to justify such an order and, whilst some hesitancy might be felt about an emergency order lasting for six weeks, the period was not so excessive as to render the detention unlawful. There was no reason to doubt the objectivity of the subsequent reports or to think that the deprivation of liberty was for any wrongful purpose. There was no breach of Article 5.1. As regards the Article 5.4 right of a detained person to take proceedings by which the lawfulness of his detention should be decided by a court, it is true that the proceedings in contemplation need not always be attended by the same guarantees as those required under Article 6.1 but none the less it is essential that the person concerned should have access to a court and the opportunity to be heard either in person or, where necessary, through some form of representation. Failing that, he will not have been afforded the fundamental guarantees of procedure applied in matters of deprivation of liberty. Mental illness may entail restricting or modifying the manner of exercise of such a right but it cannot justify impairing its very essence. The applicant was never associated, either personally or through a representative, in the proceedings leading to the various detention orders. He was never notified of the proceedings or their outcome; neither was he given the opportunity to argue his case. His requests for discharge were not dealt with by a court at all. There was a violation of Article 5.4 and also, since the effect of the orders was to deprive the applicant of capacity to deal with his property, of Article 1 of Protocol 1.

Weeks v United Kingdom (1987) 10 EHRR 293

In December 1966, the applicant was sentenced to life imprisonment for armed robbery. He was released on licence a first time in March 1976 but recalled to prison in June 1977 by decision of the Home Secretary. He was released on licence a second time in October 1982 but re-detained in April 1985, his licence having previously been revoked by the Home Secretary in November 1984. He remained in prison until September 1985 when he was once more released on licence. This licence was revoked in March 1986, although as at 27 January 1987 he was still at liberty, having fled to France.

The applicant's complaint was of a breach of Article 5. He did not dispute that his original detention following his conviction in 1966 was justified under Article 5.1 of the Convention but contended, however, that his detention subsequent to the revocation of his licence in June 1977 was not in accordance with this provision because it did not amount to lawful detention after conviction by a competent court. The Government drew a distinction between liberty, properly understood, and a life prisoner being permitted to live on licence outside prison. In the latter case, the Government explained, the prisoner was still serving his sentence, albeit outside prison as a result of a privilege granted to him by the Home Secretary, but his right to liberty had not been restored to him. In sum, it was one and the same deprivation of liberty in June 1977 as in December 1966, based on his original conviction and sentence, and no new issue arose under Article 5.

Held that the applicant did not lose his right to liberty and security of person, as guaranteed by Article 5 of the Convention, as from the moment he was sentenced to life imprisonment. Article 5 applies to "everyone". All persons, whether at liberty or in detention, are entitled to the protection of Article 5, that is to say, not to be deprived, or to continue to be deprived, of their liberty save in accordance with the conditions specified in paragraph 1 and, when arrested or detained, to receive the benefit of the various safeguards provided by paragraphs 2 to 5 so far as applicable. Whether the applicant regained his "liberty", for the purposes of Article 5 when released on licence was a question of fact, depending upon the actual circumstances of the regime to which he was subject. The freedom enjoyed by a life prisoner released on licence was more circumscribed in law and more precarious than the freedom enjoyed by the ordinary citizen. Nevertheless, the restrictions to which the applicant's freedom outside prison was subject under the law were not sufficient to prevent its being qualified as a state of "liberty" for the purposes of Article 5. Hence, when recalling the applicant to prison in 1977, the Home Secretary was ordering his removal from an actual state of liberty, albeit one enjoyed in law as a privilege and not as of right, to a state of custody. It had, therefore, to be determined whether the fresh deprivation of liberty suffered by the applicant complied with Article 5.

Following his "conviction by a competent court" in December 1966, the applicant was sentenced to life imprisonment. The issue in the present case was whether his re-detention on recall to prison some 10 years later was "in accordance with a procedure prescribed by law", "lawful" and undergone "after" that conviction. It was not contested that the re-detention was in accordance with a procedure prescribed by English law and otherwise lawful under English law. That, however, was not necessarily decisive. The "lawfulness" required by the Convention presupposes not only conformity with domestic law but also conformity with the purposes of the deprivation of liberty permitted by subparagraph (a) of Article 5.1 Furthermore, the word "after" in subparagraph (a) does not simply mean that the detention must follow the "conviction" in point of time: in addition, the "detention" must result from, "follow and depend upon" or occur "by virtue of" the "conviction". In short, there must be a sufficient causal connection between the conviction and the deprivation of liberty at issue. The contested decision of the Home Secretary was taken within the legal framework set by the life sentence passed by the "competent court" in 1966, taken together with the provisions in the legislation governing the release on licence and recall to prison of persons sentenced to life imprisonment. The objectives to be pursued by the Home Secretary in exercising his discretion to release and recall were not spelled out in the legislation. Nevertheless, the statements made by the trial judge and the judges in the Court of Appeal had made it quite plain what purpose the life sentence and any subsequent release into the community were meant to serve. The sentencing judge had said:

> "... [T]he facts of the offence and the evidence of the character and disposition of the accused ... satisfy me that ... he is a very dangerous young man ... I think an indeterminate sentence is the right sentence for somebody of this age, of this character and disposition, who is attracted to this form of conduct. That leaves the matter with the Secretary of State who can release him if and when those who have been watching him and examining him believe that with the passage of years he has become responsible ... The Secretary of State can act if and when he thinks it is safe to act."

This view was upheld in the Court of Appeal.

The Court considered that the clearly stated purpose for which the sentence was imposed, taken together with the particular facts pertaining to the offence, placed the sentence in a special category. The intention was to make the applicant, who was qualified both by the trial judge and by the Court of Appeal as a "dangerous young man", subject to a continuing security measure in the interests of public safety. The sentencing judges recognised that it was not possible for them to forecast how long his instability and personality disorders would endure. In substance, the applicant was being put at the disposal of the State because he needed continued supervision in custody for an unforeseeable length of time and, as a corollary, periodic reassessment in order to ascertain the most appropriate manner of dealing with him.

The grounds expressly relied on by the sentencing courts for ordering this form of deprivation of liberty are by their very nature susceptible of change with the passage of time, whereas the measure would remain in force for the whole of the applicant's life. Applying the principles stated in the *Van Droogenbroeck* judgment, the formal legal connection between the applicant's conviction in 1966 and his recall to prison some 10 years later was not on its own sufficient to justify the contested detention under Article 5.1. The causal link required by subparagraph (a) might eventually be broken if a position were reached in which a decision not to release or to re-detain was based on grounds that were inconsistent with the objectives of the sentencing court.

However, as a matter of English law, it was inherent in the applicant's life sentence that, whether he was inside or outside prison, his liberty was at the discretion of the executive for the rest of his life. It was not for the Court, within the context of Article 5, to review the appropriateness of the original sentence. It remained to examine the sufficiency of the grounds on which his re-detention in June 1977 and thereafter was based. In this area, as in many others, the national authorities are to be recognised as having a certain discretion since they are better placed than the international judge to evaluate the evidence in a particular case. The probation report prepared for the applicant's trial in 1966 characterised him as being susceptible to fluctuation of mood, as having a morbid interest in the literature of violence and a fascination for guns, and as displaying a high potential for aggression. His tendency towards violence and aggression continued to manifest itself periodically during his first period of imprisonment and indeed delayed his first release on licence in 1976. After being formally warned of a possible revocation of his licence, he was recalled to prison in June 1977 as a result of a series of incidents involving minor violence whilst in a drunken state, the use of an air pistol, and an attempt at suicide. In view of this unstable, disturbed and aggressive behaviour, there were grounds for the Home Secretary to have considered that the applicant's continued liberty would constitute a danger to the public and to himself. The Minister's decision to re-detain remained within the bounds of the margin of appreciation available to the responsible national authorities; it could not be regarded as arbitrary or unreasonable in terms of the objectives of the life. In the Court's view, therefore, a sufficient connection, for the purposes of subparagraph (a) of Article 5.1, existed between his conviction in 1966 and his recall to prison in 1977.

On the evidence before the Court, a similar conclusion had to be reached as regards the Home Secretary's decision not to direct any further conditional release until October 1982: the Parole Board took the view in December 1977 that the applicant was still a danger to himself and to the public and confirmed his recall; he then absconded from an open prison in 1979, surrendering himself in 1980; a provisional release date was deferred after he had, in October 1981 when residing at a prison hostel, injured a hostel warden with a knife during a violent struggle. Accordingly, the applicant's recall to prison in 1977 and the period of his subsequent detention as in issue in the present proceedings were not incompatible with Article 5.1.

The applicant's second complaint was that he had not been able, either on his recall to prison in 1977 or at reasonable intervals throughout his detention, to take proceedings satisfying the requirements of paragraph 4 of Article 5. He did not dispute that, in so far as he may have wished to challenge the lawfulness of his recall or detention in terms of English law, he at all moments had available to him a remedy before the ordinary courts in the form of an application for judicial review. However, for the purposes of Article 5.4, the "lawfulness" of an "arrest or detention" has to be determined in the light not only of domestic law but also of the text of the Convention, the general principles embodied therein and the aim of the restriction permitted by Article 5.1. The Court had held in the context of paragraph 1(a) of Article 5 that the stated purpose of social protection and rehabilitation for which the "indeterminate" sentence was passed, taken together with the particular circumstances of the offence for which he was convicted, placed the sentence in a special category: unlike the case of a person sentenced to life imprisonment because of the gravity of the offence committed, the grounds relied on by the sentencing judges for deciding that the length of the deprivation of the applicant's liberty should be subject to the discretion of the executive for the rest of his life were by their nature susceptible of change with the passage of time. The Court inferred from this that if the decisions not to release or to re-detain were based on grounds inconsistent with the objectives of the sentencing court, the applicant's detention would no longer be "lawful" for the purposes of subparagraph (a) of paragraph 1 of Article 5. It followed that, by virtue of paragraph 4 of Article 5 the applicant was entitled to apply to a "court" having jurisdiction to decide "speedily" whether or not his deprivation of liberty had become "unlawful" in this sense; this entitlement should have been exercisable by him at the moment of any return to custody after being at liberty and also at reasonable intervals during the course of his imprisonment.

The "court" referred to in Article 5.4 does not necessarily have to be a court of law of the classic kind integrated within the standard judicial machinery of the country. The term "court" serves to denote bodies which exhibit not only common fundamental features, of which the most important is independence of the executive and of the parties to the case, but also the guarantees appropriate to the kind of deprivation of liberty in question. The body in question must not have merely advisory functions but must have the competence to "decide" the "lawfulness" of the detention and to order release if the detention is unlawful. There is thus nothing to preclude a specialised body such as the Parole Board being considered as a "court" within the meaning of Article 5.4, provided it fulfils these conditions. The Court saw no reason on the facts to conclude that the Parole Board and its members were not independent and impartial.

The language of Article 5.4 speaks of the detained individual being entitled to initiate proceedings. Under the British system of parole of life prisoners, although only the Home Secretary might refer a case to the Board, referral was obligatory in recall cases except where a person recalled after a recommendation to that effect by the Board had chosen not to make written representations. In these circumstances, the recalled person could be considered as having sufficient access to the Parole Board for the purposes of Article 5.4.

There remained, however, a certain procedural weakness in the case of a recalled prisoner. The duty on the Board to act fairly, as required under English law by the principles of natural justice, did not entail an entitlement to full disclosure of the adverse material which the Board had in its possession. The procedure followed did not, therefore, allow proper participation of the individual adversely affected by the contested decision, this being one of the principal guarantees of a judicial procedure for the purposes of the Convention, and could not, then, be regarded as judicial in character. Consequently, neither in relation to consideration of the applicant's recall to prison in 1977 nor in relation to periodic examination of his detention with a view to release on licence could the Parole Board be regarded as satisfying the requirements of Article 5.4. There had, therefore, been a breach of that Article.

Lamy v Belgium (1989) 11 EHRR 529

The applicant was a director of a company which was adjudged bankrupt. On 18 February 1983, an investigating judge regional court of first instance questioned Mr Lamy and issued a warrant for his arrest. He was alleged to have committed fraudulent bankruptcy by misappropriating or concealing assets worth over 10,000,000 F and paying or favouring some creditors to the detriment of the creditors as a whole; to have forged documents; and to have kept false accounts.

On 22 February 1983, the applicant, assisted by his lawyer, appeared before the court which upheld the arrest warrant. He was remanded in custody and eventually convicted, being sentenced to three years' imprisonment, suspended for five years in respect of that part of the sentence which exceeded the time already spent in custody on remand.

The applicant claimed to be a victim of a breach of Article 5.4. In his submission, a review of the lawfulness of his detention should have been the occasion for objective, adversarial proceedings. These could not be considered to have taken place where the investigating judge and Crown Counsel had had an opportunity to make their submissions in full knowledge of the contents of a substantial file, while the defence could only argue its case on the vague charges made in the arrest warrant. Furthermore, the proceedings allegedly did not truly ensure equality of arms. After a brief interview with the investigating judge, who read the charges out to him, Mr Lamy received a copy of the warrant, which was unsigned and bore the wrong date. During the first 30 days during which he was held in custody, he was not allowed access to the investigation file; subsequently, his counsel—but not he himself— had access to it but only during the 48 hours preceding each appearance before the court.

Held that there was a breach of Article 5.4. The Court noted that during the first 30 days of custody the applicant's counsel was, in accordance with the law as judicially interpreted, unable to inspect anything in the file, and in particular the reports made by the investigating judge and the police. This applied especially on the occasion of the applicant's first appearance before the *chambre du conseil*, which had to rule on the confirmation of the arrest warrant. The applicant's counsel did not have the opportunity to effectively challenge the statements or views which the prosecution based on these documents.

Access to these documents was essential for the applicant at this crucial stage in the proceedings, when the court had to decide whether to remand him in custody or to release him. Such access would, in particular, have enabled counsel for Mr Lamy to address the court on the matter of the co-defendants' statements and attitude. In the Court's view, it was, therefore, essential to inspect the documents in question in order to challenge the lawfulness of the arrest warrant effectively.

The appraisal of the need for a remand in custody and the subsequent assessment of guilt are too closely linked for access to documents to be refused in the former case when the law requires it in the latter case.

Whereas Crown Counsel was familiar with the whole file, the procedure did not afford the applicant an opportunity of challenging appropriately the reasons relied upon to justify a remand in custody. Since it failed to ensure equality of arms, the procedure was not truly adversarial. There was, therefore, a breach of Article 5.4.

Thynne, Wilson and Gunnell v United Kingdom (1990) 13 EHRR 666

The first applicant, Thynne had a long criminal record, having served various sentences of imprisonment for theft and burglary. Within 36 hours after his release from a life sentence for rape and buggery, he gained entrance to a flat under the pretence that he was a policeman investigating a burglary. He raped and buggered the 45-year-old female occupant of the flat. In view of the nature of his personality disorder—described by a psychiatrist as "a severe psychopathic character disorder"—the Recorder considered both a hospital order and a long determinate sentence to be inappropriate. An indeterminate life sentence was imposed to enable the Home Secretary to release Mr Thynne once his condition had sufficiently improved for it to be reasonably safe to do so. The applicant was refused leave to appeal. Following representations made on the applicant's behalf, his case was referred to the Joint Parole Board–Home Office Committee. In August 1980 the Committee recommended that it should be referred to the Local Review Committee in September 1981 by which time he would have been detained for six years. Between then and 1989 the Parole Board kept his case under review but he was not released.

The second applicant, Wilson, pleaded guilty in May 1972 to one count of buggery, two counts of attempted buggery and seven counts of indecent assault on boys under 16. He had a very long history of sexual offences and was sentenced to life imprisonment for the offence of buggery and seven years on each of the other nine counts, to be served concurrently. In passing sentence the Judge said that he had a duty to the public to protect them from people like the applicant who, for one reason or another, could not control themselves. The applicant's case was first referred to the Joint Parole Board–Home Office Committee after three years of his sentence and they recommended that his case be reviewed by the Local Review Committee after seven years of his sentence had been served. Accordingly, in 1979, the Local Review Committee heard his case and referred it to the Parole Board, who, on 11 December 1981, recommended his release into a controlled protective environment with psychiatric supervision not later than December 1982. On 14 September 1982, pursuant to the Secretary of State's authorisation of 3 September 1982, the applicant was released on licence on certain conditions, one of which was that he must co-operate with his probation officer. On 11 February 1983, five months after his release on licence, the Parole Board recommended his recall and on 14 February 1983 the Secretary of State revoked his licence. The applicant on his return to prison was informed that he had been recalled because his conduct had given cause for concern and he had failed to co-operate with his supervising officer. Despite a successful judicial review and repeated reconsideration of his case by the Parole Board, he was not released.

The third applicant, Gunnell, was convicted of four offences of rape and two offences of attempted rape. He was sentenced to life imprisonment on each of the four counts of rape. On the two counts of attempted rape he was sentenced to seven years' imprisonment, such sentences to run concurrently with each other and with the life sentences. According to uncontradicted medical evidence, the applicant was suffering from a "mental disorder" within the meaning of that term in the Mental Health Act 1959 (namely psychopathy) and needed constant care and treatment in a maximum security medical setting. Nevertheless, the sentencing judge concluded that, because of the gravity of the offences, punishment had to be an element in this case, and that punishment could only be achieved by imprisonment. In December 1980 the applicant's case was reviewed by the Parole Board. They recommended his release in 15 months' time and in March 1982 the applicant was released on licence on certain conditions. However, two incidents occurred in January and February 1983 which led to the revocation of the applicant's licence and his recall to prison. He was released on licence once more in September 1988. On 24 September 1990 the applicant pleaded guilty to one charge of attempted rape, five charges of indecent assault and three charges of robbery. He was sentenced to life imprisonment, the life licence for his original offences having already been revoked.

The applicants claimed that there was no judicial procedure available under UK law to determine the continued lawfulness of their detention or, more specifically, in the case of the second and third applicants, their re-detention following release. They all invoked Article 5.4 of the Convention.

Held that in proceedings originating in an individual application, the Court has, without losing sight of the general context, to confine its attention as far as possible to the issues raised by the concrete case before it. What is of importance in this context is the nature and purpose of the detention in question, viewed in the light of the objectives of the sentencing court, and not the category to which it belongs under Article 5.1. It was clear from the judgments of the sentencing courts that in their view the three applicants, had committed offences of the utmost gravity meriting lengthy terms of imprisonment. Nevertheless, the Court was satisfied that in each case the punitive period of the discretionary life sentence had expired. Having regard to that, the Court found that the detention of the applicants after the expiry of the punitive periods of their life sentences was comparable to that at issue in the *Van Droogenbroeck* and *Weeks* cases: the factors of mental instability and dangerousness were susceptible to change over the passage of time and new issues of lawfulness might thus arise in the course of detention. It followed that at that phase in the execution of their sentences, the applicants were entitled under Article 5.4 to take proceedings to have the lawfulness of their continued detention decided by a court at reasonable intervals and to have the lawfulness of any re-detention determined by a court. Article 5.4 does not guarantee a right to judicial control of such scope as to empower the "court" on all aspects of the case, including questions of expediency, to substitute its own discretion for that of the decision-making authority; the review should, nevertheless, be wide enough to bear on those conditions which, according to the Convention, are essential for the lawful detention of a person subject to the special type of deprivation of liberty ordered against these three applicants. The Court saw no reason to depart from its finding in the *Weeks* judgment that neither the Parole Board nor judicial review proceedings—no other remedy of a judicial character being available to the three applicants—satisfy the requirements of Article 5.4. In conclusion, there had been a violation of Article 5.4 in respect of all three applicants.

ARTICLE 6

THE RIGHT TO A FAIR HEARING

1. In the determination of his civil rights and obligations or of any criminal charge against him, everyone is entitled to a fair and public hearing within a reasonable time by an independent and impartial tribunal established by law. Judgment shall be pronounced publicly but the press and public may be excluded from all or part of the trial in the interests of morals, public order or national security in a democratic society, where the interests of juveniles or the protection of the private life of the parties so require, or to the extent strictly necessary in the opinion of the court in special circumstances where publicity would prejudice the interests of justice.

2. Everyone charged with a criminal offence shall be presumed innocent until proved guilty according to law.

3. Everyone charged with a criminal offence has the following minimum rights:
   a. to be informed promptly, in a language which he understands and in detail, of the nature and cause of the accusation against him;
   b. to have adequate time and facilities for the preparation of his defence;
   c. to defend himself in person or through legal assistance of his own choosing or, if he has not sufficient means to pay for legal assistance, to be given it free when the interests of justice so require;
   d. to examine or have examined witnesses against him and to obtain the attendance and examination of witnesses on his behalf under the same conditions as witnesses against him;
   e. to have the free assistance of an interpreter if he cannot understand or speak the language used in court.

Fair Trial (General)

Teixeira de Castro v Portugal (1999) 28 EHRR 101

In connection with an operation monitoring drug-trafficking, two plain-clothes police officers approached an individual, V.S., on a number of occasions. He was suspected of petty drug-trafficking in order to pay for drugs—mainly hashish—for his own consumption. They hoped that through V.S. they would be able to identify his supplier and offered to buy several kilograms of hashish from him. Unaware that they were police officers, V.S. agreed to find a supplier. V.S. mentioned the name of the applicant as being someone who might be able to find drugs; however, he did not know the latter's address and had to obtain it from another man, F.O. All four then went to the applicant's home in the purported buyers' car. The applicant came outside at F.O.'s request and got into the car where the two officers, accompanied by V.S., were waiting. The officers said that they wished to buy 20 grams of heroin for 200,000 escudos (PTE) and produced a roll of banknotes from the Bank of Portugal. The applicant agreed to procure heroin and, accompanied by F.O., went in his own car to the home of another person, J.P.O. The latter obtained three sachets of heroin, one weighing 10 grams and the other two five grams each, from someone else and, on his return, handed them over to the applicant in exchange for a substantial payment. The applicant then took the drugs to V.S.'s home; V.S. had in the meantime returned there and the two police officers were waiting outside. The deal was to take place in the house. The officers went inside at V.S.'s invitation; the applicant then took one of the sachets out of his pocket, whereupon the two officers identified themselves and arrested the applicant, V.S. and F.O., shortly before 2 am. They searched all three and found the applicant to be in possession of another two sachets of heroin, PTE 43,000 in cash and a gold bracelet. The applicant was in due course convicted and sentenced to six years' imprisonment. He complained of a breach of Article 6.

Held that the admissibility of evidence is primarily a matter for regulation by national law and as a general rule it is for the national courts to assess the evidence before them. The Court's task under the Convention is not to give a ruling as to whether statements of witnesses were properly admitted as evidence, but rather to ascertain whether the proceedings as a whole, including the way in which evidence was taken, were fair.

The use of undercover agents must be restricted and safeguards put in place even in cases concerning the fight against drug-trafficking. While the rise in organised crime undoubtedly requires that appropriate measures be taken, the right to a fair administration of justice nevertheless holds such a prominent place that it cannot be sacrificed for the sake of expedience. The general requirements of fairness embodied in Article 6 apply to proceedings concerning all types of criminal offence, from the most straightforward to the most complex. The public interest cannot justify the use of evidence obtained as a result of police incitement.

In the earlier case of *Lüdi* v *Switzerland* (not summarised in this book) the police officer concerned had been sworn in, the investigating judge had not been unaware of his mission and the Swiss authorities, informed by the German police, had opened a preliminary investigation. The police officer's role had been confined to acting as an undercover agent. In the instant case it was necessary to determine whether or not the two police officers' activity went beyond that of undercover agents. The Court noted that the Government had not contended that the officers' intervention took place as part of an anti-drug-trafficking operation ordered and supervised by a judge. It did not appear either that the competent authorities had good reason to suspect that Mr Teixeira de Castro was a drug-trafficker; on the contrary, he had no criminal record and no preliminary investigation concerning him had been opened. Indeed, he was not known to the police officers, who only came into contact with him through the intermediaries of V.S. and F.O.

Furthermore, the drugs were not at the applicant's home; he obtained them from a third party who had in turn obtained them from another person. There was no evidence to support the Government's argument that the applicant was predisposed to committing offences. The necessary inference from these circumstances was that the two police officers did not confine themselves to investigating Mr Teixeira de Castro's criminal activity in an essentially passive manner, but exercised an influence such as to incite the commission of the offence.

In the light of all these considerations, the Court concluded that the two police officers' actions went beyond those of undercover agents because they instigated the offence and there was nothing to suggest that without their intervention it would have been committed. That intervention and its use in the impugned criminal proceedings meant that, right from the outset, the applicant was definitively deprived of a fair trial. Consequently, there had been a violation of Article 6.1.

DETERMINATION OF CIVIL RIGHTS AND OBLIGATIONS AND CRIMINAL CHARGES

Konig v Federal Republic of Germany (1979–80) 2 EHRR 170

The applicant was a doctor against whom proceedings for unprofessional conduct were commenced in October 1962. In July 1964 he was declared unfit to practise. In 1967 his authorisation to run his clinic was withdrawn. In November 1967 he commenced court action to challenge that withdrawal. In 1970, the Regional Tribunal for the medical profession, attached to the Administrative Court of Appeal, rejected his appeal against the finding that he was unfit to practise. His authorisation to practise was withdrawn in 1971. In October 1971 he commenced court action to challenge that withdrawal. Criminal proceedings were commenced against him for practising without authorisation and his action objecting to withdrawal of his authorisation to practise was suspended pending the outcome of the criminal proceedings. In July 1973, when the two actions challenging the withdrawals were still pending, he applied to the Commission, complaining that the dilatory nature of the proceedings contravened his Article 6 right to have the determination of his civil rights take place within a reasonable time. The Government argued that Article 6 covered private law disputes and that disputes between individuals and States acting in their sovereign capacity were not within the scope of the Article.

Held that the concept of a civil right is, within the Convention, autonomous and cannot be interpreted solely under reference to the domestic law of the respondent State, though that domestic law is not without importance.

Whether or not a right is a civil right within the meaning of the Convention must be determined by reference to its substantive content and effects. It is not necessary that the parties should both be private persons and where a dispute is between a private individual and a State the fact that the latter is acting in its sovereign capacity is not conclusive. The running of a medical clinic in Germany was in certain respects a commercial activity, carried on with a view to profit. It represented the exercise of a private right, akin to the right of property. The fact that there was public supervision did not mean that the running of such a clinic was a public law activity. Since the right exercised was a private right, Article 6 was applicable. It was not necessary to decide whether it would apply to rights not of a private nature. It was a matter for serious concern that more than 10 years and 10 months had elapsed without a decision on the applicant's action objecting to the withdrawal of the authorisation to run a clinic. Although the applicant's conduct of his case, which included repeatedly changing lawyer, had contributed to the delay, that did not account for more than a few months. Although the procedural history of the case was complex, it would in fact have been possible to bring it to a conclusion sooner and the reasonable time contemplated by Article 6 had been exceeded. Although the delays in the action relating to the withdrawal of authorisation to practise were not as long as those relating to the other action, they were no less serious. The suspension of the proceedings pending the outcome of the criminal proceedings was not justified in the circumstances of the case. There was, therefore, a breach of Article 6.

Ravnsborg v Sweden (1994) 18 EHRR 38

In written submissions in connection with a litigation about nursing home fees the applicant made improper remarks about his opponents (who he described as "pure rotten eggs") and certain judges (whom he called "fascist" and "tendentious"). These remarks made him liable to fines, which were imposed without an oral hearing. His application maintained that there had been a breach of Article 6.

Held that the Court had to decide whether Article 6 applied under its "criminal" head. In line with the case law of the Court there were three criteria—the classification in national law, the nature of the offence and the nature and degree of severity of the penalty. The formal classification of the fines under Swedish law was open to differing interpretations and the

Court could not find it established that the provisions belonged to criminal law under the domestic legal system. As to the nature of the offence, rules enabling a court to sanction disorderly conduct in proceedings before it are a common feature of legal systems of the Contracting States. Such rules and sanctions derive from the indispensable power of a court to ensure the proper and orderly functioning of its own proceedings. Measures ordered by courts under such rules are more akin to the exercise of disciplinary powers than to the imposition of a punishment for commission of a criminal offence. It is, of course, open to States to bring what are considered to be more serious examples of disorderly conduct within the sphere of criminal law but that had not been done in this case. The kind of conduct for which the applicant had been fined fell outside the ambit of Article 6.

As to the nature and degree of severity of the penalty, the possible amounts of the fines did not attain the level of criminal sanctions. They were not entered on the police register and a decision to convert them to imprisonment was only possible in limited circumstances and after an oral hearing. This criterion did not, therefore, warrant classifying the fines as "criminal". Article 6 did not apply and had not been violated.

RIGHT TO A COURT

Golder v United Kingdom (1979–80) 1 EHRR 524

The applicant was serving a 15-year sentence for robbery with violence. A serious disturbance occurred in a recreation area of the prison where he happened to be. Subsequently, a prison officer who had been injured in quelling the disturbance made a statement identifying his assailants, in the course of which he said that certain prisoners, including one he knew by sight and whom he thought was called Golder, had been swinging vicious blows at him. The applicant was thereupon segregated from the main body of prisoners and interviewed by police officers who told him that he would be reported for consideration of prosecution for assaulting a prison officer. He wrote to his Member of Parliament and to the Chief Constable about the disturbance and the ensuing hardships it had entailed for him but the prison governor stopped these letters since the applicant had failed to raise the issue through the authorised channels beforehand.

In a second statement, the prison officer qualified what he had said earlier, saying that he was not sure that the applicant had in fact attacked him. Another prison officer reported that at the time of the riot the applicant had been in his company and had not participated in the trouble. Accordingly, although it had been intended to charge the applicant with offences against prison discipline, the entries in his prison record were marked "charges not proceeded with".

The applicant then petitioned the Home Secretary for a transfer to a different prison and for permission to consult his solicitor on the basis that he suspected that the prison officer's statement naming him as one of his assailants was in his prison record and was interfering with his parole. He wished to commence proceedings for libel. His request was refused. He complained to the Commission about the stopping of his letters and the refusal of permission to consult a solicitor. The Government argued, *inter alia*, that Article 6 applies only where proceedings have already been commenced.

Held that by forbidding the applicant to contact his solicitor, the Home Secretary impeded the launching of the contemplated action. Hindrance can contravene the Convention just like a legal impediment. Article 6.1 does not state a right of access to the courts or tribunals in express terms. It enunciates rights which are distinct but stem from the same basic idea and which, taken together, make up a single right not specifically defined in the narrower sense of the term.

The Court's approach should be guided by Articles 31 to 33 of the Vienna Convention on the Law of Treaties. The terms of Article 6.1 taken in their context, provide reason to think that the right of access to a court is included among the guarantees set forth. The clearest indications are to be found in the French text. In the field of "contestations civiles" (civil claims) everyone has a right to proceedings instituted by or against him being conducted in a certain way—"équitablement" (fairly), "publiquement" (publicly), "dans un délai raisonnable" (within a reasonable time), etc.—but also and primarily "à ce que sa cause soit entendue" (that his case be heard) not by any authority whatever but "par un tribunal" (by a court or tribunal) within the meaning of Article 6.1.

The Government had emphasised that in French "cause" may mean "procès qui se plaide" but the noun serves also to indicate by extension "l'ensemble des intérêts à soutenir, à faire prévaloir". Moreover, the phrase "in the determination of his civil rights and obligations" does not necessarily refer only to judicial proceedings already pending; as the Commission had observed, it might be taken as synonymous with "wherever his civil rights and obligations are being determined". It too would then imply the right to have the determination of disputes relating to civil rights and obligations made by a court or "tribunal". In the present case, the most significant passage in the Preamble to the European Convention was the signatory Governments declaring that they are "resolved, as the Governments of European countries which are like-minded and have a common heritage of political traditions, ideals, freedom and the rule of law, to take the first steps for the collective enforcement of certain of the Rights stated in the Universal Declaration" of 10 December 1948.

The Commission had attached great importance to the expression "rule of law" which, in their view, elucidated Article 6.1. The Court considered, like the Commission, that it would be a mistake to see in this reference a merely "more or less rhetorical reference", devoid of relevance for those interpreting the Convention. In civil matters one could scarcely conceive of the rule of law without there being a possibility of having access to the courts. Moreover, the principle whereby a civil claim must be capable of being submitted to a judge ranks as one of the universally "recognised" fundamental principles of law. The same is true of the principle of international law which forbids the denial of justice.

Article 6.1 must be read in the light of these principles. Were it to be understood as concerning exclusively the conduct of an action which had already been initiated before a court, a Contracting State could do away with its courts, or take away their jurisdiction to determine certain classes of civil actions and entrust it to organs dependent on the Government. Such assumptions, indissociable from a danger of arbitrary power, would have serious consequences. It would be inconceivable that Article 6 should describe in detail the procedural guarantees afforded to parties in a pending lawsuit and should not first protect that which alone makes it in fact possible to benefit from such guarantees, that is, access to a court. It followed that the right of access constitutes an element which is inherent in the right stated by Article 6.1.

In petitioning the Home Secretary for leave to consult a solicitor with a view to suing the prison officer for libel, the applicant was seeking to exculpate himself of the charge made against him by that prison officer and which had entailed for him unpleasant consequences. Those proceedings would have been directed against a member of the prison staff who had made the charge in the course of his duties and who was subject to the Home Secretary's authority. It was not for the Home Secretary himself to appraise the prospects of the action contemplated; it was for an independent and impartial court to rule on any claim that might be brought. There was a breach of Article 6.1.

Malige v France (68/1997/852/1059)

The applicant was convicted of speeding. He had refused to pay the fixed penalty and stood trial. He argued unsuccessfully that the legislation which had introduced a deductible points system for driving licences was unlawful (under these provisions taken together, a driving licence has 12 points allocated to it; this number of points is automatically reduced if the licence-holder commits certain offences against the Road Traffic Code). He was fined and disqualified from driving for 15 days. On appeal, he argued unsuccessfully that the points system was not compatible with Article 6.1 of the Convention in that it excluded any possibility of challenging in court the deduction of points from the licence.

Held that it was not the task of the Court to rule on the French system of deductible-point driving licences as such, but to determine whether, in the circumstances of the case, Mr Malige's right of access to a tribunal, within the meaning of Article 6.1 of the Convention, had been respected.

In the first place, the Court had to determine whether the sanction of deducting points from driving licences was "criminal" within the meaning of Article 6.1. In order to determine whether there is a "criminal charge", the Court has regard to three criteria: the legal classification of the offence in question in national law, the very nature of the offence and the nature and degree of severity of the penalty. In the present case, it was not contested that the offence which led to the deduction of points, namely exceeding the speed limit, was criminal in nature. With regard to the classification in French law of the deduction of points, the Court noted that an examination of the relevant legislation and the case law of the Court of Cassation and the *Conseil d'Etat* clearly showed that the measure in question, considered in isolation, was regarded as an administrative sanction not connected with the criminal law. With regard to the nature of the sanction, the Court noted that points were deducted in the context of, and after the outcome of, a criminal prosecution and that the deduction of points was an automatic consequence of the conviction pronounced by the criminal court. With regard to the severity of the measure, the Court noted that the deduction of points might in time entail invalidation of the licence. The Court accordingly inferred that, although the deduction of points had a preventive character, it also had a punitive and deterrent character and was accordingly similar to a secondary penalty. The Court, therefore, concluded that Article 6.1 was applicable.

The Court noted that points were deducted when it had been established that one of the offences listed in the relevant article of the Road Traffic Code had been committed, by means of either a final conviction or payment of a fixed fine by the offender, which implied admission of the offence and tacit acceptance of the deduction of points. It observed that the applicant had not paid the fixed fine and that the partial loss of points thus depended on the criminal courts finding him guilty. In the Versailles Police Court and the Versailles Court of Appeal, criminal courts which satisfied the requirements of Article 6.1, the applicant had been able to deny that he had committed the criminal offence of exceeding the speed limit and to submit all the factual and legal arguments which he considered helpful to his case, knowing that his conviction would in addition entail the docking of a number of points.

As to the proportionality of the sanction, the Court noted that the legislation itself made provision to a certain extent for the number of points deducted to vary in accordance with the seriousness of the offence committed by the accused. In the present case the offence committed had entailed the deduction of four of the licence's 12 points, so that the measure could not be described as disproportionate to the conduct it was intended to punish. First, it did not lead immediately to disqualification. Second, the applicant could win back points, either by driving for three years without committing any further offence in respect of which a deduction of points was prescribed or by attending a special training course; he, therefore, preserved a certain latitude of action. The Court accordingly considered that a review sufficient to satisfy the requirements of Article 6.1 of the Convention was incorporated in the criminal decision convicting Mr Malige, and that it was not necessary to have a separate, additional review by a court having full jurisdiction concerning the deduction of points. The Court concluded that domestic law afforded the applicant a review by the courts of the measure in issue which was sufficient for the purposes of Article 6.1. There had accordingly been no breach of that provision.

INDEPENDENT AND IMPARTIAL TRIBUNAL

Pullar v United Kingdom (1996) 22 EHRR 391

The applicant was an elected member of Tayside Regional Council who was indicted with another man in Perth Sheriff Court on a charge that they contravened section 1(1) of the Public Bodies Corrupt Practices Act 1889 by offering, in exchange for money, to use their influence to support a particular planning application. An architect and a quantity surveyor, who were involved in that application, were key prosecution witnesses.

One of those called for jury service was a man called Forsyth, who was a junior clerk in the architect's firm, though he had just been given a redundancy notice. He walked to the court with the architect, who was to be a witness. He told the sheriff clerk about his connection with the witness but said that he knew nothing of the particular matter with which the trial was concerned. The clerk did not tell the sheriff, the procurator fiscal or the defence. Forsyth was balloted and empanelled as a juror. When the architect saw that Forsyth was on the jury, he told the clerk about the connection. Once again, the clerk took no action.

The applicant was in due course convicted by majority. Thereafter, the defence learned of the connection between Forsyth and the witness and appealed on the ground that the sheriff ought to have directed the jury at the start of the trial that any of them who knew anyone named in the indictment should declare it and that Forsyth's involvement in the deliberations of the jury amounted to a miscarriage of justice. That appeal failed when the High Court of Justiciary held that, whilst the clerk should have told the sheriff about his conversation with Forsyth and that the sheriff would probably have discharged Forsyth, a mere suspicion that a juror was biased was insufficient to justify quashing a verdict; it was necessary to show that a miscarriage of justice had in fact taken place. The applicant complained of a breach of Article 6.

Held that the view taken by the accused with regard to the impartiality of the tribunal could not be conclusive. What mattered was whether his doubts could be held to be objectively justified. Although the principle of impartiality is an important element in support of the confidence which the courts must inspire in a democratic society, it does not necessarily follow from the fact that a member of a tribunal has some personal knowledge of one of the witnesses in a case that he would be prejudiced in favour of that person's testimony. In each individual case it has to be decided whether the familiarity in question is of such a nature and degree as to indicate a lack of impartiality on the part of the tribunal. Forsyth was only one of 15 jurors, the jury was directed to dispassionately assess the credibility of all the witnesses before them and all of the jurors took an oath to similar effect. There was no breach of Article 6.1.

A HEARING WITHIN A REASONABLE TIME

Eckle v Germany (1982) 5 EHRR 1

The applicants were husband and wife and they ran a builders' merchant type of business in the course of which they extended substantial credit and ultimately got into financial difficulties which led them into dishonesty. The trade practices of the applicants from 1959 to 1967 were the subject of three separate sets of prosecutions in Trier, Saarbrücken and Cologne. The first and last of these were in issue in the instant case: the applicants complained that their duration exceeded the "reasonable time" referred to in Article 6.1 of the Convention. In the Trier proceedings, acting on a complaint lodged on 28 October 1959 by a bank, the public prosecutor's office began, in November 1959, a preliminary investigation in respect of Mr Eckle. On 22 February 1960, after it had obtained information as to the existence of maximum prices in the building materials trade and without having questioned either the applicants or any witnesses, the prosecutor's office stopped the investigation. Examination of the complaint was resumed with a fresh preliminary investigation prompted by a complaint from the Trier Chamber of Industry and Commerce. Forty witnesses were interviewed between 1960 and 1962, 36 in 1963 and 133 in 1964. Also in 1964, the applicant's business premises were searched and business records seized. In 1965, 325 witnesses were heard. One of the 12 public prosecutors at Trier, who was in charge of the investigation, was relieved of his other duties in January 1965 in order to allow him to devote himself entirely to the Eckle case and a special commission of five officers from the criminal police began assisting the public prosecutor from this date onwards so that the investigation could be intensified.

In October 1966 the "bill of indictment" was lodged with the court. It filled four volumes and comprised 793 pages in all. It alleged a total of 474 offences of fraud and extortion, listed almost 500 witnesses and mentioned more than 250 documents produced in evidence. The trial and related appeals took between them until 23 January 1978.

Meanwhile, on 21 March 1967, the Cologne public prosecutor's office began a preliminary investigation of Mr Eckle, who was suspected of having committed various frauds. The police searched the business premises of the Eckle company on 11 and 12 May 1967. They seized four metric tons of documents which the public prosecutor's office made available to an accountant whom it had appointed as a consultant the previous month.

Also in May a special commission was set up composed of a public prosecutor and three police officers who were specialists in investigating economic crime; this commission worked exclusively on the Eckle case and continued in existence until May 1972. During that period, it made numerous searches of premises. Between March 1967 to August 1968 statements were taken from about 832 creditors, from the majority of some 3,500 purchasers of building materials from the Eckle company and from a large number of other witnesses or employees; and the Eckle company's accounts with some 25 credit institutions were examined. The investigative stage lasted until 25 September 1973, when the public prosecutor's office preferred the "bill of indictment" before the Cologne Regional Court. The "indictment", which ran to 432 pages, mentioned three experts and 143 witnesses. The trial and related appeals took until 21 September 1977. During both sets of proceedings, as also in the Saarbrücken proceedings, the applicants increasingly resorted to actions—including the systematic recourse to challenge of judges—likely to delay matters; some of these actions could even be interpreted as illustrating a policy of deliberate obstruction.

Held that in criminal matters, the "reasonable time" referred to in Article 6.1 begins to run as soon as a person is "charged"; this may occur on a date prior to the case coming before the trial court, such as the date of arrest, the date when the person concerned was officially notified that he would be prosecuted or the date when preliminary investigations were opened. "Charge", for the purposes of Article 6.1, may be defined as "the official notification given to an individual by the competent authority of an allegation that he has committed a criminal offence", a definition that also corresponds to the test whether "the situation of the [suspect] has been substantially affected". Applying these principles to the facts of the case, the Court considered that the date put forward by the applicants in respect of the Trier proceedings could not be the relevant one because documents produced by the Government showed that the complaint lodged on 28 October 1959 did not lead to any formal measures of inquiry being ordered. A true preliminary investigation was begun only in August 1960 when numerous witnesses were interviewed in connection with the allegations made against Mr Eckle. Having been unable to ascertain as from what moment the applicants officially learned of the investigation or began to be affected by it, the Court took as the starting point for the "time" the date of 1 January 1961. As regards the end of the "time", in criminal matters the period governed by Article 6.1 covers the whole of the proceedings in issue, including appeal proceedings. In the event of conviction, there is no "determination ... of any criminal charge", within the meaning of Article 6.1, as long as the sentence is not definitively fixed. The length of time to be examined thus amounted to seventeen years and three weeks (1 January 1961–23 January 1978) as regards the Trier proceedings and ten years, four months and ten days as regards the Cologne proceedings (11 May 1967–21 September 1977).

Drawing attention to the fact that the applicants had continued their illegal activities during the course of the investigation of the case at Trier, the Government requested the Court to deduct from the total length of those proceedings the periods during which the fresh offences were being committed. The Court viewed this factor as simply one of the elements that are of importance for reviewing the "reasonableness" of the "time". The reasonableness of the length of the proceedings must be assessed in each instance according to the particular circumstances. In this exercise, the Court had regard to, among other things, the complexity of the case, the conduct of the applicants and the conduct of the judicial authorities.

The present case concerned sets of proceedings that endured 17 years and 10 years respectively. Such a delay was undoubtedly inordinate and was, as a general rule, to be regarded as exceeding the "reasonable time" referred to in Article 6. In such circumstances, it falls to the respondent State to come forward with explanations. Article 6 does not require the applicants actively to cooperate with the judicial authorities and no reproach could be levelled against the applicants for having made full use of the remedies available under the domestic law, though their conduct constituted an objective fact, not capable of being attributed to the respondent State, which was to be taken into account when determining whether or not the proceedings lasted longer than the reasonable time referred to in Article 6. The Court had come to the conclusion that the competent authorities did not act with the necessary diligence and expedition. The enormous number of cases subjected to inquiry was not without effect in prolonging the preliminary investigation. In the Government's submission, the principle of obligatory prosecution of all criminal offences required that examination; but the Government could not, in relation to the fulfilment of the engagements undertaken by them by virtue of Article 6, seek refuge behind the possible failings of their own domestic law. The Court considered that the competent authorities did not act with the necessary diligence and expedition. On the basis of all the various factors taken into account, the Court reached the conclusion that the difficulties of investigation and the behaviour of the applicants did not on their own account for the length of the proceedings: one of the main causes, therefore, was to be found in the manner in which the judicial authorities conducted the case. There was a breach of Article 6.1.

Silva Pontes v Portugal (1994) 18 EHRR 156

In 1975 the applicant was severely injured in a road traffic accident. He commenced civil proceedings in December 1977. Portuguese law divided such proceedings into declaratory proceedings (establishing the right to compensation) and enforcement proceedings. The two parts of the proceedings, and all relevant appeals, took until December 1989 to resolve. The applicant contended that the determination of the case had not taken place within the "reasonable time" specified in Article 6. The government argued that the application was out of time so far as it related to the declaratory proceedings.

Held that it was not for the Court to express a view on the difference of opinion between legal writers as to whether under Portuguese law enforcement proceedings are autonomous. The moment at which there is determination of a civil right has to be ascertained with reference to the Convention and not on the basis of national law. It is reasonable to consider that the right has not been determined until the amount has been decided. The determination of a right entails deciding not only on the existence of that right, but also on its scope or the manner in which it may be exercised, which would evidently include the calculation of the amount due. The reasonableness of the length of proceedings is to be determined in the light of the circumstances of the case and with reference to the criteria laid down in the Court's case law, in particular the complexity of the case, the conduct of the applicant and of the relevant authorities and what was at stake for the applicant in the dispute. In connection with the latter point, special diligence is called for in determining compensation for the victims of road accidents. There had been a violation of Article 6.1.

Portington v Greece (109/1997/893/1105)

Early in 1986 the applicant was arrested in Greece and charged with murder. On 17 February 1988, the Criminal Court of Thessaloniki composed of jurors and professional judges convicted the applicant of murder and sentenced him to death. The applicant appealed. On 6 October 1989 the applicant's appeal came for hearing before the Criminal Court of Appeal of Thessaloniki. Nine prosecution witnesses were not present. According to the Government, the defence asked for an adjournment on the ground that, while none of the witnesses present had first-hand information about the murder, there was a person in England with information about the case who should be called to testify. The court decided to adjourn the case *sine die*. The applicant disputed that and maintained that he did not instruct his lawyer to apply for an adjournment and that the Court of Appeal adjourned the case on the ground that it was necessary to hear the testimony of all the witnesses, including the nine who were absent at the appeal hearing.

The applicant's appeal came up for hearing again on 19 April 1991. According to the Government, the applicant asked for the adjournment of the case on the ground that his lawyer was not present in court. The court decided to adjourn *sine die* to enable the applicant to be represented. The applicant maintained that he did not request that the court adjourn *sine die* but merely sought a brief adjournment to enable him to arrange his legal representation.

On 8 February 1993 the applicant appeared again before the appeal court. The defence asked for an adjournment on the basis that six prosecution witnesses were absent. The prosecution agreed and the court adjourned *sine die*.

Between 27 May 1993 and 30 June 1994 on several occasions the lawyers were on strike. The applicant's appeal was finally heard on 12 February 1996. The appeal court upheld his conviction but commuted his sentence to life imprisonment. The applicant appealed on points of law. In March 1998 he was transferred to the UK under the Council of Europe Convention on the Transfer of Sentenced Persons. He complained to the Commission of a breach of Article 6.1 in that the criminal appeal proceedings in his case were not concluded within a reasonable time.

Held that, even though the case was of some complexity, having regard to the serious nature of the conviction and the applicant's grounds of appeal, it could not be said that this in itself had justified the length of the proceedings on appeal. Even if all the adjournments had been attributable to requests made by the applicant and he might be considered on that account to be responsible for some of the delay which resulted, this could not justify the length of the periods in between individual hearings and certainly not the total length of the appeal proceedings—almost eight years. In view of the importance of what was at stake for the applicant who had been sentenced to the death penalty by the trial court, a total lapse of time in hearing his appeal of approximately eight years could not be regarded as reasonable. There had, accordingly, been a breach of Article 6.1 of the Convention.

PRESUMPTION OF INNOCENCE AND THE RIGHT TO SILENCE

Adolf v Austria (1982) 4 EHRR 313

The applicant had been accused of a trivial assault, which he denied committing. After certain investigations, the public prosecutor asked the court to close the proceedings. The order closing the proceedings was made without taking into account the applicant's version of events and supporting evidence. It narrated that the applicant had done the act constituting the assault. The applicant appealed to the Supreme Court, which held that the procedure used to close the proceedings did not require verification of the elements of the offence but only that suspicion existed. It regretted that the lower court had not made that clear. A limited amount of publicity followed. The applicant complained that the order of the lower court had breached Article 6.2 because it had contained findings on the facts and on his alleged guilt without any hearing.

Held that (contrary to the argument of the Government) the circumstances had amounted to a criminal charge against the applicant; the decision to discontinue the proceedings could not alter their nature retrospectively. However, the proceedings in the lower court had to be read in conjunction with the decision of the Supreme Court, which cleared the applicant of any finding of guilt. There had, accordingly, been no breach of Article 6.

Barbera, Messegue and Jabardo v Spain (1989) 11 EHRR 360

The three applicants had been convicted of a terrorist murder. They had been incriminated by a man called Martinez Vendrell who had been arrested in connection with terrorism but who had been released and was untraced at the time of the proceedings against the applicants. On arrest, the applicants were held incommunicado and not allowed to have the assistance of a lawyer. While in custody they signed a statement in which they admitted having taken part in the murder, though their account differed from Vendrell's. They appeared before an investigating judge, who questioned them without any defence lawyer being present. They retracted their confessions to the police and two of them complained of being subjected to physical and psychological torture while in police custody. The case was committed for trial and the court instructed the prosecution to make their interim submissions. They offered as evidence the examination of the defendants, the hearing of eye-witnesses and the production of the entire case file; no mention was made of Mr Martinez Vendrell.

The applicants were held in Barcelona and the trial was to take place in Madrid. The applicants stated that they left Barcelona on the evening before the trial and arrived in Madrid at four o'clock the following morning, when the hearing was due to commence at 10.30; they said that they were in very poor shape after travelling more than 600 kms in a prison van. That same morning, the presiding judge had to leave Madrid suddenly as his brother-in-law had been taken ill. Another judge took his place. In accordance with the legislation in force, the parties were not warned of this substitution or of the replacement of another judge in the case.

The trial was held on the appointed day in a high-security courtroom; in particular, the defendants appeared in a glass cage and were kept in hand-cuffs for most of the time. The prosecution offered for examination only the three witnesses who had been present at the time of the crime. Two of them were very old and could not travel to Madrid but the prosecution asked that their statements to the police on the day after the crime should be taken into account. The single witness who did give evidence in court did not recognise any of the applicants. The only documentary evidence produced by the prosecution was a copy of the file on the investigation. All the parties agreed to treat the documentary evidence as if it had been produced (*por reproducida*). The whole proceedings were concluded within the space of a single day. The applicants complained of breaches of Article 6.

Held that, as a general rule, it is for the national courts, and in particular the court of first instance, to assess the evidence before them as well as the relevance of the evidence which the accused seeks to adduce. The Court must, however, determine whether the proceedings considered as a whole, including the way in which prosecution and defence evidence was taken, were fair as required by Article 6.1. As a result of the late transfer from Barcelona, the applicants had to face a trial that was vitally important for them, in view of the seriousness of the charges against them and the sentences that might be passed, in a state which must have been one of lowered physical and mental resistance. That undoubtedly weakened their position at a vital moment when they needed all their resources to defend themselves, and in particular, to face up to questioning at the very start of the trial and to consult effectively with their counsel. They were given no notice of the change in the judges and could legitimately fear that the new presiding judge was unfamiliar with an unquestionably complex case. In criminal cases, the whole matter of the taking and presentation of evidence must be looked at in the light of paragraphs 2 and 3 of Article 6 of the Convention.

Paragraph 2 embodies the principle of the presumption of innocence. It requires, *inter alia*, that when carrying out their duties, the members of a court should not start with the preconceived idea that the accused has committed the offence charged; the burden of proof is on the prosecution, and any doubt should benefit the accused. It also follows that it is for the prosecution to inform the accused of the case that will be made against him, so that he may prepare and present his defence accordingly, and to adduce evidence sufficient to convict him.

Paragraph 1 of Article 6, taken together with paragraph 3, also requires the Contracting States to take positive steps in particular to inform the accused promptly of the nature and cause of the accusation against him, to allow him adequate time and facilities for the preparation of his defence, to secure him the right to defend himself in person or with legal assistance, and to enable him to examine or have examined witnesses against him and to obtain the attendance and examination of witnesses on his behalf under the same conditions as witnesses against him. The latter right not only entails equal treatment of the prosecution and the defence in this matter but also means that the hearing of witnesses must in general be adversarial. In addition, the object and purpose of Article 6 and the wording of some of the subparagraphs in paragraph 3 show that a person charged with a criminal offence is entitled to take part in the hearing and to have his case heard in his presence by a "tribunal". The Court inferred that all the evidence must in principle be produced in the presence of the accused at a public hearing with a view to adversarial argument.

The trial began with the questioning of the applicants. The use of the *por reproducida* procedure had the consequence that much of the evidence was admitted without being exposed to public scrutiny. The Government had argued that there was nothing to prevent counsel for the applicants from requesting that certain documents from the investigation file or indeed the whole file should be read out at the trial. As they had not done this, they had waived their right to do so.

According to the Court's established case law, waiver of the exercise of a right guaranteed by the Convention—in so far as it is permissible—must be established in an unequivocal manner. While the use of the *por reproducida* procedure showed that the defence accepted that the contents of the file need not be read out in public, it could not be inferred from this that it agreed not to challenge the contents even where the prosecution relied on them. In Spain the adversarial nature of criminal proceedings extends to the investigation stage: the Code of Criminal Procedure enables an accused, with the assistance of his advocate, to intervene in respect of steps affecting him, as regards both his own and the prosecution's evidence or measures taken by the investigating judge. In the applicants' case, however, the investigation had commenced well before their arrest. They obviously could not have played any part in it before then.

The trial court had before it only the written text of Mr Martinez Vendrell's statements. The evidence of Mr Martinez Vendrell would have been of crucial importance, but the central investigating judge did not even attempt to hear Mr Martinez Vendrell's evidence after the arrest of the applicants on 14 October 1980, not only to confirm his identification of them but also to compare his successive statements with theirs and arrange a confrontation with the applicants. In the end, the applicants never had an opportunity to examine a person whose evidence—which was vital—had been taken in their absence and was deemed to have been read out at the trial.

The statements made by the accused themselves constituted another important item of evidence. When they made their confessions to the police, they had already been charged but did not have the assistance of a lawyer, although they did not appear to have waived their right to one. Accordingly, these confessions, which were moreover obtained during a long period of custody in which they were held incommunicado, gave rise to reservations on the part of the Court. They were nevertheless appended to the police report and were pivotal in the questioning of the defendants by the investigating judges in Barcelona and by the private prosecutor at the trial.

The central investigating judge in Madrid never heard evidence from the defendants in person—even after the temporary transfer of one of them to the capital—despite the obvious contradictions in their successive statements; he proceeded by way of letters rogatory. The weapons, other items and documents found at the applicants' homes, and subsequently at the places indicated by Mr Barbera and Mr Messegue, were not produced in court at the trial, although they were relied upon by the prosecution as evidence. That being so, the defence was unable to challenge their identification or relevance in a fully effective manner. Having regard to the belated transfer of the applicants from Barcelona to Madrid, the unexpected change in the court's membership immediately before the hearing opened, the brevity of the trial and, above all, the fact that very important pieces of evidence were not adequately adduced and discussed at the trial in the applicants' presence and under the watchful eye of the public, the Court concluded that the proceedings in question, taken as a whole, did not satisfy the requirements of a fair and public hearing. Consequently, there was a violation of Article 6.1.

Murray v United Kingdom (1996) 22 EHRR 29

The applicant had been convicted of terrorist offences. Police officers had gone to a house where a man referred to as "L" was being held captive by the IRA. They entered the house some appreciable time after they had knocked on the door and found the accused coming down the stairs. L gave evidence that, whilst in the house, he had been blindfolded and forced to make a aped "confession". After the arrival of the police at the house, his blindfold had been removed and he had seen the applicant at the top of the stairs. L had been told to go downstairs and watch television. The applicant was pulling a tangled tape out of a cassette recorder. The tape was later found by police in the house.

The applicant maintained silence throughout questioning. During the first 48 hours of his detention he was denied access to a solicitor in terms of section 15 of the Northern Ireland (Emergency Provisions) Act 1987 on the basis that the police had reasonable grounds to believe that the exercise of the right of access to a solicitor would interfere with the gathering of information about acts of terrorism or make it more difficult to prevent such acts.

The trial proceeded before a judge alone (in a "Diplock" Court) and that judge drew strong inferences against the applicant by reason of his failure to give an account of his presence in the house when interrogated by the police and by reason of his refusal to give evidence in his own defence when asked by the court to do so.

The applicant complained that to permit the drawing of inferences from silence amounted to infringements of the right to silence, the right not to incriminate oneself and the principle that the prosecution must bear the burden of proving the case without assistance from the accused, all of which are guaranteed by Article 6 ECHR.

Held that there could be no doubt that the right to remain silent under police questioning and the privilege against self-incrimination are generally recognised international standards which lie at the heart of the notion of a fair procedure under Article 6. The Court did not consider it necessary to give an abstract analysis of the scope of these rights. Rather, it considered, the question before it was whether they are absolute, so that the exercise by the accused of the right to silence cannot under any circumstances be used against him at trial. On the one hand it is self-evident that it is incompatible with the immunities under consideration to base a conviction solely or mainly on the accused's silence or on a refusal to answer questions or to give evidence himself. On the other hand, it is equally obvious that these immunities cannot and should not prevent that the accused's silence, in situations which clearly call for an explanation from him, be taken into account in assessing the persuasiveness of evidence adduced by the prosecution.

The right to silence is not absolute. Having regard to the weight of the case against the applicant, the Court considered that the drawing of inferences from his refusal at arrest, at police questioning and at trial to provide an explanation for his presence in the house was a matter of commonsense and could not be regarded as unfair or unreasonable. Nor could it be regarded as shifting the burden of proof. In a considerable number of European countries, in which the free evaluation of proof applies, the courts, in evaluating the evidence in a given case, can have regard to all relevant circumstances, including the manner in which the accused has behaved or has conducted his defence.

That having been said, Article 6 will normally require that the accused be allowed to benefit from the assistance of a lawyer even at the initial stages of police interrogation. This right is not explicitly set out in the Convention but is derived from Article 6. It may be restricted where there is good cause to do so; and the considerations addressed by section 15 of the Northern Ireland (Emergency Provisions) Act 1987 are capable of amounting to such cause. However, although it is an important element to be taken into account, even a lawfully exercised power of restriction is capable of depriving an accused, in some circumstances, of a fair procedure.

Where silence may found inferences, the suspect is, at the beginning of police interrogation, confronted with a fundamental dilemma relating to his defence. If he chooses to remain silent, adverse inferences may be drawn against him. If he opts to break his silence during the course of interrogation, he runs the risk of prejudicing his defence without necessarily removing the risk of inferences being drawn against him. Under such conditions the concept of fairness enshrined in Article 6 requires that the accused has the benefit of the assistance of a lawyer already at the initial stages of police interrogation. There had been a breach of Article 6 as regards the denial of access to a lawyer during the first 48 hours of detention.

Saunders v United Kingdom (1996) 23 EHRR 313

The applicant had been a director and chief executive of Guinness PLC. In early 1986 Guinness was competing with another public company, Argyll Group PLC, to take over a third public company, the Distillers Company PLC. The take-over battle resulted in victory for Guinness. Guinness's offer to Distillers' shareholders, like Argyll's, included a substantial share exchange element, and accordingly the respective prices at which Guinness and Argyll shares were quoted on the Stock Exchange was a critical factor for both sides. During the course of the bid the Guinness share price rose dramatically, but once the bid had been declared unconditional it fell significantly. The substantial increase in the quoted Guinness share price during the bid was achieved as a result of an unlawful share-support operation. This involved certain persons ("supporters") purchasing Guinness shares in order to maintain, or inflate, its quoted share price. Supporters were offered secret indemnities against any losses they might incur, and, in some cases, also large success fees, if the Guinness bid was successful. Such inducements were unlawful (1) because they were not disclosed to the market under the City Code on Take-overs and Mergers and (2) because they were paid out of Guinness's own moneys in breach of section 151 of the Companies Act 1985 ("the 1985 Act"), which prohibits a company from giving financial assistance for the purpose of the acquisition of its own shares.

Allegations and rumours of misconduct during the course of the bid led the Secretary of State for Trade and Industry to appoint inspectors some months after the events pursuant to sections 432 and 442 of the 1985 Act. The inspectors were empowered to investigate the affairs of Guinness.

On 12 January 1987, the inspectors informed the Department of Trade and Industry that there was concrete evidence of criminal offences having been committed. On the same date the DTI contacted the Director of Public Prosecutions' office. It was decided that the proper thing to do was to permit the inspectors to carry on with their inquiry and to pass the transcripts on to the Crown Prosecution Service.

On 30 January 1987, a meeting was held attended by the inspectors, the solicitor to and other officials of the DTI, a representative of the DPP and a representative from the CPS. Amongst other matters, potential accused were identified—including the applicant—possible charges were discussed and it was stated that a decision had to be made as to when to start a criminal investigation. All concerned agreed on the need to work closely together in preparing the way for bringing charges as soon as possible. The inspectors indicated their readiness to co-operate although they reserved the right to conduct their investigations as they thought right.

The applicant was thereafter interviewed by the inspectors on nine occasions. He was accompanied by his legal representatives throughout these interviews.

He was subsequently charged with numerous offences relating to the illegal share-support operation and, together with his co-defendants, was arraigned before the Crown Court. The trial involved 75 days of evidence, 10 days of speeches by counsel and a five-day summing-up to the jury by the trial judge. The applicant faced 15 counts including, *inter alia*, eight counts of false accounting contrary to section 17(1)b of the Theft Act 1968 and two counts of theft and several counts of conspiracy. In the course of his trial the applicant, who was the only accused to give evidence—after the reading of the transcripts—testified that he knew nothing about the giving of indemnities or the paying of success fees and that he had not been consulted on such matters. He asserted that he had been guilty of no wrongdoing. The Crown relied heavily on the evidence of Guinness's finance director who had been granted immunity from prosecution. It also referred to the statements made by the applicant in the course of interviews to the DTI inspectors. The transcripts of the interviews were referred to by prosecuting counsel in his opening speech; they were read to the jury by the prosecution over a three-day period during the trial. They were used in order to establish the state of the applicant's knowledge and to refute evidence given by the applicant to the jury. In his cross-examination of the applicant, counsel for the prosecution referred to the answers in the transcripts to contradict Mr Saunders's testimony. He made further such reference in his closing speech to the jury. In his summing-up to the jury, the judge also compared and contrasted what the applicant had said in court with the answers which he had given to the inspectors. On 22 August 1990 the applicant was convicted of 12 counts in respect of conspiracy, false accounting and theft. He received an overall prison sentence of five years.

The applicant contended that he was denied a fair trial in breach of Article 6.1. He complained of the fact that statements made by him under compulsion to the inspectors appointed by the Department of Trade and Industry during their investigation were admitted as evidence against him at his subsequent criminal trial.

Held that, although not specifically mentioned in Article 6 of the Convention, the right to silence and the right not to incriminate oneself are generally recognised international standards which lie at the heart of the notion of a fair procedure under Article 6. Their rationale lies, *inter alia*, in the protection of the accused against improper compulsion by the authorities thereby contributing to the avoidance of miscarriages of justice and to the fulfilment of the aims of Article 6. The right not to incriminate oneself, in particular, presupposes that the prosecution in a criminal case seek to prove their case against the accused without resort to evidence obtained through methods of coercion or oppression in defiance of the will of the accused. In this sense the right is closely linked to the presumption of innocence contained in Article 6.2.

The right not to incriminate oneself is primarily concerned, however, with respecting the will of an accused person to remain silent. As commonly understood in the legal systems of the Contracting Parties to the Convention and elsewhere, it does not extend to the use in criminal proceedings of material which may be obtained from the accused through the use of compulsory powers but which has an existence independent of the will of the suspect such as, *inter alia*, documents acquired pursuant to a warrant, breath, blood and urine samples and bodily tissue for the purpose of DNA testing.

It had not been disputed by the Government that the applicant was subject to legal compulsion to give evidence to the inspectors. He was obliged under sections 434 and 436 of the Companies Act 1985 to answer the questions put to him by the inspectors in the course of nine lengthy interviews of which seven were admissible as evidence at his trial. A refusal by the applicant to answer the questions put to him could have led to a finding of contempt of court and the imposition of a fine or committal to prison for up to two years and it was no defence to such refusal that the questions were of an incriminating nature. However, the Government had emphasised that nothing said by the applicant in the course of the interviews was self-incriminating and that he had merely given exculpatory answers or answers which, if true, would serve to confirm his defence. In their submission only statements which are self-incriminating could fall within the privilege against self-incrimination.

The Court did not accept the Government's premise on this point since some of the applicant's answers were in fact of an incriminating nature in the sense that they contained admissions to knowledge of information which tended to incriminate him. In any event, bearing in mind the concept of fairness in Article 6, the right not to incriminate oneself cannot reasonably be confined to statements of admission of wrongdoing or to remarks which are directly incriminating. Testimony obtained under compulsion which appears on its face to be of a non-incriminating nature—such as exculpatory remarks or mere information on questions of fact—may later be deployed in criminal proceedings in support of the prosecution case, for example, to contradict or cast doubt upon other statements of the accused or evidence given by him during the trial or to otherwise undermine his credibility. Where the credibility of an accused must be assessed by a jury the use of such testimony may be especially harmful. It follows that what is of the essence in this context is the use to which evidence obtained under compulsion is put in the course of the criminal trial. In this regard, the Court observes that part of the transcript of answers given by the applicant was read to the jury by counsel for the prosecution over a three-day period despite objections by the applicant. The fact that such extensive use was made of the interviews strongly suggested that the prosecution must have believed that the reading of the transcripts assisted their case in establishing the applicant's dishonesty. This interpretation of the intended impact of the material was supported by certain remarks made by the trial judge. Moreover, there were clearly instances where the statements were used by the prosecution to incriminating effect in order to establish the applicant's knowledge of payments to persons involved in the share-support operation and to call into question his honesty. In sum, the evidence available to the Court supported the claim that the transcripts of the applicant's answers, whether directly self-incriminating or not, were used in the course of the proceedings in a manner which sought to incriminate the applicant.

The general requirements of fairness contained in Article 6, including the right not to incriminate oneself, apply to criminal proceedings in respect of all types of criminal offences without distinction from the most simple to the most complex. The public interest cannot be invoked to justify the use of answers compulsorily obtained in a non-judicial investigation to incriminate the accused during the trial proceedings. It was noteworthy in this respect that under the relevant legislation statements obtained under compulsory powers by the Serious Fraud Office cannot, as a general rule, be adduced in evidence at the subsequent trial of the person concerned. Moreover the fact that statements were made by the applicant prior to his being charged did not prevent their later use in criminal proceedings from constituting an infringement of the right. Accordingly, there has been an infringement in the present case of the right not to incriminate oneself.

ADEQUATE FACILITIES FOR THE PREPARATION OF THE DEFENCE

Edwards v United Kingdom (1992) 15 EHRR 417

The applicant was convicted at Sheffield Crown Court, *inter alia*, of one count of robbery and two counts of burglary; he was sentenced to imprisonment. The evidence against him consisted of detailed oral admissions that he had allegedly made to the police concerning his involvement in the three offences. His defence during the trial was to maintain that these statements had been concocted by the police.

The applicant petitioned the Secretary of State for the Home Department with complaints against police officers who had investigated his case and given evidence at his trial. An independent police investigation was ordered, following which the Home Secretary referred the applicant's case to the Court of Appeal (Criminal Division).

The applicant submitted to the Court of Appeal that the verdict should be set aside as unsafe and unsatisfactory because of certain shortcomings in the prosecution case, in particular, that certain information had been withheld by the police. At the trial one of the police witnesses had stated under cross-examination that no fingerprints were found at the scene of the crime. In fact two fingerprints had been found which later turned out to be those of the next door neighbour who was a regular visitor to the house. The applicant had not been informed of this by the prosecution before his trial. A further shortcoming complained of by the applicant related to the fact that the police had shown two volumes of photographs of possible burglars (including a photograph of the applicant) to the elderly victim of the robbery who said that she had caught a fleeting glimpse of the burglar. Her statement, read to the jury, said that she thought she would be able to recognise her assailant. Yet she did not pick out the applicant from the photographs. This fact was not, however, mentioned by one of the police witnesses who had made a written statement which was read out to the jury and had not been indicated to the applicant before or during his trial. Counsel for the applicant submitted to the Court of Appeal that this omission cast such doubt on the evidence of the prosecution that it might have led the jury to believe that the confession statements had indeed been "manufactured" by the police as the applicant alleged.

The Court of Appeal rejected these arguments and concluded as follows:

> "It is clear that there was some slipshod police work in the present case, no doubt because they took the view that here was a man who had admitted these crimes fully, and consequently there was very little need for them to indulge in a further verification of whether what he said was true. Although this is a matter which perhaps casts the police in a somewhat lazy or idle light, we do not think in the circumstances there was anything unsafe or unsatisfactory in the end about these convictions."

The applicant complained that he did not receive a fair trial, in breach of Article 6.1 and 3(d).

Held that the guarantees in Article 6.3 are specific aspects of the right to a fair trial. In the circumstances of the case it was unnecessary to examine the relevance of paragraph 3(d) to the case since the applicant's allegations, in any event, amounted to a complaint that the proceedings had been unfair. The Court, therefore, confined its examination to this point. In so doing, it had to consider the proceedings as a whole including the decision of the appellate court. Moreover it was not within the province of the European Court to substitute its own assessment of the facts for that of the domestic courts and, as a general rule, it is for these courts to assess the evidence before them. The Court's task was to ascertain whether the proceedings in their entirety, including the way in which evidence was taken, were fair. The Court considered that it is a requirement of fairness under Article 6.1, indeed one which is recognised under English law, that the prosecution authorities disclose to the defence all material evidence for or against the accused and that the failure to do so in the present case gave rise to a defect in the trial proceedings.

However, when this was discovered, the Secretary of State, following an independent police investigation, referred the case to the Court of Appeal which examined the transcript of the trial including the applicant's alleged confession and considered in detail the impact of the new information on the conviction. In the proceedings before the Court of Appeal the applicant was represented by senior and junior counsel who had every opportunity to seek to persuade the court that the conviction should not stand in view of the evidence of non-disclosure.

Admittedly the police officers who had given evidence at the trial were not heard by the Court of Appeal. It was, none the less, open to counsel for the applicant to make an application to the Court—which they chose not to do—that the police officers be called as witnesses. Having regard to all of this, the Court concluded that the defects of the original trial were remedied by the subsequent procedure before the Court of Appeal. There was no indication that the proceedings before the Court of Appeal were in any respect unfair. Accordingly, there had been no breach of Article 6.

THE RIGHT TO DEFEND ONESELF IN PERSON
OR THROUGH LEGAL ASSISTANCE

Artico v Italy (1981) 3 EHRR 1

The applicant was sentenced to a total of 29 months' imprisonment and a fine for fraud. He challenged the conviction and sentence and requested free legal aid in connection with the applications to quash. The court appointed for the purpose Mr Della Rocca, a lawyer from Rome. Subsequently, by letter, Mr

Della Rocco advised the applicant that it was only on his return from holiday that he learned of the appointment, stated that other commitments prevented him from accepting it and gave the name of a colleague whose services he strongly recommended the applicant to utilise. The applicant asked Mr Della Rocca to apply for the appointment of a substitute in accordance with the procedure laid down by law. Mr Della Rocca replied that he had submitted a formal request to that effect, indicating therein that for health reasons he was unable to undertake a task which he described as very demanding and onerous; he considered that in this way he had fulfilled his obligations and expressed the wish to be left in peace. The registry of the court subsequently wrote to the applicant to say that Mr Della Rocco was still acting, since a lawyer appointed for legal aid purposes was not in law entitled to refuse the appointment. Protracted correspondence failed to resolve the situation and in the end the applicant's application to quash was heard and declared to be inadmissible without the applicant being represented.

The applicant complained of a violation of Article 6.3(c) of the Convention. The Government asserted that the obligation was satisfied by the nomination of a lawyer for legal aid purposes, contending that what occurred thereafter was in no way the concern of the Italian Republic. According to them, although Mr Della Rocca declined to undertake the task entrusted to him, he continued to the very end and "for all purposes" to be the applicant's lawyer.

Held that paragraph 3 of Article 6 contains an enumeration of specific applications of the general principle stated in paragraph 1 of the Article. The various rights of which a non-exhaustive list appears in paragraph 3 reflect certain of the aspects of the notion of a fair trial in criminal proceedings. When compliance with paragraph 3 is being reviewed, its basic purpose must not be forgotten, nor must it be severed from its roots. Subparagraph (c) guarantees the right to an adequate defence either in person or through a lawyer, this right being reinforced by an obligation on the part of the State to provide free legal assistance in certain cases. The Convention is intended to guarantee not rights that are theoretical or illusory but rights that are practical and effective; this is particularly so of the rights of the defence in view of the prominent place held in a democratic society by the right to a fair trial, from which they derive. Article 6.3(c) speaks of "assistance" and not of "nomination". Mere nomination does not ensure effective assistance, since the lawyer appointed for legal aid purposes may die, fall seriously ill, be prevented for a protracted period from acting or shirk his duties. If they are notified of the situation, the authorities must either replace him or cause him to fulfil his obligations. Adoption of the Government's restrictive interpretation would lead to results that are unreasonable and incompatible with both the wording of subparagraph (c) and the structure of Article 6 taken as a whole; in many instances free legal assistance might prove to be worthless.

In the applicant's case, the interests of justice did require the provision of effective assistance. The task would, according to Mr Della Rocca, have been demanding and onerous. A qualified lawyer would have been able to clarify the grounds adduced by Mr Artico. Only a lawyer could have countered the pleadings of the public prosecutor's department by causing the Court of Cassation to hold a public hearing. Although the Government had argued that, for there to be a violation of Article 6.3(c), the lack of assistance must have actually prejudiced the person charged with a criminal offence, there is nothing in Article 6.3(c) indicating that proof of prejudice is necessary; and interpretation that introduced this requirement into the subparagraph would deprive it in large measure of its substance. More generally, following *Marckx v Belgium* the existence of a violation is conceivable even in the absence of prejudice. Admittedly, a State cannot be responsible for every shortcoming on the part of a lawyer appointed for legal aid purposes but, in the particular circumstance, it was for the competent Italian authorities to take steps to ensure that the applicant enjoyed effectively the right to which they had recognised he was entitled. Two courses were open to the authorities: either to replace Mr Della Rocca or, if appropriate, to cause him to fulfil his obligations. They chose a third course—remaining passive—whereas compliance with the Convention called for positive action on their part. There had been a breach of the requirements of Article 6.3(c).

Ekbatani v Sweden (1988) 13 EHRR 504

The applicant was a US citizen who had gone to Sweden to do certain research work at the University of Gothenburg. However, his initial plans did not come to fruition and his financial situation forced him to look for other work. He found a job at the Gothenburg Tramway Company but failed the Swedish driving test. This led to an angry exchange of views between the applicant and the traffic assistant who had been in charge of the test and he was in due course convicted of threatening a civil servant. He appealed, seeking a reconsideration of the facts of the case. In his first written statement of evidence to the Court of Appeal, the applicant took it for granted that a hearing would be held. The public prosecutor, however, applied for the case to be dealt with without a hearing in the Court of Appeal. In the event, the Court of Appeal held no hearing and simply confirmed the City Court's judgment.

Held that criminal proceedings form an entity and the protection afforded by Article 6 does not cease with the decision at first instance. The manner of application of Article 6 to proceedings before courts of appeal does, however, depend on the special features of the proceedings involved; account must be taken of the entirety of the proceedings in the domestic legal order and of the role of the appellate court therein. Thus, leave-to-appeal proceedings and proceedings involving only questions of law, as opposed to questions of fact, may comply with the requirements of Article 6 although the appellant was not given an opportunity of being heard in person by the appeal court. The underlying reason was that the courts concerned did not have the task of establishing the facts of the case, but only of interpreting the legal rules involved.

Here, however, the Court of Appeal was called upon to examine the case as to the facts and the law. In particular, it had to make a full assessment of the question of the applicant's guilt or innocence. The only limitation on its jurisdiction was that it did not have the power to increase the sentence imposed by the City Court. In the circumstances of the case that question could not, as a matter of fair trial, have been properly determined without a direct assessment of the evidence given in person by the applicant—who claimed that he had not committed the act alleged to constitute the criminal offence—and by the complainant. Accordingly, the Court of Appeal's re-examination of Mr Ekbatani's conviction at first instance ought to have comprised a full rehearing of the applicant and the complainant. Having regard to the entirety of the proceedings before the Swedish courts, to the role of the Court of Appeal, and to the nature of the issue submitted to it, the Court reached the conclusion that there were no special features to justify a denial of a public hearing and of the applicant's right to be heard in person. Accordingly, there had been a violation of Article 6.1.

Tripodi v Italy (1994) 18 EHRR 295

The applicant had been convicted of a number of offences and a suspended sentence had been imposed on her. She appealed to the Court of Cassation, whose proceedings were primarily written. At the hearing an appellant's lawyer was only entitled to present argument in relation to submissions already made in the memorials. The applicant's lawyer duly submitted her written argument. Three weeks before the oral hearing he wrote requesting an adjournment on the ground that he had undergone an operation and was not fit to attend the hearing. The adjournment was refused and the appeal was decided—against the applicant—on the basis of the written submissions.

Held that the lawyer could and should have taken steps to ensure that he was replaced for the hearing. The Court could not hold the state responsible for the shortcomings of the applicant's lawyer. In view of the emphasis on written submissions and the conduct of the lawyer, there was no breach of Article 6.3(c).

T v United Kingdom (24724/94)

When he was 10 years old, the applicant and another 10-year-old boy, "V." had played truant from school and abducted a two-year-old boy from a shopping precinct, taken him on a journey of over two miles and then battered him to death and left him on a railway line to be run over. Their trial for this offence took place over three weeks in public, at Preston Crown Court before a judge and 12 jurors. In the two months preceding the trial each applicant was taken by social workers to visit the courtroom and was introduced to trial procedures and personnel by way of a "child witness pack" containing books and games. The trial was preceded and accompanied by massive national and international publicity. Throughout the criminal proceedings, the arrival of the defendants was greeted by a hostile crowd. On occasion, attempts were made to attack the vehicles bringing them to court. In the courtroom, the press benches and public gallery were full. The trial was conducted with the formality of an adult criminal trial. The judge and counsel wore wigs and gowns.

The procedure was, however, modified to a certain extent in view of the defendants' age. They were seated next to social workers in a specially raised dock. Their parents and lawyers were seated nearby. The hearing times were shortened to reflect the school day (10.30 am to 3.30 pm, with an hour's lunch break), and a 10-minute interval was taken every hour. During adjournments the defendants were allowed to spend time with their parents and social workers in a play area. The judge made it clear that he would adjourn whenever the social workers or defence lawyers told him that one of the defendants was showing signs of tiredness or stress. This occurred on one occasion.

At the opening of the trial on 1 November 1993 the judge made an order that there should be no publication of the names, addresses or other identifying details of the applicant or V. or publication of their photographs. On the same day, the applicant's counsel made an application for a stay of the proceedings, on the grounds that the trial would be unfair due to the nature and extent of the media coverage. After hearing argument, the judge found that it was not established that the defendants would suffer serious prejudice to the extent that no fair trial could be held. He referred to the warning that he had given to the jury to put out of their minds anything which they might have heard or seen about the case outside the courtroom.

The jury convicted V. and the applicant of murder and abduction. Neither applicant made any appeal to the Court of Appeal against his conviction. Following the applicant and V.'s conviction for murder, the judge sentenced them, as required by law, to detention during Her Majesty's pleasure. He subsequently recommended that a period of eight years be served by the boys to satisfy the requirements of retribution and deterrence. The Lord Chief Justice recommended a tariff of 10 years. The applicant's representatives made written representations to the Home Secretary, who was to fix the tariff period.

By a letter the Home Secretary informed the applicant that the family of the deceased child had submitted a petition signed by 278,300 people urging him to take account of their belief that the boys should never be released, accompanied by 4,400 letters of support from the public; that a Member of Parliament had submitted a petition signed by 5,900 people calling for a minimum of 25 years to be served; that 21,281 coupons from the *Sun* newspaper supporting a whole life tariff and a further 1,357 letters and small petitions had been received of which 1,113 wanted a higher tariff than the judicial recommendations. The applicant's solicitors were given an opportunity to submit further representations to the Secretary of State. By a further letter, the Secretary of State informed the applicant that he should serve a period of 15 years in respect of retribution and deterrence.

Held that Article 3 enshrines one of the most fundamental values of democratic society. It prohibits in absolute terms torture or inhuman or degrading treatment or punishment, irrespective of the victim's conduct. Ill-treatment must attain a minimum level of severity if it is to fall within the scope of Article 3. The assessment of this minimum is, in the nature of things, relative; it depends on all the circumstances of the case, such as the nature and context of the treatment or punishment, the manner and method of its execution, its duration, its physical or mental effects and, in some instances, the sex, age and state of health of the victim. Treatment has been held by the Court to be "inhuman" because, *inter alia*, it was premeditated, was applied for hours at a stretch and caused either actual bodily injury or intense physical and mental suffering, and also "degrading" because it was such as to arouse in its victims feelings of fear, anguish and inferiority capable of humiliating and debasing them. In order for a punishment or treatment associated with it to be "inhuman" or "degrading", the suffering or humiliation involved must in any event go beyond that inevitable element of suffering or humiliation connected with a given form of legitimate treatment or punishment. The question whether the purpose of the treatment was to humiliate or debase the victim is a further factor to be taken into account but the absence of any such purpose cannot conclusively rule out a finding of violation of Article 3.

The Court had considered first whether the attribution to the applicant of criminal responsibility in respect of acts committed when he was 10 years old could, in itself, give rise to a violation of Article 3. In this connection, the Court observed that there was not yet a commonly accepted minimum age for the imposition of criminal responsibility in Europe. While most of the Contracting States have adopted an age-limit which is higher than that in force in England and Wales, other States attributed criminal responsibility from a younger age. Moreover, no clear tendency could be ascertained from examination of the relevant international texts and instruments. The Court did not consider that there was any clear common standard amongst the Member States of the Council of Europe as to the minimum age of criminal responsibility. Even if England and Wales was among the few European jurisdictions to retain a low age of criminal responsibility, the age of 10 could not be said to be so young as to differ disproportionately from the age-limit followed by other European States. The Court concluded that the attribution of criminal responsibility to the applicant did not in itself give rise to a breach of Article 3 of the Convention.

The second part of the applicant's complaint under Article 3 concerning the trial related to the fact that the criminal proceedings took place over three weeks in public in an adult Crown Court with attendant formality, and that, after his conviction, his name was permitted to be published. The Court noted in this connection that several international instruments stipulated that children accused of crimes should have their privacy fully respected at all stages of the proceedings. The Court considered that this demonstrated an international tendency in favour of the protection of the privacy of juvenile defendants. Moreover, Article 6.1 of the Convention states that "the press and public may be excluded from all or part of the trial ... where the interests of juveniles ... so require". However, whilst the existence of such a trend was one factor to be taken into account when assessing whether the treatment of the applicant could be regarded as acceptable under the other Articles of the Convention, it could not be determinative of the question whether the trial in public amounted to ill-treatment attaining the minimum level of severity necessary to bring it within the scope of Article 3. The Court recognised that the criminal proceedings against the applicant were not motivated by any intention on the part of the State authorities to humiliate him or cause him suffering. Indeed, special measures were taken to modify the Crown Court procedure in order to attenuate the rigours of an adult trial in view of the defendants' young age. Even if there was evidence that proceedings such as those applied to the applicant could be expected to have a harmful effect on an 11-year-old child, the Court considered that any proceedings or inquiry to determine the circumstances of the acts committed by V. and the applicant, whether such inquiry had been carried out in public or in private, attended by the formality of the Crown Court or informally in the Youth Court, would have provoked in the applicant feelings of guilt, distress, anguish and fear. Whilst the public nature of the proceedings may have exacerbated to a certain extent these feelings in the applicant, the Court was not convinced that the particular features of the trial process as applied to him caused, to a significant degree, suffering going beyond that which would inevitably have been engendered by any attempt by the authorities to deal with the applicant following the commission by him of the offence in question. The Court, therefore, did not consider that the applicant's trial gave rise to a violation of Article 3 of the Convention. However, the Court noted that Article 6, read as a whole, guarantees the right of an accused to participate effectively in his criminal trial. It could not be said that the trial on criminal charges of a child, even one as young as 11, as such violates the fair trial guarantee under Article 6.1 but it is essential that a child charged with an offence is dealt with in a manner which takes full account of his age, level of maturity and intellectual and emotional capacities, and that steps are taken to promote his ability to understand and participate in the proceedings. It follows that, in respect of a young child charged with a grave offence attracting high levels of media and public interest, it would be necessary to conduct the hearing in such a way as to reduce as far as possible his or her feelings of intimidation and inhibition.

It was noteworthy that in England and Wales children charged with less serious crimes were dealt with in special Youth Courts, from which the general public is excluded and in relation to which there are imposed automatic reporting restrictions on the media. Whilst public trials might (as the Government had argued) serve the general interest in the open administration of justice, where appropriate in view of the age and other characteristics of the child and the circumstances surrounding the criminal proceedings, this general interest could be satisfied by a modified procedure providing for selected attendance rights and judicious reporting.

Although special measures were taken in view of the applicant's young age and to promote his understanding of the proceedings, the formality and ritual of the Crown Court must nevertheless at times have seemed incomprehensible and intimidating for a child of 11, and there was evidence that certain of the modifications to the courtroom, in particular the raised dock which was designed to enable the defendants to see what was going on, had the effect of increasing the applicant's sense of discomfort during the trial, since he felt exposed to the scrutiny of the press and public. The trial generated extremely high levels of press and public interest, both inside and outside the courtroom, to the extent that the judge in his summing-up referred to the problems caused to witnesses by the blaze of publicity and asked the jury to take this into account when assessing their evidence.

Psychiatric evidence in relation to the applicant had been that the post-traumatic stress disorder suffered by the applicant, combined with the lack of any therapeutic work since the offence, had limited his ability to instruct his lawyers and testify adequately in his own defence. Moreover, the applicant in his memorial had stated that due to the conditions in which he was put on trial, he was unable to follow the trial or take decisions in his own best interests.

In such circumstances the Court did not consider that it was sufficient for the purposes of Article 6.1 that the applicant was represented by skilled and experienced lawyers. Although the applicant's legal representatives were seated, as the Government put it, "within whispering distance", it was highly unlikely that the applicant would have felt sufficiently uninhibited, in the tense courtroom and under public scrutiny, to have consulted with them during the trial or, indeed, that, given his immaturity and his disturbed emotional state, he would have been capable outside the courtroom of co-operating with his lawyers and giving them information for the purposes of his defence.

In conclusion, the Court considered that the applicant was unable to participate effectively in the criminal proceedings against him and was, in consequence, denied a fair hearing in breach of Article 6.1.

As regards sentence, the applicant argued that, in view of his age at the time of the offence, the sentence of detention during Her Majesty's pleasure was severely disproportionate and in breach of Article 3 of the Convention. In assessing whether the above facts constitute ill-treatment of sufficient severity to violate Article 3, the Court had regard to the fact that Article 37 of the UN Convention on the Rights of the Child 1989 prohibits life imprisonment without the possibility of release in respect of offences committed by persons below the age of 18 and provides that the detention of a child "shall be used only as a measure of last resort and for the shortest appropriate period of time". The Court recalled that States have a duty under the Convention to take measures for the protection of the public from violent crime and did not consider that the punitive element inherent in the tariff approach itself gave rise to a breach of Article 3, or that the Convention prohibits States from subjecting a child or young person convicted of a serious crime to an indeterminate sentence allowing for the offender's continued detention or recall to detention following release where necessary for the protection of the public. The applicant had not yet reached the stage in his sentence where he was able to have the continued lawfulness of his detention reviewed with regard to the question of dangerousness, and although he had not yet been notified of any new tariff, it could be assumed that he was currently detained for the purposes of retribution and deterrence. Until a new tariff had been set, it was not possible to draw any conclusions regarding the length of puni-tive detention to be served by the applicant. At the time of adoption of the present judgment he had been detained for six years since his conviction in November 1993. The Court did not consider that, in all the circumstances of the case including the applicant's age and his conditions of detention, a period of punitive detention of this length could be said to amount to inhuman or degrading treatment. It followed that there had been no violation of Article 3 in respect of the applicant's sentence.

Since the applicant had been detained following conviction by a competent court his detention fell within the scope of Article 5.1(a) of the Convention. There could be no question but that the sentence of detention during Her Majesty's pleasure was lawful under English law and was imposed in accordance with a procedure prescribed by law. Moreover, it could not be said that the applicant's detention was not in conformity with the purposes of the deprivation of liberty permitted by Article 5.1(a), so as to be arbitrary. It followed that there had been no violation of Article 5.1 of the Convention.

However, the Court recalled that Article 6.1 guarantees certain rights in respect of the "determination of ... any criminal charge ...". In criminal matters, it was clear that Article 6(1) covers the whole of the proceedings in issue, including appeal proceedings and the determination of sentence. In contrast to the mandatory life sentence imposed on adults convicted of murder which constitutes punishment for life, the sentence of detention during Her Majesty's pleasure was open-ended. A period of detention, "the tariff", was served to satisfy the requirements of retribution and deterrence, and thereafter it was legitimate to continue to detain the offender only if this appeared to be necessary for the protection of the public. It followed that the fixing of the tariff amounts to a sentencing exercise. Article 6.1 was, accordingly, applicable to this procedure. That Article guarantees, *inter alia*, "a fair ... hearing ... by an independent and impartial tribunal ...". "Independent" in this context means independent of the parties to the case and also of the executive. The Home Secretary, who set the applicant's tariff, was clearly not independent of the executive, and it followed that there had been a violation of Article 6.1.

Moreover, the Court recalled that where a national court, after convicting a person of a criminal offence, imposes a fixed sentence of imprisonment for the purposes of punishment, the supervision required by Article 5.4 is incorporated in that court decision. That was not the case, however, in respect of any ensuing period of detention in which new issues affecting the lawfulness of the detention might arise. Since the failure to have the applicant's tariff set by an independent tribunal gave rise to a violation of Article 6.1 and given that the sentence of detention during Her Majesty's pleasure was indeterminate and that the tariff was initially set by the Home Secretary rather than the sentencing judge, it could not be said that the supervision required by Article 5.4 was incorporated in the trial court's sentence. It followed that the applicant had been deprived, since his conviction, of the opportunity to have the lawfulness of his detention reviewed by a judicial body in accordance with Article 5.4 and there was a violation of that Article.

EXAMINATION OF WITNESSES

Unterpertinger v Austria (1991) 13 EHRR 175

The applicant had been prosecuted for assaults on his stepdaughter and his wife. At the trial, the wife and stepdaughter availed themselves of their right under Austrian law to refuse to give evidence. At the request of the Public Prosecutor's Department, however, the documents it had mentioned in its application for leave to prosecute including the police reports, the accused's criminal record and two files relating to previous convictions of his, were read out. These documents thus included the various statements made by the wife and stepdaughter to the police. The applicant was convicted and was sentenced to six months' imprisonment. His appeal was unsuccessful. He complained of a breach of Article 6.3(d) and asserted that because the two women had refused, as close relatives, to give evidence at the trial, he had not had an opportunity to examine them or to have them examined at any stage of the proceedings.

Held that the guarantees contained in Article 6.3 are specific aspects of the general concept of a fair trial set forth in paragraph 1. The Court would consider the applicant's complaints from the angle of paragraph 1 taken together with the principles inherent in paragraph 3(d).

In itself, the reading out of statements could not be regarded as being inconsistent with Article 6.1 and 3(d) of the Convention, but the use made of them as evidence must nevertheless comply with the rights of the defence, which it is the object and purpose of Article 6 to protect. This is especially so where the person "charged with a criminal offence", who has the right under Article 6.3(d) to "examine or have examined" witnesses against him, has not had an opportunity at any stage in the earlier proceedings to question the persons whose statements are read out at the hearing. By refusing to give evidence in court, the wife and stepdaughter prevented the applicant from examining them or having them examined on their statements. Admittedly, he was able to submit his comments freely during the hearing, but the Court of Appeal had refused to admit the evidence he sought to adduce in order to put his former wife's stepdaughter's credibility in doubt.

It was true that the statements were not the only evidence before the courts. They also had before them, *inter alia*, the police reports, the medical reports appended thereto and the file on the couple's divorce proceedings; in addition, the Court of Appeal had heard a sister-in-law of Mr Unterpertinger as a witness. However, it was clear from the judgment of 4 June 1980 that the Court of Appeal based the applicant's conviction mainly on the statements made by the wife and stepdaughter. It did not treat these simply as items of information but as proof of the truth of the accusations made by the women at the time. Mr Unterpertinger was convicted on the basis of "testimony" in respect of which his defence rights were appreciably restricted. That being so, the applicant did not have a fair trial and there was a breach of paragraph 1 of Article 6 of the Convention, taken together with the principles inherent in paragraph 3(d).

Asch v Austria (1993) 15 EHRR 597

A dispute broke out between the applicant and his cohabitee. She left the house and took refuge at her mother's home. The following morning she consulted a doctor. He found her to be suffering from multiple bruising and headaches. A report drawn up by the hospital stated that she claimed to have been struck with a belt and that she had several bruises on her body and one on her head. She reported the incident to the police and alleged that the applicant had threatened to use violence on her if she did not get out immediately. As she refused to obey, he had hit her with a belt on her back, her arms and her legs. Seeing him seize a rifle, she had tried to reason with him and then taken advantage of a moment of calm to escape.

She subsequently returned to the police station to inform the relevant officers that she and the applicant had been reconciled and that she had returned to live with him. She expressed her wish to withdraw her complaint. However, the prosecutor proceeded with the case. The cohabitee refused to give evidence and her statement was read out by a police officer. The applicant was convicted. He complained of a breach of Article 6 of the Convention.

Held that as the guarantees in paragraph 3 of Article 6 are specific aspects of the right to a fair trial set forth in paragraph 1, the Court would consider the complaint under the two provisions taken together. Although she refused to testify at the hearing she should, for the purposes of Article 6.3(d), be regarded as a witness—a term to be given an autonomous interpretation—because her statements, as taken down in writing by a police officer and then related orally by him at the hearing, were in fact before the court, which took account of them.

The admissibility of evidence is primarily a matter for regulation by national law and, as a rule, it is for the national courts to assess the evidence before them. The Court's task is to ascertain whether the proceedings considered as a whole, including the way in which evidence was taken, were fair. All the evidence must normally be produced in the presence of the accused at a public hearing with a view to adversarial argument. This does not mean, however, that the statement of a witness must always be made in court and in public if it is to be admitted in evidence; in particular, this may prove impossible in certain cases.

The use in this way of statements obtained at the pre-trial stage is not in itself inconsistent with paragraphs 3(d) and 1 of Article 6, provided that the rights of the defence have been respected. As a rule, these rights require that the defendant be given an adequate and proper opportunity to challenge and question a witness against him, either when he was making his statements or at a later stage of the proceedings. In this instance, before the trial court only the police officer recounted the facts of the case as the cohabitee had described them to him on the very day of the incident. It would clearly have been preferable if it had been possible to hear her in person, but the right on which she relied in order to avoid giving evidence could not be allowed to block the prosecution, the appropriateness of which it was, moreover, not for the European Court to determine. Subject to the rights of the defence being respected, it was, therefore, open to the national court to have regard to this statement, in particular in view of the fact that it could consider it to be corroborated by other evidence before it, including the two medical certificates attesting to the injuries. Furthermore, the applicant had the opportunity to discuss the cohabitee's version of events and to put his own, first to the police and later to the court. However, on each occasion he gave a different version, which tended to undermine his credibility.

It was clear from the file that the cohabitee's statements did not constitute the only item of evidence on which the first instance court based its decision. It also had regard to the personal assessment made by the police officer as a result of his interviews with the cohabitee and the applicant, to the two concurring medical certificates, to the police investigation and to the other evidence appearing in the applicant's file. The fact that it was impossible to question the cohabitee at the hearing did not, therefore, in the circumstances of the case, violate the rights of the defence and did not deprive the accused of a fair trial. Accordingly, there had been no breach of paragraphs 1 and 3(d) of Article 6, taken together.

Doorson v The Netherlands (1996) 22 EHRR 330

The police received information that the applicant was engaged in drug-trafficking. A number of drug addicts subsequently stated to the police that they recognised the applicant from his photograph and that he had sold drugs. Some of these drug addicts remained anonymous.

The applicant was arrested on suspicion of having committed drug offences. A preliminary judicial investigation was opened, during which the applicant's lawyer submitted a request for an examination of the witnesses referred to in the police report in the applicant's case. The investigating judge accordingly ordered the police to bring these witnesses before him on 30 May 1988 between 9.30 am and 4.00 pm. The applicant's lawyer was notified and invited to attend the questioning of these witnesses before the investigating judge. However, after an hour and a half had elapsed and none of the witnesses had appeared, he concluded that no questioning would take place. He, therefore, left for another appointment. After the lawyer had left, two of the eight witnesses referred to in the police report turned up and were heard by the investigating judge in the absence of the lawyer.

The case proceeded and the applicant was ultimately convicted and sentenced to imprisonment. He appealed to the Amsterdam Court of Appeal and his lawyer requested that the anonymous witnesses should be summoned to give evidence. The Court of Appeal decided to verify the necessity of maintaining the anonymity of the witnesses and referred the case back to the investigating judge for this purpose. The Court of Appeal also requested the investigating judge to examine the witnesses with respect to the facts imputed to the applicant, and to offer his lawyer the opportunity both to attend this examination in the room in which it would take place and to put questions to the witnesses. This was done and the lawyer was given the opportunity to put questions to the witnesses but was not informed of their identity. The identity of both witnesses was known to the investigating judge.

The Court of Appeal ultimately quashed the Regional Court's judgment and substituted a conviction for the deliberate sale of quantities of heroin and cocaine. This finding was based on the following evidence: (a) the fact, as appeared from the police records, that upon information that the applicant was engaged in drug-trafficking his photograph was added to the collection of photographs of persons suspected of that offence; (b) the statements made before the investigating judge by the anonymous witnesses; (c) the fact that the applicant had recognised himself on the police photograph; and (d) statements made to the police by named witnesses. The applicant was sentenced to 15 months' imprisonment. The time which he had spent in police custody and detention on remand was deducted from the sentence. A further appeal, to the Supreme Court, was unsuccessful.

The applicant complained that he had been a victim of violations of Article 6.1 and 3(d) of the Convention in that he had been convicted on the evidence of witnesses who had not been heard in his presence and whom he had not had the opportunity to question, in that the Court of Appeal had accepted the evidence of the anonymous witnesses on the basis of the statement of an investigating judge who at a previous stage of the proceedings had participated in a decision to prolong his detention on remand, and in that the Court of Appeal had refused to hear an expert brought forward by the defence but had agreed to hear an expert brought forward by the prosecution.

Held that, as the requirements of Article 6.3 are to be seen as particular aspects of the right to a fair trial guaranteed by Article 6.1 the Court would examine the complaints under Article 6.1 and 3(d) taken together.

The admissibility of evidence is primarily a matter for regulation by national law and as a general rule it is for the national courts to assess the evidence before them. The Court's task under the Convention is not to give a ruling as to whether statements of witnesses were properly admitted as evidence, but rather to ascertain whether the proceedings as a whole, including the way in which evidence was taken, were fair. The Convention does not preclude reliance, at the investigation stage, on sources such as anonymous informants. The subsequent use of their statements by the trial court to found a conviction is however capable of raising issues under the Convention. But such use is not under all circumstances incompatible with the Convention.

It is true that Article 6 does not explicitly require the interests of witnesses in general, and those of victims called upon to testify in particular, to be taken into consideration. However, their life, liberty or security of person may be at stake, as may interests coming generally within the ambit of Article 8 of the Convention. Such interests of witnesses and victims are in principle protected by other, substantive provisions of the Convention, which imply that Contracting States should organise their criminal proceedings in such a way that those interests are not unjustifiably imperilled. Against this background, principles of fair trial also require that in appropriate cases the interests of the defence are balanced against those of witnesses or victims called upon to testify. As the Amsterdam Court of Appeal made clear, its decision not to disclose the identity of witnesses to the defence was inspired by the need, as assessed by it, to obtain evidence from them while at the same time protecting them against the possibility of reprisals by the applicant. This was certainly a relevant reason to allow them anonymity. Although there had been no suggestion that witnesses were ever threatened by the applicant himself, the decision to maintain their anonymity could not be regarded as unreasonable *per se*. Regard must be had to the fact, as established by the domestic courts and not contested by the applicant, that drug dealers frequently resorted to threats or actual violence against persons who gave evidence against them. Furthermore, the statements made by the witnesses concerned to the investigating judge showed that one of them had apparently on a previous occasion suffered violence at the hands of a drug dealer against whom he had testified, while the other had been threatened. In sum, there was sufficient reason for maintaining the anonymity of witnesses.

The maintenance of the anonymity of the witnesses presented the defence with difficulties which criminal proceedings should not normally involve. Nevertheless, no violation of Article 6.1 taken together with Article 6.3(d) of the Convention can be found if it is established that the handicaps under which the defence laboured were sufficiently counterbalanced by the procedures followed by the judicial authorities. In the instant case the anonymous witnesses were questioned at the appeals stage in the presence of Counsel by an investigating judge who was aware of their identity, even if the defence was not. She noted, in the official record of her findings dated 19 November 1990, circumstances on the basis of which the Court of Appeal was able to draw conclusions as to the reliability of their evidence. Counsel was not only present, but he was put in a position to ask the witnesses whatever questions he considered to be in the interests of the defence except in so far as they might lead to the disclosure of their identity, and these questions were all answered. While it would clearly have been preferable for the applicant to have attended the questioning of the witnesses, the Court considered, on balance, that the Amsterdam Court of Appeal was entitled to consider that the interests of the applicant were in this respect outweighed by the need to ensure the safety of the witnesses. More generally, the Convention does not preclude identification, for the purposes of Article 6.3(d), of an accused with his counsel.

It followed that in the circumstances the "counterbalancing" procedure followed by the judicial authorities in obtaining the evidence of witnesses must be considered sufficient to have enabled the defence to challenge the evidence of the anonymous witnesses and attempt to cast doubt on the reliability of their statements. Finally, it should be recalled that, even when "counterbalancing" procedures are found to compensate sufficiently the handicaps under which the defence labours, a conviction should not be based either solely or to a decisive extent on anonymous statements.

In summary, the Court could not find that the proceedings as a whole were unfair. Accordingly, there had been no violation of Article 6.1 taken together with Article 6.3(d) of the Convention.

THE FREE ASSISTANCE OF AN INTERPRETER

Luedicke, Belkacem and Koc v Federal Republic of Germany (1980) 2 EHRR 149

Each of the applicants was a foreign national with limited command of German who had been prosecuted and convicted of an offence in Germany and ordered to pay the costs of the proceedings, including the interpretation costs. Each applied to the Commission on the basis that the requirement to pay for the interpreter to whose services the Convention entitled them constituted a breach of Article 6.3(e).

Held that in interpreting Article 6.3(e) the Court would be guided by the Vienna Convention on the Law of Treaties 1969. In both French and English (the Court's two official languages) the terms "gratuitement" and "free", which Article 6.3(e) uses to describe the basis on which the interpreter's services are to be provided, are unqualified, denoting a once and for all exemption or exoneration. It had to be determined whether context and object and purpose negatived that literal interpretation. To read the Article as allowing the domestic court to require a person who has been convicted to meet inter-pretation costs would be to limit Article 6.3(e) in time and in practice to deny its benefit to a person who is eventually convicted. This might have implications for fair trial. The ordinary meaning of "gratuitement" and "free" is not contradicted by context or by object and purpose and the requirement to pay interpretation costs, therefore, amounted to a breach of the Convention.

ARTICLE 7

THE RIGHT NOT TO BE SUBJECTED
TO RETROSPECTIVE CRIMINALISATION

1. No one shall be held guilty of any criminal offence on account of any act or omission which did not constitute a criminal offence under national or international law at the time when it was committed. Nor shall a heavier penalty be imposed than the one that was applicable at the time the criminal offence was committed.

2. This article shall not prejudice the trial and punishment of any person for any act or omission which, at the time when it was committed, was criminal according to the general principles of law recognised by civilised nations.

Welch v United Kingdom (1995) 20 EHRR 247

The applicant was arrested and charged in November 1986 in relation to drug-trafficking offences. In January 1987 the Drug Trafficking Offences Act 1986 came into force, making it possible for the first time for English courts to impose confiscation orders. In February and May 1987 the applicant was charged with further drug-trafficking offences. In August 1988 he was convicted of five counts. He was imprisoned and a confiscation order was imposed in the sum of £66,914 (subsequently reduced on appeal to £59,914). He complained under Article 7 that the imposition of a confiscation order constituted a retroactive criminal penalty. The Government argued that the true purpose of a confiscation order was two-fold: first, to deprive a person of the profits which he had received from drug-trafficking and second, to remove the value of the proceeds from future use in the drugs trade. On this basis, the Government argued, confiscation was not a penalty.

Held that the concept of a penalty in Article 7 is an autonomous Convention concept. The wording of Article 7.1 indicates that the starting point for the assessment of the existence of a penalty is whether the measure is imposed following conviction for a criminal offence. Other factors that may be taken into account are the nature and purpose of the measure in question, its characterisation under national law, the procedures involved in the making and implementation of the measure and its severity. Before a confiscation

order can be made in English law, the accused must have been convicted of a
drug-trafficking offence. This link is not diminished by the fact that, due to
the operation of the statutory presumptions concerning the extent to which
the accused has benefited from drug-trafficking, the court order may affect
proceeds which are not directly related to the facts underlying the criminal
conviction. The 1986 Act was introduced to overcome the inadequacy of existing powers of forfeiture. Although the provisions were designed to ensure
that proceeds were not available for use in future drug-trafficking and that
crime does not pay, the legislation also pursues the aim of punishing the
offender. The aims of prevention and reparation are consistent with a punitive
purpose and may be seen as constituent elements of the very notion of
punishment.

Several aspects of the making of an order under the 1986 Act were in keeping
with the idea of a penalty even though they were essential to the preventive scheme inherent in the 1986 Act. These included the sweeping statutory
assumptions that all property passing through the offender's hands during
a six-year period is the fruit of drug-trafficking unless he can prove otherwise, the fact that the confiscation order is directed to proceeds and not
restricted to actual enrichment or profit, the discretion of the trial judge in
fixing the order to take account of the degree of culpability of the accused
and the possibility of imprisonment in default of payment. These elements,
considered together, provide a strong indication of, *inter alia*, a regime of
punishment. Looking behind appearances at the reality of the situation,
whatever the characterisation of the measure of confiscation, the fact remains
that the applicant faced more far-reaching detriment as a result of the order
than that to which he was exposed at the time of the commission of the offences
of which he was convicted. There was, therefore, a breach of Article 7; but the
Court stressed that its conclusion related only to the retrospective application
of the legislation and did not call into question in any respect the powers of
confiscation conferred on the courts as a weapon in the fight against the
scourge of drug-trafficking.

C.R. v United Kingdom; S.W. v United Kingdom (1995) 21 EHRR 363

These two cases raised the same issue and were heard by the Court on the
same day.

C.R. was separated from his wife. She had returned to live with her parents
and had left a letter for the applicant in which she informed him that she intended to petition for divorce. However, no legal proceedings had been taken
by her before the occurrence of the incident which gave rise to criminal
proceedings. Twenty-two days after his wife had returned to live with her
parents, and while the parents were out, the applicant forced his way into the
parents' house and attempted to have sexual intercourse with the wife against
her will. In the course of that attempt he assaulted her, in particular by

squeezing her neck with both hands. He was in due course convicted of (*inter alia*) attempted rape. He appealed on the ground that the trial judge had made a wrong decision in law in ruling that a man may rape his wife when the consent to intercourse which his wife gave on entering marriage had been revoked neither by a court order nor by agreement between the parties. His appeal was unsuccessful and the Court of Appeal remarked that:

> "It seems to us that where the common law rule [as relied on by the applicant] no longer even remotely represents what is the true position of a wife in present-day society, the duty of the court is to take steps to alter the rule if it can legitimately do so ... We take the view that the time has now arrived when the law should declare that a rapist remains a rapist subject to the criminal law, irrespective of his relationship with his victim."

The Court of Appeal granted the applicant leave to appeal to the House of Lords, which unanimously upheld the Court of Appeal's judgment and pointed out that:

> "the common law is ... capable of evolving in the light of changing social, economic and cultural developments. Hale's proposition reflected the state of affairs in these respects at the time it was enunciated. Since then the status of women, and particularly of married women, has changed out of all recognition in various ways which are very familiar and upon which it is unnecessary to go into detail. Apart from property matters and the availability of matrimonial remedies, one of the most important changes is that marriage is in modern times regarded as a partnership of equals, and no longer one in which the wife was the subservient chattel of the husband. Hale's proposition involves that by marriage a wife gives her irrevocable consent to sexual intercourse with her husband under all circumstances and irrespective of the state of her health or how she happens to be feeling at the time. In modern times any reasonable person must regard that conception as quite unacceptable".

S.W.'s wife had told him that for some weeks she had been thinking of leaving him and that she regarded the marriage as over. Prior to that date they had been sleeping separately—according to the applicant, for one night, or according to his wife, for five nights. The applicant did not accept that his wife meant what she said and they had a row following which he ejected her from the house, bruising her arm. She went to her next door neighbours and called the police, who subsequently visited and spoke to both the applicant and his wife separately. Later the same evening she re-entered the house and the applicant had sexual intercourse with her. Shortly afterwards she left the house, having first tried to take their child with her. She went to the neighbours crying and distressed, complaining to them and to the police, whom she telephoned, that she had been raped at knife-point. S.W. was prosecuted for rape and maintained unsuccessfully that the retrospective effect of the change in the law effected by the Court of Appeal and House of Lords in the case against C.R. should be pronounced incompatible with Article 7 of the Convention.

Both C.R. and S.W. complained of a breach of Article 7.

Held that the guarantee enshrined in Article 7, which is an essential element of the rule of law, occupies a prominent place in the Convention system of protection, as is underlined by the fact that no derogation from it is permissible under Article 15. It should be construed and applied, as follows from its object and purpose, in such a way as to provide effective safeguards against arbitrary prosecution, conviction and punishment. As the Court said in *Kokkinakis* v *Greece*, Article 7 is not confined to prohibiting the retrospective application of the criminal law to an accused's disadvantage: it also embodies, more generally, the principle that only the law can define a crime and prescribe a penalty (*nullum crimen, nulla poena sine lege*) and the principle that the criminal law must not be extensively construed to an accused's detriment, for instance by analogy. From these principles it follows that an offence must be clearly defined in the law. This requirement is satisfied where the individual can know from the wording of the relevant provision and, if need be, with the assistance of the courts' interpretation of it, what acts and omissions will make him criminally liable. The Court thus indicated that when speaking of "law" Article 7 alludes to the very same concept as that to which the Convention refers elsewhere when using that term, a concept which comprises written as well as unwritten law and implies qualitative requirements, notably those of accessibility and foreseeability.

However clearly drafted a legal provision may be, in any system of law, including criminal law, there is an inevitable element of judicial interpretation. There will always be a need for elucidation of doubtful points and for adaptation to changing circumstances. Indeed, in the UK, as in the other Convention States, the progressive development of the criminal law through judicial law-making is a well-entrenched and necessary part of legal tradition. Article 7 of the Convention cannot be read as outlawing the gradual clarification of the rules of criminal liability through judicial interpretation from case to case, provided that the resultant development is consistent with the essence of the offence and could reasonably be foreseen.

It is in the first place for the national authorities, notably the courts, to interpret and apply national law. The decisions of the Court of Appeal and then the House of Lords did no more than continue a perceptible line of case law development dismantling the immunity of a husband from prosecution for rape upon his wife. There was no doubt under the law as it stood that a husband who forcibly had sexual intercourse with his wife could, in various circumstances, be found guilty of rape. Moreover, there was an evident evolution, which was consistent with the very essence of the offence, of the criminal law through judicial interpretation towards treating such conduct generally as within the scope of the offence of rape. This evolution had reached a stage where judicial recognition of the absence of immunity had become a reasonably foreseeable development of the law.

The essentially debasing character of rape is so manifest that the result of the decisions of the Court of Appeal and the House of Lords—that the applicant could be convicted of attempted rape, irrespective of his relationship with the victim—could not be said to be at variance with the object and purpose of Article 7 of the Convention, namely to ensure that no one should be subjected to arbitrary prosecution, conviction or punishment. What is more, the abandonment of the unacceptable idea of a husband being immune against prosecution for rape of his wife was in conformity not only with a civilised concept of marriage but also, and above all, with the fundamental objectives of the Convention, the very essence of which is respect for human dignity and human freedom.

There was no breach of Article 7 in either case.

ARTICLE 8

THE RIGHT TO RESPECT FOR PRIVATE LIFE

1. Everyone has the right to respect for his private and family life, his home and his correspondence.
2. There shall be no interference by a public authority with the exercise of this right except such as is in accordance with the law and is necessary in a democratic society in the interests of national security, public safety or the economic well-being of the country, for the prevention of disorder or crime, for the protection of health or morals, or for the protection of the rights and freedoms of others.

PRIVATE LIFE

Halford v United Kingdom (1997) 24 EHRR 523

The applicant was Assistant Chief Constable with the Merseyside police and, as such, the most senior-ranking female police officer in the UK. However, Home Office approval for her promotion to Deputy Chief Constable was consistently withheld on the recommendation of the Chief Constable of the Merseyside police, who objected to her commitment to equality of treatment between men and women. She commenced Industrial Tribunal proceedings against the Chief Constable and the Home Secretary, claiming that she had been discriminated against on grounds of sex. In due course, the Industrial Tribunal proceedings were settled on terms favourable to the applicant. She complained to the Commission that calls made on her office telephones were intercepted with a view to securing material for use in relation to the Industrial Tribunal, so that there had been, *inter alia*, breaches of Articles 8 and 13.

Held that telephone calls made from business premises as well as from the home may be covered by the notions of "private life" and "correspondence" within the meaning of Article 8. There was no evidence of any warning having been given that calls from the applicant's office would be liable to interception. She would have had a reasonable expectation of privacy for such calls, especially because one of her office phones was specifically designated for her private use and because she had been given an assurance that she could use her office telephones for the purposes of her sex discrimination case.

The evidence justified the conclusion that there was a reasonable likelihood that calls made by Ms Halford from her office were intercepted by the Merseyside police with the primary aim of gathering material to assist in the defence of the sex discrimination proceedings brought against them. This interception constituted an "interference by a public authority", within the meaning of Article 8, with the exercise of Ms Halford's right to respect for her private life and correspondence.

The requirement that any interference must be "in accordance with the law" does not only necessitate compliance with domestic law, but also relates to the quality of that law, requiring it to be compatible with the rule of law. In the context of secret measures of surveillance or interception of communications by public authorities, because of the lack of public scrutiny and the risk of misuse of power, the domestic law must provide some protection to the individual against arbitrary interference with Article 8 rights. Thus, the domestic law must be sufficiently clear in its terms to give citizens an adequate indication as to the circumstances in and conditions on which public authorities are empowered to resort to any such secret measures.

The Government had accepted that if, contrary to their submission, the Court were to conclude that there had been an interference with the applicant's rights under Article 8 in relation to her office telephones, such interference was not "in accordance with the law" since domestic law did not provide any regulation of interceptions of calls made on telecommunications systems outside the public network. It followed that there had been a violation of Article 8. Moreover, since there was no provision in domestic law to regulate interceptions of telephone calls made on internal communications systems operated by public authorities, such as the Merseyside police, the applicant was unable to seek relief at national level in relation to her complaint. It followed that there had been a violation of Article 13.

FAMILY

Keegan v Ireland (1994) 18 EHRR 342

After the applicant had been cohabiting with his girlfriend for about 10 months, they decided to have a child. Subsequently, they became engaged to be married and about a week later it was confirmed that the girlfriend was pregnant. Shortly after this the relationship broke down and they ceased cohabiting. The day after the birth of their daughter the applicant visited and saw the baby. Two weeks later he visited the girlfriend's parents' home but was not permitted to see either her or the child. During her pregnancy, the girlfriend had made arrangements to have the child adopted and in due course she had the child placed by a registered adoption society with the prospective adopters. She informed the applicant of this by letter a week later.

The applicant subsequently instituted court proceedings to be appointed guardian, which would have enabled him to challenge the proposed adoption. However, it was ultimately held that the first and paramount consideration in the exercise of the court's discretion was the welfare of the child, and the blood link between child and father as merely one of the many relevant factors which may be viewed by the court as relevant to that question. It was said that regard should not be had to the objective of satisfying the wishes and desires of the father to be involved in the guardianship of and to enjoy the society of his child unless the court had first concluded that the quality of welfare which would probably be achieved for the infant by its custody with the prospective adoptive parents, as compared with the quality of welfare which would probably be achieved by custody with the father was not to an important extent better. There was evidence that the child would suffer trauma if moved to the applicant's custody. It could not be said that the quality of welfare likely to be achieved with the prospective adopters would not be to an important extent better than that likely to be achieved by custody with the father. An adoption order was made in respect of the child.

Held that the notion of the "family" in Article 8 is not confined solely to marriage-based relationships and may encompass other *de facto* "family" ties where the parties are living together outside of marriage. A child born out of such a relationship is *ipso iure* part of that "family" unit from the moment of his birth and by the very fact of it. There thus exists between the child and his parents a bond amounting to family life even if at the time of his or her birth the parents are no longer cohabiting or if their relationship has then ended. In the present case, the relationship between the applicant and the child's mother lasted for two years during one of which they cohabited. Moreover, the conception of their child was the result of a deliberate decision and they had also planned to get married. Their relationship at this time had thus the hallmark of family life for the purposes of Article 8. The fact that it subsequently broke down did not alter this conclusion any more than it would for a couple who were lawfully married and in a similar situation. It followed that from the moment of the child's birth there existed between the applicant and his daughter a bond amounting to family life.

The essential object of Article 8 is to protect the individual against arbitrary action by the public authorities. There might be, in addition, positive obligations inherent in an effective "respect" for family life. The boundaries between the State's positive and negative obligations under this provision do not lend themselves to precise definition. The applicable principles are similar. In both contexts regard must be had to the fair balance that has to be struck between the competing interests of the individual and of the community as a whole; and in both contexts the State enjoys a certain margin of appreciation.

Where the existence of a family tie with a child has been established, the State must act in a manner calculated to enable that tie to be developed and legal safeguards must be created that render possible as from the moment of birth the child's integration in his family. The mutual enjoyment by parent and child of each other's company constitutes a fundamental element of family life even when the relationship between the parents has broken down.

In the present case the obligations inherent in Article 8 were closely intertwined, bearing in mind the State's involvement in the adoption process. The fact that Irish law permitted the secret placement of the child for adoption without the applicant's knowledge or consent, leading to the bonding of the child with the proposed adopters and to the subsequent making of an adoption order, amounted to an interference with his right to respect for family life.

Such interference is permissible only if the conditions set out in paragraph 2 of Article 8 are satisfied. It was clear that the decision to place the child for adoption without the father's knowledge or consent was in accordance with Irish law as were the decisions taken by the courts concerning the welfare of the child. It was also evident that they pursued the legitimate aim of protecting the rights and freedoms of the child. The essential problem in the present case was with the fact that Irish law permitted the applicant's child to have been placed for adoption shortly after her birth without his knowledge or consent. Such a state of affairs not only jeopardised the proper development of the applicant's ties with the child but also set in motion a process which was likely to prove to be irreversible, thereby putting the applicant at a significant disadvantage in his contest with the prospective adopters for the custody of the child. The Government had advanced no reasons relevant to the welfare of the applicant's daughter to justify such a departure from the principles that govern respect for family ties. That being so, the Court could not consider that the interference which it had found with the applicant's right to respect for family life was necessary in a democratic society. There had thus been a violation of Article 8.

Hokkanen v Finland (1994) 19 EHRR 139

Following the death of his wife, the applicant's daughter was looked after by her maternal grandparents. According to the applicant, he had agreed to this as a provisional arrangement so that he could deal with various problems caused by his wife's death. The grandparents, however, refused to return the child to him and the authorities refused to order her return on the basis that he had consented to the arrangement leaving the child in the care of the grandparents and that, in view of the lapse of time and of the little contact the child had had with the applicant, returning her could be contrary to her own interests.

Custody proceedings were commenced in court and a provisional order was made that the child should remain with her grandparents but that the applicant should have certain access rights. The grandparents refused to respect those access rights. In due course, the court awarded custody to the applicant but the grandparents refused to comply with that order. Little was done by the authorities to secure compliance and what was done was ineffective.

Held that the child of a marriage is *ipso iure* part of that "family" unit from the moment of birth and by the very fact of it. The applicant remained the child's legal guardian and had continuously sought to have access to her and to have her returned to him. He had met her on a number of occasions. These links were undoubtedly sufficient to establish "family life" within the meaning of Article 8.

The essential object of Article 8 is to protect the individual against arbitrary interference by the public authorities. There might in addition be positive obligations inherent in an effective "respect" for family life. Whilst the boundaries between the State's positive and negative obligations under this provision do not lend themselves to precise definition, the applicable principles are similar. In particular, in both contexts regard must be had to the fair balance that has to be struck between the competing interests of the individual and the community as a whole, and in both contexts the State is recognised as enjoying a certain margin of appreciation. The Court's role was not to substitute itself for the competent Finnish authorities in regulating custody and access issues in Finland, but rather to review under the Convention the decisions that those authorities have taken in the exercise of their power of appreciation. In so doing, it must determine whether the reasons purporting to justify the actual measures adopted with regard to the applicant's enjoyment of his right to respect for family life were relevant and sufficient under Article 8.

Article 8 includes a right for the parent to have measures taken with a view to his or her being reunited with the child and an obligation for the national authorities to take such action. This principle had to be taken as also applying to cases such as the present where the origin of the provisional transfer of care was a private agreement. The obligation of the national authorities to take measures to facilitate reunion was not absolute, since the reunion of a parent with a child who has lived for some time with other persons might not be able to take place immediately and might require preparatory measures being taken to this effect. The nature and extent of such preparation would depend on the circumstances of each case, but the understanding and co-operation of all concerned would always be an important ingredient. Whilst national authorities must do their utmost to facilitate such co-operation, any obligation to apply coercion in this area had to be limited since the interests as well as the rights and freedoms of all concerned must be taken into account, and more particularly the best interests of the child and his or her rights under Article 8. Where contacts with the parent might appear to threaten those interests or interfere with those rights, it was for the national authorities to strike a fair balance between them. What was decisive was whether the national authorities had taken all necessary steps to facilitate reunion as can reasonably be demanded in the special circumstances of each case.

In the present case, it could not be said that the competent authorities made reasonable efforts to facilitate reunion. On the contrary, the inaction of the authorities placed the burden on the applicant to have constant recourse to a succession of time-consuming and ultimately ineffectual remedies to enforce his rights. Accordingly, notwithstanding the margin of appreciation enjoyed by the competent authorities, the non-enforcement of the applicant's right of access constituted a breach of his right to respect for his family life under Article 8.

Kroon and Others v The Netherlands (1994) 19 EHRR 263

The first applicant, whilst separated from but still married to her husband bore a son to the second applicant. She obtained a divorce some months later. Although they did not cohabit, the applicants sought to have the second applicant registered as the father of the child but, because the first applicant had still been married when the child was born, such registration was not possible unless the husband brought proceedings to deny paternity.

Held that the notion of "family life" in Article 8 is not confined solely to marriage-based relationships. Although, as a rule, living together may be a requirement for such a relationship, exceptionally other factors may also serve to demonstrate that a relationship has sufficient constancy to create *de facto* "family ties"; such was the case here, as four children had since been born to the applicants. A child born of such a relationship is *ipso iure* part of that "family unit" from the moment of its birth and by the very fact of it. There thus existed between the boy and the second applicant a bond amounting to family life, whatever the contribution of the latter to his son's care and up-bringing. Article 8 was, therefore, applicable.

The essential object of Article 8 is to protect the individual against arbitrary action by the public authorities. There might, in addition, be positive obligations inherent in effective "respect" for family life. The boundaries between the State's positive and negative obligations under this provision do not lend themselves to precise definition but the applicable principles are none the less similar. In both contexts regard must be had to the fair balance that has to be struck between the competing interests of the individual and of the community as a whole; and in both contexts the State enjoys a certain margin of appreciation.

According to the principles set out by the Court in its case law, where the existence of a family tie with a child has been established, the State must act in a manner calculated to enable that tie to be developed and legal safeguards must be established that render possible as from the moment of birth or as soon as practicable thereafter the child's integration in his family. In the instant case it had been established that the relationship between the applicants qualified as "family life". There was thus a positive obligation on the part of the competent authorities to allow complete legal family ties to be formed between the first applicant and his son as expeditiously as possible. The Government suggested that the option of "step-parent adoption", which was available, would make the boy the "legitimate" child of the applicants; but it would have required them to marry each other, which they did not wish to do. A solution which only allowed a father to create a legal tie with a child with whom he has a bond amounting to family life if he marries the child's mother could not be regarded as compatible with the notion of "respect" for family life. "Respect" for "family life" required that biological and social reality prevail over a legal presumption which, as in the present case, flew in the face of both established fact and the wishes of those concerned without actually benefiting anyone. Accordingly, even having regard to the margin of appreciation left to the State, The Netherlands had failed to secure to the applicants the "respect" for their family life to which they were entitled under the Convention. There had accordingly been a violation of Article 8.

HOME

Gillow v United Kingdom (1986) 11 EHRR 339

The applicants had been born in England. When the first applicant was appointed to an official position on Guernsey, they built and occupied a house on the island. After he resigned from that position they had retained ownership of the house, to which they always intended to return, and kept their furniture in it. Since the first applicant's work required them to live elsewhere, they let the house to tenants. When the last tenant left, the applicants proposed to return and live in the house but were told by the Guernsey authorities that they could not do so without a licence under the Housing (Control of Occupation) (Guernsey) Law 1975. That was the latest in a series of pieces of legislation passed to deal with intense pressure on the island's housing stock. It operated by requiring the satisfaction of certain qualifications for residence. The application for a licence was refused in the light of the "present adverse housing situation" and because, even assuming that Mrs Gillow took up employment considered essential to the community, the applicants would not be permitted to stay in their property after her retirement, because she was too old to complete a minimum of 10 consecutive years in such employment, as required by the Housing Law 1975.

Because repairs were required, the applicants nevertheless moved into the property. They were in due course prosecuted for so doing. The first applicant was convicted and fined. The applicants finally sold the property for a price which in their view was less than its actual value. Before the Court, the Government conceded that, since the applicants had not established a home elsewhere, the property on Guernsey had to be regarded as their home and that there were special circumstances affecting the applicants' position which rendered the refusal of licences disproportionate.

Held the Court's responsibilities extended to pronouncing on the non-contested allegation of violation of Article 8. Although the applicants had been absent from Guernsey for almost 19 years, they had in the circumstances retained sufficient continuing links with the house there for it to be considered their "home", for the purposes of Article 8. The fact that, on pain of prosecution, the applicants were obliged to obtain a licence to live in their own house, the refusal of the licences applied for, the institution of criminal proceedings against them for unlawful occupation of the property and, in Mr Gillow's case, his conviction and the imposition of a fine constituted interferences with the exercise of the applicants' right to respect for their home. The interferences were in accordance with the law and, since the island is very limited in area, it was legitimate for the authorities to try to maintain the population within limits that permit the balanced economic development of the island. It was also legitimate, in this connection, to show a certain preference for persons who had strong attachments to the island or were engaged in an employment essential to the community when considering whether to grant licences to occupy premises. The relevant legislation was thus designed to promote the economic well-being of the island.

The notion of necessity in a democratic society implies a pressing social need; in particular, the measure employed must be proportionate to the legitimate aim pursued. In addition, the scope of the margin of appreciation enjoyed by the national authorities will depend not only on the nature of the aim of the restriction but also on the nature of the right involved. In the instant case, the economic well-being of Guernsey had to be balanced against the applicants' right to respect for their "home", a right which is pertinent to their own personal security and well-being. The importance of such a right to the individual must be taken into account in determining the scope of the margin of appreciation allowed to the Government.

The Guernsey legislature was better placed than the international judge to assess the effects of any relaxation of the housing controls. Furthermore, when considering whether to grant a licence, the Housing Authority could exercise its discretion so as to avoid any disproportionality in a particular case. It followed that the statutory obligation imposed on the applicants to seek a licence to live in their "home" could not be regarded as disproportionate to the legitimate aim pursued. There had, accordingly, been no breach of Article 8 as far as the terms of the contested legislation are concerned. There remained, however, the question whether the manner in which the Housing Authority exercised its discretion in the applicants' case—refusal of permanent and temporary licences, and referral of the matter to the Law Officers with a view to prosecution—corresponded to a pressing social need and, in particular, was proportionate to the legitimate aim pursued. The Court considered that insufficient weight had been given to the applicants' particular circumstances. They had built the house as a residence for themselves and their family. At that time, they possessed "residence qualifications". Thereafter, they had retained ownership of the house and left furniture there. By letting it over a period of 18 years to persons approved by the Housing Authority, they contributed to the Guernsey housing stock. On their return in 1979, they had no other "home" in the UK or elsewhere; the house was vacant and there were no prospective tenants. Moreover, the house needed repairs after 18 years of rented use, with the result that it could not be occupied in the meantime by anyone other than the applicants. The Court, therefore, concluded that the decisions by the Housing Authority to refuse the applicants permanent and temporary licences to occupy the house, as well as the conviction and fining of Mr Gillow, constituted interferences with the exercise of their right to respect for their "home" which were disproportionate to the legitimate aim pursued. There had, accordingly, been a breach of Article 8.

(*Note*: The question of Protocol 1 Article 1 was not available for consideration by the Court because the UK had not extended the application of that Protocol to Guernsey.)

Niemietz v Germany (1992) 16 EHRR 97

A letter, bearing to be from a pressure group, was sent to Judge Miosga of the Freising District Court. It related to criminal proceedings pending before that court. It accused the judge of abuse of office, threatened to use every avenue to bring the matter to public attention and informed the judge that he was expected to "abandon the path of terrorisation" upon which he had embarked "and to reach the only decision appropriate in this case—an acquittal".

The applicant was a lawyer with links to the pressure group concerned. A number of premises, including the applicant's office, were subjected to wide-ranging searches under warrant with a view to identifying the author of the letter. The applicant complained of a breach of Article 8. The Government argued that Article 8 did not protect business premises.

Held that it was not possible or necessary to attempt an exhaustive definition of the notion of "private life". However, it would be too restrictive to limit the notion to an "inner circle" in which the individual may live his own personal life as he chooses and to exclude therefrom entirely the outside world not encompassed within that circle. Respect for private life must also comprise to a certain degree the right to establish and develop relationships with other human beings. There appeared to be no reason of principle why this understanding of the notion of "private life" should be taken to exclude activities of a professional or business nature since it is, after all, in the course of their working lives that the majority of people have a significant, if not the greatest, opportunity of developing relationships with the outside world. This view was supported by the fact that it is not always possible to distinguish clearly which of an individual's activities form part of his professional or business life and which do not. Thus, especially in the case of a person exercising a liberal profession, his work in that context may form part and parcel of his life to such a degree that it becomes impossible to know in what capacity he is acting at a given moment of time.

As regards the word "home", appearing in the English text of Article 8, in certain Contracting States it had been accepted as extending to business premises. Such an interpretation is fully consonant with the French text, since the word "domicile" has a broader connotation than the word "home" and may extend, for example, to a professional person's office. More generally, to interpret the words "private life" and "home" as including certain professional or business activities or premises would be consonant with the essential object and purpose of Article 8, namely to protect the individual against arbitrary interference by the public authorities.

The search of the applicant's office constituted an interference with his rights under Article 8. It was not in dispute that it pursued aims that were legitimate, namely the prevention of crime and the protection of the rights of others, that is the honour of Judge Miosga; but the Court considered that what was done was not proportionate to those aims. Whilst attempting to bring pressure on a judge is not a minor offence, the warrant was drawn in broad terms, in that it ordered a search for and seizure of "documents", without any limitation, revealing the identity of the author of the offensive letter; this point is of special significance where, as in Germany, the search of a lawyer's office is not accompanied by any special procedural safeguards, such as the presence of an independent observer. The search impinged on professional secrecy to an extent that appeared disproportionate in the circumstances; it had, in this connection, to be recalled that, where a lawyer is involved, an encroachment on professional secrecy may have repercussions on the proper administration of justice and hence on the rights guaranteed by Article 6 of the Convention. In addition, the attendant publicity must have been capable of affecting adversely the applicant's professional reputation, in the eyes both of his existing clients and of the public at large. There had been a breach of Article 8.

López Ostra v Spain (1994) 20 EHRR 277

Several tanneries in the home town of the applicant, all belonging to a limited company called SACURSA, had a plant for the treatment of liquid and solid waste built with a State subsidy on municipal land 12 metres away from the applicant's home. The plant began to operate without the licence from the municipal authorities required for activities classified as causing nuisance and being unhealthy, noxious and dangerous and without having followed the procedure for obtaining such a licence. Owing to a malfunction, its start-up released gas fumes, pestilential smells and contamination, which immediately caused health problems and nuisance to many people, particularly those living in the applicant's district.

The town council evacuated the local residents and rehoused them free of charge in the town centre for three months. Following numerous complaints and in the light of reports from the health authorities and the Environment and Nature Agency, the town council ordered cessation of one of the plant's activities while permitting the continuation of others. Certain nuisances continued and, according to some expert opinion, might endanger the health of those living nearby. The applicant and her family required to move house as a result.

Held that severe environmental pollution may affect individuals' well-being and prevent them from enjoying their homes in such a way as to affect their private and family life adversely, without, however, seriously endangering their health. Whether the question was analysed in terms of a positive duty on the State—to take reasonable and appropriate measures to secure the applicant's rights under paragraph 1 of Article 8—or in terms of an "interference by a public authority" to be justified in accordance with paragraph 2, the applicable principles were broadly similar. In both contexts regard must be had to the fair balance that has to be struck between the competing interests of the individual and of the community as a whole, and in any case the State enjoys a certain margin of appreciation. Furthermore, even in relation to the positive obligations flowing from the first paragraph of Article 8 in striking the required balance the aims mentioned in the second paragraph might be of a certain relevance. Admittedly, the Spanish authorities, and in particular the municipality, were theoretically not directly responsible for the emissions in question. However, the town allowed the plant to be built on its land and the State subsidised the plant's construction. The town council could not be unaware that the environmental problems continued after the partial shutdown. Even supposing that the municipality did fulfil the functions assigned to it by domestic law the Court need only establish whether the national authorities took the measures necessary for protecting the applicant's right to respect for her home and for her private and family life under Article 8. The municipality not only failed to take steps to that end but also resisted judicial decisions to that effect. In proceedings instituted by the applicant's sisters-in-law it appealed against a judicial decision ordering temporary closure of the plant, and that measure was suspended as a result.

Other State authorities also contributed to prolonging the situation. Crown Counsel had appealed against an investigating judge's decision temporarily to close the plant in the prosecution for an environmental health offence, with the result that the enforcement of the order was delayed. The family had to bear the nuisance caused by the plant for over three years before moving house with all the attendant inconveniences. They moved only when it became apparent that the situation could continue indefinitely and on medical advice. Despite the margin of appreciation left to the respondent State, the State did not succeed in striking a fair balance between the interest of the town's economic well-being—that of having a waste-treatment plant—and the applicant's effective enjoyment of her right to respect for her home and her private and family life. There had accordingly been a violation of Article 8.

POSITIVE OBLIGATION

Marckx v Belgium (1979–80) 2 EHRR 330

The applicants were a journalist and her illegitimate daughter. Under Belgian law, no legal bond between an unmarried mother and her child resulted from the mere fact of birth. Whilst the birth certificate recorded at the register office sufficed to prove the maternal affiliation of a married woman's children, the maternal affiliation of an illegitimate child required further procedure before it was established.

The establishment of maternal affiliation had certain consequences for the extent of the child's family relationships and consequent rights of access and maintenance, and for her inheritance rights. To place the child on the same footing as a legitimate child, the mother had to adopt her. The applicants complained of breaches of Articles 8 and 14.

Held that the complaint was not merely theoretical even though none of the disadvantages consequent upon illegitimacy had affected the child in a practical way between her birth and her adoption by her mother 13 days later. Rather, the applicants challenged a legal position which affected them personally. Since the word "victim" denotes "the person directly affected by the act or omission which is in issue", the applicants could claim to be within that category and the merits required to be examined to determine whether they actually were victims of a breach.

The Court had to consider Articles 8 and 14. It was necessary to clarify the meaning and purport of the words "respect for . . . private and family life". Article 8 presupposes the existence of a family but makes no distinction between the legitimate and the illegitimate family. The Court noted that the Committee of Ministers had (in Resolution (70) 15) in 1970 regarded the unmarried woman and her child as a family. Accordingly, the applicants were a family for the purposes of Article 8.

By proclaiming the right to respect for family life, Article 8 signifies that the State cannot interfere with the exercise of that right otherwise than in accordance with Article 8.2; but in addition to this primarily negative undertaking there may be positive obligations inherent in an effective "respect" for family life. This means, among other things, that the State must act in a manner calculated to allow those concerned to lead a normal family life. Respect for family life implies in particular the existence in domestic law of legal safeguards that render possible, from the moment of birth, the child's integration in its family.

Under Article 14, a distinction is discriminatory if it has no objective and reasonable justification; that is, if it does not pursue a legitimate aim or if there is not a reasonable relationship of proportionality between the means employed and the aim sought to be realised. The necessity for a particular procedure to establish the maternal affiliation of an illegitimate child derived from a refusal fully to acknowledge the mother's maternity from the moment of birth and was attended with disadvantages in relation to patrimonial rights. There had, therefore, been a breach of Article 8.

The Government had sought to justify the differences in the situations of married and unmarried mothers on the basis that some unmarried mothers do not wish to keep their children; but such an attitude is not a general feature of relationships between unmarried mothers and their children and is a feature of the relationship between some married mothers and their children. Although there was a history of distinction between legitimate and illegitimate relationships in many European States in the great majority of countries the law had evolved and was continuing to evolve towards full juridical recognition of the maxim *mater semper certa est*. There was a breach of Article 8 alone and in combination with Article 14.

X and Y v The Netherlands (1985) 8 EHRR 235

The applicants were Mr X and his daughter Y. She was mentally handicapped and had been living since 1970 in a privately-run home for mentally handicapped children. On the night after her 16th birthday, she was woken up by a certain Mr B, the son-in-law of the directress; he lived with his wife on the premises of the institution although he was not employed there. Mr B forced the girl to follow him to his room, to undress and to have sexual intercourse with him. The incident had traumatic consequences for Miss Y, causing her major mental disturbance.

Mr X went to the local police station to file a complaint and to ask for criminal proceedings to be instituted. The police officer said that since Mr X considered his daughter unable to sign the complaint because of her mental condition, he could do so himself. The statement lodged by Mr X read as follows: "In my capacity as father I denounce the offences committed by Mr B on the person of my daughter. I am doing this because she cannot do so herself, since, although sixteen years of age, she is mentally and intellectually still a child."

The public prosecutor's office provisionally decided not to open proceedings against Mr B, provided that he did not commit a similar offence within the next two years. Mr X appealed against the decision of the public prosecutor's office to the Arnhem Court of Appeal; he requested the court to direct that criminal proceedings be instituted. That Court dismissed the appeal. It considered it doubtful whether a charge of rape could be proved. There existed an offence which applied to a person who "through gifts or promises . . . , through abuse of a dominant position resulting from factual circumstances, or through deceit, deliberately causes a minor of blameless conduct to commit indecent acts with him or to suffer such acts from him" but in a case of that kind, the offender could be prosecuted only on complaint by the actual victim.

According to the applicants, the impossibility of having criminal proceedings instituted against Mr B violated Article 8 of the Convention.

Held that the facts underlying the application to the Commission concerned a matter of "private life", a concept which covers the physical and moral integrity of the person, including his or her sexual life. The Court recalled that although the object of Article 8 is essentially that of protecting the individual against arbitrary interference by the public authorities, it does not merely compel the State to abstain from such interference: in addition to this primarily negative undertaking, there may be positive obligations inherent in an effective respect for private or family life. These obligations may involve the adoption of measures designed to secure respect for private life even in the sphere of the relations of individuals between themselves. The choice of the means calculated to secure compliance with Article 8 in the sphere of the relations of individuals between themselves is in principle a matter that falls within the Contracting States' margin of appreciation. In this connection, there are different ways of ensuring "respect for private life", and the nature of the State's obligation will depend on the particular aspect of private life that is at issue. Recourse to the criminal law is not necessarily the only answer. However, the protection afforded by the civil law in the case of wrongdoing of the kind inflicted on Miss Y is insufficient. This was a case where fundamental values and essential aspects of private life were at stake. Effective deterrence is indispensable in this area and it can be achieved only by criminal law provisions; indeed, it is by such provisions that the matter is normally regulated. The Criminal Code did not provide Miss Y with practical and effective protection. It had, therefore, to be concluded, taking account of the nature of the wrongdoing in question, that she was the victim of a violation of Article 8 of the Convention.

Johnston v Ireland (1986) 9 EHRR 203

There were three applicants in the case. The first was a man who had married in 1952. He had parted from his wife in 1965. In 1976 he began to cohabit with the second applicant. The third applicant was their daughter, born in 1978. There was in Ireland a constitutional prohibition on the dissolution of marriage so that the first applicant could not divorce from his wife. He could not, therefore, marry the second applicant as a result of which she could not obtain the security provided by marriage in matters such as a right to be maintained by the first applicant and rights of succession on intestacy. Moreover, the third applicant was, as a result of the irregularity of her parents' relationship, illegitimate. This placed her in a less advantageous position as regards succession and maintenance rights against her father than would have been the case had she been legitimate and carried with it the risk of stigma if it became known. They applied to the Commission, complaining of breaches of, *inter alia*, Articles 8 and 12. They argued that the central issue was not whether the Convention guarantees the right to divorce but rather whether the fact that they were unable to marry each other was compatible with the rights to marry and to respect for family life enshrined in Articles 12 and 8. The Government maintained by way of preliminary objection that the applicants' domestic circumstances were in fact tranquil and that they had raised problems that were purely hypothetical, so that they could not be said to be victims for the purposes of the Convention. The Government also opposed the application on its merits.

Held that the Convention entitled individuals to contend that a law violates their rights by itself, in the absence of individual measures of implementation, if they run the risk of being directly affected by it. It does not require actual detriment before a person can claim to be a victim for the purposes of the Convention.

However, the Court did not consider that the issues could be separated out in the watertight way urged by the applicants. In any society espousing monogamy it was inconceivable that the first applicant would be able to remarry before the dissolution of his existing marriage. The second applicant was not prevented in general from marrying but only from marrying the first applicant. The situation arose precisely because the first applicant could not obtain a divorce. Consequently, the case could not be examined in isolation from the problem of the non-availability of divorce. In order to determine whether the applicants could derive a right to divorce from Article 12 the Court had to seek to ascertain the ordinary meaning of the terms of that provision in their context and in the light of its object and purpose. The ordinary meaning of the words "right to marry" are clear in the sense that they cover the formation of marital relationships but not their dissolution. This interpretation of Article 12 is consistent with what was revealed by the *travaux préparatoires*. The provision was explained to the Consultative Assembly as only guaranteeing the right to marry. Although the Convention fell to be interpreted in light of present-day conditions, the Court could not, by means of an evolutive interpretation, derive from the Convention a right that was not included therein at the outset.

It was clear that the applicants constituted a family for the purposes of Article 8 and the question was whether an effective respect for their family life imposed on Ireland a positive obligation to introduce measures that would permit divorce. Although Article 8, with its somewhat vague notion of respect for family life, might appear to lend itself more readily to evolutive interpretation than does Article 12, the Convention must be read as a whole and the Court did not consider that a right to divorce, which it had found to be excluded from Article 12, could with consistency be derived from Article 8. However the third applicant's position was significantly less advantageous than that of a legitimate child. It was recorded in the preamble to the European Convention on the Legal Status of Children born out of Wedlock that "in a great number of Member States efforts have been or are being made to improve the legal status of children born out of wedlock by reducing the differences between their legal status and that of children born in wedlock". The Court could not but be influenced by these developments. Respect for family life implies an obligation for the State to act in a manner calculated to allow ties between near relatives to develop normally, which meant that the third applicant should be placed, legally and socially, in a position akin to that of a legitimate child. Notwithstanding the wide margin of appreciation enjoyed by Ireland in this area, the absence of an appropriate legal regime reflecting the third applicant's natural family ties amounted to a failure to respect her family life. Moreover, the close relationship between the third applicant and her parents meant that there was a resultant failure to respect the family life of each of the latter. This did not amount to an indirect finding that the first applicant should be entitled to divorce and remarry—Ireland itself was proposing to improve the legal situation of illegitimate children whilst maintaining the constitutional prohibition on divorce.

INTERFERENCE BY A PUBLIC AUTHORITY

Beldjoudi v France (1992) 14 EHRR 801

The first applicant was an Algerian citizen, born in France. His parents were Algerian and he lost his French citizenship as a consequence of Algerian independence. The second applicant was the wife of the first and she was a French national. Other members of his family lived in France. Over the years the first applicant acquired a significant criminal record. In 1979 a deportation order was issued against him on the ground that his presence on French territory was a threat to public order. He made repeated but unsuccessful requests for the order to be withdrawn. Only one of them even received a reply, after the Commission had found the application admissible. That reply said that the order would not be withdrawn but that a compulsory residence order had been issued, requiring the applicant to live in the department where he had his habitual residence. It was said that the order, which carried with it permission to work, could continue depending on the applicant's conduct. The applicant's appeals against the deportation order were unsuccessful.

Held that enforcement of the deportation order would constitute an interference by a public authority with the exercise of the applicants' right to respect for their family life. There was no doubt that the order was made lawfully and for the prevention of crime.

The Court acknowledged that it is for the Contracting States to maintain public order, in particular by exercising their right, as a matter of well-established international law and subject to their treaty obligations, to control the entry, residence and expulsion of aliens. However, their decisions in this field must, in so far as they may interfere with a right protected under paragraph 1 of Article 8, be necessary in a democratic society, that is to say, justified by a pressing social need and, in particular, proportionate to the legitimate aim pursued. The first applicant's criminal record was a bad one and it was necessary to examine whether the other circumstances of the case, relating to both applicants or to one of them only, were enough to compensate for this important fact. They were married in France over 20 years before and had always had their matrimonial home there. The periods when Mr Beldjoudi was in prison undoubtedly prevented them from living together for a considerable time, but did not terminate their family life, which remained under the protection of Article 8.

Mr Beldjoudi, the person immediately affected by the deportation, was born in France of parents who were then French. He had French nationality until 1 January 1963. He was deemed to have lost it on that date, as his parents had not made a declaration of recognition before 27 March 1967. It should not be forgotten, however, that he was a minor at the time and unable to make a declaration personally. Moreover, as early as 1970, a year after his first conviction but over nine years before the adoption of the deportation order, he manifested the wish to recover French nationality; after being registered at his request in 1971, he was declared by the French military authorities to be fit for national service. Furthermore, Mr Beldjoudi married a Frenchwoman. His close relatives all kept French nationality until 1 January 1963, and had resided in France for several decades. Finally, he had spent his whole life—over 40 years—in France, was educated in French and appeared not to know Arabic. He did not seem to have any links with Algeria apart from that of nationality.

Mrs Beldjoudi for her part was born in France of French parents, had always lived there and had French nationality. Were she to follow her husband after his deportation, she would have to settle abroad, presumably in Algeria, a State whose language she probably did not know. To be uprooted like this could cause her great difficulty in adapting, and there might be real practical or even legal obstacles. The interference in question might, therefore, imperil the unity or even the very existence of the marriage. Having regard to these various circumstances, it appeared, from the point of view of respect for the applicants' family life, that the decision to deport Mr Beldjoudi, if put into effect, would not be proportionate to the legitimate aim pursued and would, therefore, violate Article 8.

A v France (1993) 17 EHRR 462

A man informed a senior police officer that the applicant had hired him to carry out a murder. That officer recorded a telephone conversation between the informer and the applicant and disclosed the existence of that recording to the investigating judge after the commencement of proceedings against the applicant. He handed the recording over to that investigating judge. The criminal proceedings were in due course discontinued on the ground that there was no case to answer. Meanwhile, the applicant had laid a complaint against the informer and the police officer for invasion of privacy and breach of the confidentiality of telephone communications, together with an application to join the proceedings as *partie civile*. That complaint was unsuccessful. The applicant complained of a breach of Article 8. The Government argued that there had been a failure to exhaust domestic remedies, because the applicant had not commenced civil proceedings. It further argued that there had been no breach of Article 8 because one of the persons involved in the conversation had agreed to the recording and because the conversation had related to the planning of a crime rather than any private matter. Finally, it argued that the police officer was not an official of the State and not acting on its behalf in what he did, so that what was done was not done by a public authority.

Held that civil proceedings would have been directed to the same end as the complaint which the applicant did make and would not have offered better chances of success. The objection that there had been a failure to exhaust domestic remedies had, therefore, to be dismissed. Although the police officer had acted without authorisation either from his superiors or from an investigating judge, he had been acting in the performance of his duties as a high ranking police officer. The public authorities were, therefore, involved to such an extent that State responsibility under the Convention was engaged. The recording had, furthermore, constituted an interference with the applicant's correspondence. There had been a breach of Article 8. Costs and expenses were awarded to the applicant but the finding of a breach was sufficient just satisfaction for any non-pecuniary damage which she had sustained.

IN ACCORDANCE WITH LAW

Malone v United Kingdom (1984) 7 EHRR 14

The applicant was an antique dealer who was tried and acquitted in relation to the dishonest handling of stolen goods. During his trial, it emerged that details of a telephone conversation to which he had been a party were contained in the notebook of the police officer in charge of the investigations. Counsel for the prosecution then accepted that this conversation had been intercepted on the authority of a warrant issued by the Home Secretary. The applicant alleged that his telephone had been tapped repeatedly and that his mail had also been intercepted. He complained of breaches of Article 8. The Government declined to disclose to what extent, if at all, his telephone calls and mail had been intercepted otherwise on behalf of the police. They did, however, concede that, as a suspected receiver of stolen goods, he was a member of a class of persons against whom measures of postal and telephone interception were liable to be employed.

Held that as telephone conversations are covered by the notions of "private life" and "correspondence" within the meaning of Article 8, the admitted measure of interception involved an "interference by a public authority" with the exercise of a right guaranteed to the applicant under paragraph 1 of Article 8. The existence in England and Wales of laws and practices which permitted and established a system for effecting secret surveillance of communications amounted in itself to an interference with the exercise of the applicant's rights under Article 8, apart from any measures actually taken against him. This being so, the Court did not consider it necessary to inquire into the applicant's further claims that both his mail and his telephone calls were intercepted for a number of years.

The principal issue of contention was whether the interferences found were justified under the terms of paragraph 2 of Article 8, notably whether they were "in accordance with the law" and "necessary in a democratic society" for one of the purposes enumerated in that paragraph. The phrase "in accordance with the law" does not merely refer back to domestic law but also relates to the quality of the law, requiring it to be compatible with the rule of law, which is expressly mentioned in the preamble to the Convention. The phrase thus implies that there must be a measure of legal protection in domestic law against arbitrary interferences by public authorities with the rights safeguarded by paragraph 1.

Especially where a power of the executive is exercised in secret, the risks of arbitrariness are evident. The requirement of foreseeability cannot mean that an individual should be enabled to foresee when the authorities are likely to intercept his communications so that he can adapt his conduct accordingly. Nevertheless, the law must be sufficiently clear in its terms to give citizens an adequate indication as to the circumstances in which, and the conditions on which, public authorities are empowered to resort to this secret and potentially dangerous interference with the right to respect for private life and correspondence.

Since the implementation in practice of measures of secret surveillance of communications is not open to scrutiny by the individuals concerned or the public at large, it would be contrary to the rule of law for the legal discretion granted to the executive to be expressed in terms of an unfettered power. Consequently, the law must indicate the scope of any such discretion conferred on the competent authorities and the manner of its exercise with sufficient clarity, having regard to the legitimate aim of the measure in question, to give the individual adequate protection against arbitrary interference.

It was common ground that the settled practice of intercepting communications on behalf of the police in pursuance of a warrant issued by the Secretary of State for the purposes of detecting and preventing crime, and hence the admitted interception of one of the applicant's telephone conversations, were lawful under the law of England and Wales. The issue to be determined was, therefore, whether, under domestic law, the essential elements of the power to intercept communications were laid down with reasonable precision in accessible legal rules that sufficiently indicated the scope and manner of exercise of the discretion conferred on the relevant authorities. On the evidence before the Court, at the very least, the law in England and Wales governing interception of communications for police purposes was somewhat obscure and open to differing interpretations. It could not be said with any reasonable certainty what elements of the powers to intercept were incorporated in legal rules and what elements remained within the discretion of the executive.

In view of the attendant obscurity and uncertainty as to the state of the law in this essential respect, the Court could not but reach the conclusion that the law of England and Wales did not indicate with reasonable clarity the scope and manner of exercise of the relevant discretion conferred on the public authorities. To that extent, the minimum degree of legal protection to which citizens are entitled under the rule of law in a democratic society was lacking. The interferences with the applicant's right under Article 8 to respect for his private life and correspondence were not "in accordance with the law". There was a breach of Article 8.

Kruslin v France (1990) 12 EHRR 528

An investigating judge who was inquiring into a murder issued a warrant to tap the telephone of a suspect, Mr Dominique Terrieux. The gendarmes intercepted 17 telephone calls in all. The applicant, who was staying with Mr Terrieux at the time and occasionally used his telephone, had been a party to several of the telephone conversations, during one of which there had been a conversation in veiled terms about a different unsolved murder. As a result of that he was investigated, tried and convicted in respect of that murder. He complained of a breach of Article 8.

Held that although it was Mr Terrieux's line that they were tapping, the police in consequence intercepted and recorded several of the applicant's conversations, and one of these led to proceedings being taken against him. The telephone tapping, therefore, amounted to an "interference by a public authority" with the exercise of the applicant's right to respect for his "correspondence" and his "private life". Such an interference contravenes Article 8 unless it is "in accordance with the law", pursues one or more of the legitimate aims referred to in Article 8.2 and furthermore is "necessary in a democratic society" in order to achieve them.

The expression "in accordance with the law", within the meaning of Article 8.2, requires that the impugned measure should have some basis in domestic law; it also refers to the quality of the law in question, requiring that it should be accessible to the person concerned, who must moreover be able to foresee its consequences for him, and compatible with the rule of law. It was a matter of dispute whether the first condition was satisfied in the instant case but for many years the French courts had regarded certain Articles of the Code of Criminal Procedure as providing a legal basis for telephone tapping carried out by a senior police officer under a warrant issued by an investigating judge. Settled case law of this kind could not be disregarded.

In relation to Article 8.2 and other similar clauses, the Court had always understood the term "law" in its "substantive" sense, not its "formal" one; it has included both enactments of lower rank than statutes and unwritten law. In sum, the interference complained of had a legal basis in French law.

The requirement of the accessibility of the law did not raise any problem in the instant case but the same was not true of the third requirement, the law's "foreseeability" as to the meaning and nature of the applicable measures. The law must be sufficiently clear in its terms to give citizens an adequate indication as to the circumstances in which and the conditions on which public authorities are empowered to resort to this secret and potentially dangerous interference with the right to respect for private life and correspondence. Tapping and other forms of interception of telephone conversations represent a serious interference with private life and correspondence and must accordingly be based on a "law" that is particularly precise. It is essential to have clear, detailed rules on the subject, especially as the technology available for use is continually becoming more sophisticated.

The Articles of the Code of Criminal Procedure on which the action was based provided some safeguards. Others had been laid down piecemeal in judgments given over the years, the great majority of them after the interception complained of by the applicant. Some had not yet been expressly laid down in the case law at all; the Government appeared to infer them either from general enactments or principles or else from an analogical interpretation of legislative provisions—or court decisions—concerning investigative measures different from telephone tapping, notably searches and seizure of property.

Although plausible in itself, such extrapolation did not provide sufficient legal certainty in the present context. Above all, the system did not for the time being afford adequate safeguards against various possible abuses. For example, the categories of people liable to have their telephones tapped by judicial order and the nature of the offences which might give rise to such an order were nowhere defined. Nothing obliged a judge to set a limit on the duration of telephone tapping. Similarly unspecified were the procedure for drawing up the summary reports containing intercepted conversations; the precautions to be taken in order to communicate the recordings intact and in their entirety for possible inspection by the judge (who could hardly verify the number and length of the original tapes on the spot) and by the defence; and the circumstances in which recordings might or must be erased or the tapes be destroyed, in particular where an accused has been discharged by an investigating judge or acquitted by a court. In short, French law, written and unwritten, did not indicate with reasonable clarity the scope and manner of exercise of the relevant discretion conferred on the public authorities. There had, therefore, been a breach of Article 8 of the Convention.

Necessary

Klass v Germany (1979–80) 2 EHRR 214

The applicants complained that certain legislation, which permitted surveillance without obliging the authorities in every case to notify the persons concerned after the event, and which excluded any remedy before the courts against the ordering and execution of such measures, was contrary to the Convention. Before lodging their application with the Commission, the applicants had appealed unsuccessfully to the Federal Constitutional Court. At no time had surveillance measures provided for by the legislation been ordered or implemented against the applicants. The Government argued, *inter alia*, that the applicants were not "victims" for the purposes of the Convention.

Held that the Convention requires that an individual applicant should claim to have been actually affected by the violation he alleges and does not institute for individuals a kind of *actio popularis* for the interpretation of the Convention; it does not permit individuals to complain against a law *in abstracto* simply because they feel that it contravenes the Convention. In principle, it does not suffice for an individual applicant to claim that the mere existence of a law violates his rights under the Convention; it is necessary that the law should have been applied to his detriment. Nevertheless, a law may by itself violate the rights of an individual if the individual is directly affected by the law in the absence of any specific measure of implementation.

The question arose whether an individual was to be deprived of the opportunity of lodging an application with the Commission because, owing to the secrecy of the measures objected to, he could not point to any concrete measure specifically affecting him. In the Court's view, the effectiveness of the Convention implied in such circumstances some possibility of having access to the Commission. If this were not so, the efficiency of the Convention's enforcement machinery would be materially weakened. The procedural provisions of the Convention must, in view of the fact that the Convention and its institutions were set up to protect the individual, be applied in a manner which serves to make the system of individual applications efficacious. The Court, therefore, accepted that an individual might, under certain conditions, claim to be the victim of a violation occasioned by the mere existence of secret measures or of legislation permitting secret measures, without having to allege that such measures were in fact applied to him. The relevant conditions are to be determined in each case according to the Convention right or rights alleged to have been infringed, the secret character of the measures objected to, and the connection between the applicant and those measures. Where a State institutes secret surveillance, the existence of which remains unknown to the persons being controlled, with the effect that the surveillance remains unchallengeable, Article 8 could to a large extent be reduced to a nullity. It is possible in such a situation for an individual to be treated in a manner contrary to Article 8, or even to be deprived of the right granted by that Article, without his being aware of it and, therefore, without being able to obtain a remedy either at the national level or before the Convention institutions. As to the facts of the particular case, the contested legislation instituted a system of surveillance under which all persons in the Federal Republic of Germany could potentially have their mail, post and telecommunications monitored, without their ever knowing this. To that extent, the disputed legislation directly affected all users or potential users of the postal and telecommunication services in the Federal Republic of Germany. That surveillance could be claimed in itself to restrict free communication through the postal and telecommunication services, thereby constituting for all users or potential users a direct interference with the right guaranteed by Article 8.

Having regard to the specific circumstances of the case, the Court concluded that each of the applicants was entitled to claim to be the victim of a violation of the Convention. Although telephone conversations are not expressly mentioned in paragraph 1 of Article 8, the Court considered that such conversations are covered by the notions of "private life" and "correspondence" referred to by this provision. Clearly, any of the permitted surveillance measures, once applied to a given individual, would result in an interference by a public authority with the exercise of that individual's right to respect for his private and family life and his correspondence.

Furthermore, in the mere existence of the legislation itself there was involved, for all those to whom the legislation could be applied, a menace of surveillance; this menace necessarily struck at freedom of communication between users of the postal and telecommunication services and thereby constituted an "interference by a public authority" with the exercise of the applicants' right to respect for private and family life and for correspondence. Powers of secret surveillance of citizens, characterising as they do the police state, are tolerable under the Convention only in so far as strictly necessary for safeguarding the democratic institutions. In order for the "interference" not to infringe Article 8 it must, according to paragraph 2, first of all have been "in accordance with the law". This requirement was fulfilled in the present case since the "interference" resulted from Acts passed by Parliament. It remained to be determined whether the other requisites laid down in paragraph 2 of Article 8 were also satisfied. According to the Government and the Commission, the interference permitted by the contested legislation was "necessary in a democratic society in the interests of national security" and/or "for the prevention of disorder or crime". The Government also submitted that the interference was additionally justified "in the interests of . . . public safety" and "for the protection of the rights and freedoms of others".

The Court found that the aim was indeed to safeguard national security and/or to prevent disorder or crime in pursuance of Article 8.2. In those circumstances, the Court did not deem it necessary to decide whether the further purposes cited by the Government were also relevant. The Court had to accept that the existence of some legislation granting powers of secret surveillance over the mail, post and telecommunications is, under exceptional conditions, necessary in a democratic society in the interests of national security and/or for the prevention of disorder or crime. As concerns the fixing of the conditions under which the system of surveillance is to be operated, the domestic legislature enjoys a certain discretion and it was not for the Court to substitute for the assessment of the national authorities any other assessment of what might be the best policy in this field. Nevertheless, the Court stressed that this did not mean that the Contracting States enjoy an unlimited discretion to subject persons within their jurisdiction to secret surveillance. The Court, being aware of the danger such a law poses of undermining or even destroying democracy on the ground of defending it, affirmed that the Contracting States may not, in the name of the struggle against espionage and terrorism, adopt whatever measures they deem appropriate. The Court must be satisfied that, whatever system of surveillance is adopted, there exist adequate and effective guarantees against abuse. This assessment has only a relative character: it depends on all the circumstances of the case, such as the nature, scope and duration of the possible measures, the grounds required for ordering such measures, the authorities competent to permit, carry out and supervise such measures, and the kind of remedy provided by the national law.

Under the legislation complained of, the permissible restrictive measures were confined to cases in which there were factual indications for suspecting a person of planning, committing or having committed certain serious criminal acts; measures might only be ordered if the establishment of the facts by another method was without prospects of success or considerably more difficult; even then, the surveillance could cover only the specific suspect or his presumed "contact-persons". So-called exploratory or general surveillance was not permitted by the contested legislation. Surveillance might be ordered only on written application giving reasons, and such an application may be made only by the head, or his substitute, of certain services; the decision thereon had to be taken by a Federal Minister empowered for the purpose by the Chancellor.

Accordingly, under the law there existed an administrative procedure designed to ensure that measures were not ordered haphazardly, irregularly or without due and proper consideration. The measures in question remained in force for a maximum of three months and might be renewed only on fresh application; the measures had to be discontinued immediately once the required conditions had ceased to exist or the measures themselves were no longer necessary; knowledge and documents thereby obtained might not be used for other ends, and documents must be destroyed as soon as they were no longer needed to achieve the required purpose. As regards the implementation of the measures, an initial control was carried out by an official qualified for judicial office. That official examined the information obtained before transmitting to the competent services such information as might be used in accordance with the Act and was relevant to the purpose of the measure; he destroyed any other intelligence that might have been gathered. While recourse to the courts in respect of the ordering and implementation of measures of surveillance was excluded, subsequent control or review was provided instead by two bodies appointed by the people's elected representatives and to which the competent Minister was required to make frequent reports. The rule of law implies, *inter alia*, that an interference by the executive authorities with an individual's rights should be subject to an effective control which should normally be assured by the judiciary, at least in the last resort, judicial control offering the best guarantees of independence, impartiality and a proper procedure. Nevertheless, having regard to the nature of the supervisory and other safeguards provided for, the Court concluded that the exclusion of judicial control did not exceed the limits of what might be deemed necessary in a democratic society. There was no breach of Article 8 and the possibility of challenging the legislation in the Federal Constitutional Court, aggregated with other remedies available in the German system, amounted to an effective remedy for the purposes of Article 13. An "effective remedy" under Article 13 must mean a remedy that is as effective as can be having regard to the restricted scope for recourse inherent in any system of secret surveillance.

Dudgeon v United Kingdom (1981) 4 EHRR 149

The applicant was a homosexual and his complaints were directed primarily against the existence in Northern Ireland of laws which had the effect of making certain homosexual acts between consenting adult males criminal offences. He and others have been conducting a campaign aimed at bringing the law in Northern Ireland into line with that in force in England and Wales and, if possible, achieving a minimum age of consent lower than 21 years.

The police had searched the applicant's house under the Misuse of Drugs Act 1971 and found a quantity of cannabis which subsequently led to another person being charged with drug offences. Personal papers, including correspondence and diaries, belonging to the applicant in which were described homosexual activities were also found and seized. As a result, he was asked to go to a police station where for about four and a half hours he was questioned, on the basis of these papers, about his sexual life. The police investigation file was sent to the Director of Prosecutions where it was considered with a view to instituting criminal proceedings. It was decided that it would not be in the public interest for proceedings to be brought. Mr Dudgeon was so informed and his papers, with annotations marked over them, were returned to him.

He complained, *inter alia,* that the existence, in the criminal law in force in Northern Ireland, of various offences capable of relating to male homosexual conduct and the police investigation in January 1976 constituted an unjustified interference with his right to respect for his private life, in breach of Article 8 of the Convention.

Held that although it was not homosexuality itself which was prohibited but particular acts, there could be no doubt but that male homosexual practices whose prohibition was the subject of the applicant's complaints came within the scope of the offences punishable under the impugned legislation. The maintenance in force of the impugned legislation constituted a continuing interference with the applicant's right to respect for his private life (which included his sexual life) within the meaning of Article 8. An interference with the exercise of an Article 8 right will not be compatible with paragraph 2 unless it is "in accordance with the law", has an aim or aims that is or are legitimate under that paragraph and is "necessary in a democratic society" for the aim or aims.

The interference was plainly "in accordance with the law" since it resulted from legislative provisions and the common law. The general aim pursued by the legislation was the protection of morals in the sense of moral standards obtaining in Northern Ireland, though it was somewhat artificial to draw a rigid distinction between "protection of the rights and freedoms of others" and "protection of morals". The latter may imply safeguarding the moral ethos or moral standards of a society as a whole but may also cover protection of the moral interests and welfare of a particular section of society, for example, schoolchildren. Thus, "protection of the rights and freedoms of others", when meaning the safeguarding of the moral interests and welfare of certain individuals or classes of individuals who are in need of special protection for reasons such as lack of maturity, mental disability or state of dependence, amounts to one aspect of "protection of morals".

The cardinal issue arising under Article 8 in this case was to what extent, if at all, the maintenance in force of the legislation was "necessary in a democratic society" for those aims.

There could be no denial that some degree of regulation of male homosexual conduct, as indeed of other forms of sexual conduct, by means of the criminal law could be justified as "necessary in a democratic society". The overall function served by the criminal law in this field is to preserve public order and decency and to protect the citizen from what is offensive or injurious. The necessity for some degree of control may even extend to consensual acts committed in private, notably where there is call to provide sufficient safe-guards against exploitation and corruption of others, particularly those who are specially vulnerable because they are young, weak in body or mind, inexperienced, or in a state of special physical, official or economic dependence.

It being accepted that some form of legislation is "necessary" to protect particular sections of society as well as the moral ethos of society as a whole, the question in the present case was whether the contested provisions of the law of Northern Ireland and their enforcement remained within the bounds of what, in a democratic society, might be regarded as necessary in order to accomplish those aims. A number of principles are relevant to the assessment of the necessity in a democratic society of a measure taken in furtherance of an aim that is legitimate under the Convention. "Necessary" in this context does not have the flexibility of such expressions as "useful", "reasonable", or "desirable", but implies the existence of a "pressing social need" for the inter-ference in question. It is for the national authorities to make the initial assessment of the pressing social need in each case; accordingly, a margin of appreciation is left to them. However, their decision remains subject to review by the Court.

The scope of the margin of appreciation is not identical in respect of each of the aims justifying restrictions on a right. The present case concerned a most intimate aspect of private life. Accordingly, there must exist particularly serious reasons before interferences on the part of the public authorities could be legitimate.

Finally, the notion of "necessity" is linked to that of a "democratic society". A restriction on a Convention right cannot be regarded as "necessary in a democratic society"—two hallmarks of which are tolerance and broad-mindedness—unless, amongst other things, it is proportionate to the legitimate aim pursued. The Government had drawn attention to profound differences of attitude and public opinion between Northern Ireland and Great Britain in relation to questions of morality. The Court acknowledged that such differences did exist and were a relevant factor. The fact that similar measures were not considered necessary in other parts of the UK or in other Member States of the Council of Europe did not mean that they could not be necessary in Northern Ireland. However, as compared with the era when the legislation was enacted, there was now a better understanding and, in consequence, an increased tolerance, of homosexual behaviour to the extent that in the great majority of the Member States of the Council of Europe it was no longer considered to be necessary or appropriate to treat homosexual practices of the kind in question as in themselves a matter to which the sanctions of the criminal law should be applied. In Northern Ireland itself, the authorities had refrained in recent years from enforcing the law in respect of private homosexual acts between consenting males over the age of 21 years. No evidence had been adduced to show that this had been injurious to moral standards in Northern Ireland or that there had been any public demand for stricter enforcement of the law. It could not be maintained in these circum-stances that there was a "pressing social need" to make such acts criminal offences, there being no sufficient justification provided by the risk of harm to vulnerable sections of society requiring protection or by the effects on the public.

On the issue of proportionality, the Court considered that such justifications as there were for retaining the law in force unamended were outweighed by the detrimental effects which the very existence of the legislative provisions in question could have on the life of a person of homosexual orientation like the applicant. Although members of the public who regard homosexuality as immoral might be shocked, offended or disturbed by the commission by others of private homosexual acts, this could not on its own warrant the application of penal sanctions when it was consenting adults alone who were involved. There was accordingly a breach of Article 8.

Olsson v Sweden (1988) 11 EHRR 259

The applicants were a married couple. Both of them had spent time in a home for the mentally retarded. The male applicant had retired early. Relations between the applicants were bad. They had separated for a long period and, after a reconciliation, had separated again. They had two sons and a daughter.

The family had moved four times in two and a half years. Their sons showed clear signs of backwardness. There was a lack of care for the children on the part of the parents, and the children's behaviour was disturbed.

The relevant authorities decided to take the children into care. They were placed first in children's homes and then in separate foster homes. The applicants' access to them was limited, partly to protect the children's chances of settling down, partly because the applicants had twice removed one of the boys from the children's home and hidden him and partly because of the applicants' hostility towards the foster parents. The applicants complained that the decision to take the children into care, the manner in which it had been implemented and the authorities' refusals to terminate care had given rise to violations of Article 8.

Held that the mutual enjoyment by parent and child of each other's company constitutes a fundamental element of family life; furthermore, the natural family relationship is not terminated by reason of the fact that the child is taken into public care. It followed that the measures at issue amounted to interferences with the applicants' right to respect for their family life. Such an interference entails a violation of Article 8 unless it was "in accordance with the law", had an aim or aims that is or are legitimate under Article 8.2 and was "necessary in a democratic society" for the aim or aims.

A norm cannot be regarded as a "law" unless it is formulated with sufficient precision to enable the citizen—if need be, with appropriate advice—to foresee, to a degree that is reasonable in the circumstances, the consequences which a given action may entail; however, experience shows that absolute precision is unattainable and the need to avoid excessive rigidity and to keep pace with changing circumstances means that many laws are inevitably couched in terms which, to a greater or lesser extent, are vague. The phrase "in accordance with the law" does not merely refer back to domestic law but also relates to the quality of the law, requiring it to be compatible with the rule of law; it thus implies that there must be a measure of protection in domestic law against arbitrary interferences by public authorities with the rights safeguarded by, *inter alia*, paragraph 1 of Article 8. A law which confers a discretion is not in itself inconsistent with the requirement of foreseeability, provided that the scope of the discretion and the manner of its exercise are indicated with sufficient clarity, having regard to the legitimate aim of the measure in question, to give the individual adequate protection against arbitrary interference.

The Swedish legislation applied in the present case was admittedly rather general in terms and conferred a wide measure of discretion, especially as regards the implementation of care decisions. In particular, it provided for intervention by the authorities where a child's health or development was jeopardised or in danger, without requiring proof of actual harm to him. On the other hand, the circumstances in which it might be necessary to take a child into public care and in which a care decision may fall to be implemented are so variable that it would scarcely be possible to formulate a law to cover every eventuality. To confine the authorities' entitlement to act to cases where actual harm to the child has already occurred might well unduly reduce the effectiveness of the protection which he requires. Moreover, in interpreting and applying the legislation, there was guidance as to the exercise of the discretion it conferred. Again, safeguards against arbitrary interference were provided by the fact that the exercise of nearly all the statutory powers was either entrusted to or is subject to review by the administrative courts at several levels.

Taking these safeguards into consideration, the scope of the discretion conferred on the authorities by the laws in question appeared to the Court to be reasonable and acceptable for the purposes of Article 8. The Court thus concluded that the interferences in question were "in accordance with the law". The legislation was clearly designed to protect children and there was nothing to suggest that it was applied in the present case for any other purpose. The interferences in question, therefore, had legitimate aims.

The notion of necessity implies that the interference corresponds to a pressing social need and, in particular, that it is proportionate to the legitimate aim pursued; in determining whether an interference is "necessary in a democratic society", the Court will take into account that a margin of appreciation is left to the Contracting States. The Court's review is not limited to ascertaining whether a respondent State exercised its discretion reasonably, carefully and in good faith; and in exercising its supervisory jurisdiction the Court cannot confine itself to considering the impugned decisions in isolation, but must look at them in the light of the case as a whole; it must determine whether the reasons adduced to justify the interferences at issue are "relevant and sufficient".

It is an interference of a very serious order to split up a family. Such a step must be supported by sufficiently sound and weighty considerations in the interests of the child; it is not enough that the child would be better off if placed in care.

The primary reason for taking the Olsson children into care was the inability of the parents to provide them with proper care, as vouched by medical reports. The impugned decision was, therefore, supported by "sufficient" reasons and, having regard to their margin of appreciation, the Swedish authorities were reasonably entitled to think that it was necessary to take the children into care, especially since preventive measures had proved unsuccessful. For similar reasons, they were entitled to think it necessary to continue to keep the children in care.

However, there appeared to have been no question of the children's being adopted. The care decision should, therefore, have been regarded as a temporary measure, to be discontinued as soon as circumstances permitted, and any measures of implementation should have been consistent with the ultimate aim of reuniting the Olsson family. In point of fact, the steps taken by the Swedish authorities ran counter to such an aim. The ties between members of a family and the prospects of their successful reunification will perforce be weakened if impediments are placed in the way of their having easy and regular access to each other. The children were placed at a significant distance from their parents and from each other, which must have adversely affected the possibility of contacts between them. This situation was compounded by the restrictions imposed by the authorities on parental access. Whilst those restrictions might to a certain extent have been warranted by the applicants' attitude towards the foster families it was not to be excluded that the failure to establish a harmonious relationship was partly due to the distances involved.

There was nothing to suggest that the Swedish authorities did not act in good faith in implementing the care decision. However, this did not suffice to render a measure "necessary" in Convention terms. An objective standard had to be applied in this connection. Examination of the Government's arguments suggested that it was partly administrative difficulties that prompted the authorities' decisions; yet, in so fundamental an area as respect for family life, such considerations could not be allowed to play more than a secondary role. In conclusion, in the respects indicated and despite the applicants' unco-operative attitude, the measures taken in implementation of the care decision were not supported by "sufficient" reasons justifying them as proportionate to the legitimate aim pursued. They were therefore, notwithstanding the domestic authorities' margin of appreciation, not "necessary in a democratic society".

Norris v Ireland (1998) 13 EHRR 186

The applicant was an active homosexual and a campaigner for homosexual rights. He objected in particular to the existence in Ireland of laws which made certain homosexual practices between consenting adult men criminal offences. Although prosecutions had been confined in practice to cases involving minors, there was no bar to prosecution in the case of such consenting adults.

Held that, since there was a possibility of prosecution, the applicant qualified as a victim for the purposes of the Convention. Otherwise, the case was indistinguishable from the *Dudgeon* case. It was true that, unlike Mr Dudgeon, the applicant was not the subject of any police investigation. However, the Court's finding in the *Dudgeon* case that there was an interference with the applicant's right to respect for his private life was not dependent upon this additional factor. As was held in that case, the maintenance in force of the impugned legislation constituted a continuing interference with the applicant's right to respect for his private life within the meaning of Article 8.1. In the personal circumstances of the applicant, the very existence of this legislation continuously and directly affected his private life. The Court, therefore, found that the impugned legislation interfered with the applicant's right to respect for his private life under Article 8.

It was common ground that the interference was in accordance with the law and that it had a legitimate aim, namely the protection of morals. It remained to be determined whether the maintenance in force of the impugned legislation was necessary in a democratic society for that aim. According to the Court's case law, this will not be so unless, *inter alia*, the interference in question answers a pressing social need and in particular is proportionate to the legitimate aim pursued. It was argued by the Government that a wider view of necessity should be taken in an area in which the Contracting States enjoy a wide margin of appreciation and that the identification of "necessity" with "pressing social need" in the context of moral values is too restrictive and produces a distorting result, while the test of proportionality involves the evaluation of a moral issue and this was something that the Court should avoid if possible.

The Court was not convinced by this line of argument. As early as 1976, the Court declared in its *Handyside* judgment that, in investigating whether the protection of morals necessitated the various measures taken, it had to make an "assessment of the reality of the pressing social need implied by the notion of 'necessity' in this context" and stated that "every 'restriction' imposed in this sphere must be proportionate to the legitimate aim pursued". It confirmed this approach in its *Dudgeon* judgment. The Government offered no viable alternative tests of their own and appeared to be contending that the State's discretion in the field of the protection of morals is unfettered. Whilst national authorities do enjoy a wide margin of appreciation in matters of morals, this is not unlimited. It was for the Court, in this field also, to give a ruling on whether an interference was compatible with the Convention. To do otherwise would run counter to the terms of Article 19 of the Convention, under which the Court was set up in order "to ensure the observance of the engagements undertaken by the High Contracting Parties".

The present case concerned a most intimate aspect of private life. Accordingly, there must exist particularly serious reasons before interferences on the part of public authorities could be legitimate for the purposes of paragraph 2 of Article 8. Yet, the Government had adduced no evidence which would point to the existence of factors justifying the retention of the impugned laws which were additional to or are of greater weight than those present in the *Dudgeon* case. Applying the same tests to the present case, the Court considered that it could not be maintained that there was a "pressing social need" to make such acts criminal offences. There was a breach of Article 8.

Campbell v United Kingdom (1992) 15 EHRR 137

The applicant was serving a life sentence for murder in Scotland. He was involved in several sets of legal proceedings in the civil courts and two applications to the Commission in Strasbourg. In terms of Prison Rules, his correspondence was opened and read by the prison authorities. This included correspondence with his solicitor and with the European Commission of Human Rights. The particular rule provided that correspondence with a legal adviser about legal proceedings to which an inmate was already a party or, about a forthcoming adjudication, might not be read or stopped unless the Governor had reason to suppose it contained other material. Such a letter might be examined for illicit enclosures, but should only be opened for that purpose in the presence of the inmate by whom it is sent or to whom it is addressed. The Government stated that, in practice, as regards correspondence between prisoners and the Commission, outgoing letters if sealed would normally go unopened. Incoming letters from the Commission were opened; the contents were examined to confirm that they were what they purported to be but they were not read; they were thereafter issued promptly to the prisoner.

Before the Commission, it was not disputed between the parties that the measure complained of was in conformity with law; but before the Court, the applicant questioned the legal validity of the power to open correspondence.

Held that it is not, in principle, for the Court to examine the validity of secondary legislation. This is primarily a matter which falls within the competence of national courts which in the present case had examined and upheld the validity of the prison rule providing for the opening and reading of prisoners' correspondence. In the circumstances the Court saw no reason to call into question the findings of the national court. Accordingly, the Court found that the interference was "in accordance with the law" within the meaning of Article 8.2.

There was no reason to doubt that the control of the applicant's correspondence was carried out under the Prison Rules and Standing Orders to ensure, *inter alia*, that it did not contain material which was harmful to prison security or the safety of others or was otherwise of a criminal nature. The interference thus pursued the legitimate aim of "the prevention of disorder or crime".

The notion of necessity implies that the interference corresponds to a pressing social need and, in particular, that it is proportionate to the legitimate aim pursued. Some measure of control over prisoners' correspondence is called for and is not of itself incompatible with the Convention, regard being paid to the ordinary and reasonable requirements of imprisonment. In assessing the permissible extent of such control in general, the fact that the opportunity to write and to receive letters is sometimes the prisoner's only link with the outside world should, however, not be overlooked.

It is clearly in the general interest that any person who wishes to consult a lawyer should be free to do so under conditions which favour full and un-inhibited discussion. It is for this reason that the lawyer–client relationship is, in principle, privileged. That such correspondence be susceptible to routine scrutiny, particularly by individuals or authorities who may have a direct interest in the subject-matter contained therein, is not in keeping with the principles of confidentiality and professional privilege attaching to relations between a lawyer and his client. Admittedly, as the Government pointed out, the borderline between mail concerning contemplated litigation and that of a general nature is especially difficult to draw and correspondence with a lawyer may concern matters which have little or nothing to do with litigation.

Nevertheless, the Court saw no reason to distinguish between the different categories of correspondence with lawyers which, whatever their purpose, concern matters of a private and confidential character. In principle, such letters are privileged under Article 8.

This means that the prison authorities may open a letter from a lawyer to a prisoner when they have reasonable cause to believe that it contains an illicit enclosure which the normal means of detection have failed to disclose. The letter should, however, only be opened and should not be read. Suitable guarantees preventing the reading of the letter should be provided—for example, opening the letter in the presence of the prisoner. The reading of a prisoner's mail to and from a lawyer, on the other hand, should only be permitted in exceptional circumstances when the authorities have reasonable cause to believe that the privilege is being abused in that the contents of the letter endanger prison security or the safety of others or are otherwise of a criminal nature.

What may be regarded as "reasonable cause" will depend on all the circumstances but it presupposes the existence of facts or information which would satisfy an objective observer that the privileged channel of communication was being abused. It had not been suggested that there was any reason to suspect that the applicant's solicitor was not complying with the rules of his profession. In sum, the mere possibility of abuse is outweighed by the need to respect the confidentiality attached to the lawyer–client relationship. There being no further room for allowing for a margin of appreciation, the Court found that there was no pressing social need for the opening and reading of the applicant's correspondence with his solicitor and that, accordingly, this interference was not "necessary in a democratic society".

Moreover, the Court considered that it was of importance to respect the confidentiality of mail from the Commission since it might concern allegations against the prison authorities or prison officials. The opening of letters from the Commission undoubtedly gave rise to the possibility that they would be read and might also conceivably, on occasions, create the risk of reprisals by the prison staff against the prisoner concerned. There was no compelling reason why such letters from the Commission should be opened. The risk, adverted to by the Government, of Commission stationery being forged in order to smuggle prohibited material or messages into prison, was so negligible that it must be discounted. Accordingly, there had been breaches of Article 8.

Funke v France (1993) 16 EHRR 297

Acting on information received from the tax authorities, customs and police officers visited the applicant to obtain particulars of assets held abroad. The suspicion was that he had committed certain offences. They searched his home and, as the law entitled them to do, they required him to produce certain bank statements. He did not do so and was in due course summoned to Strasbourg police court which convicted him of failing to produce the documents, fined him 1,200 FF and ordered him to produce them, under penalty of 20 FF per day's delay. His appeals within the domestic system were unsuccessful. He applied to the Commission on the basis that his conviction had infringed his right to a fair trial and that the search had breached Article 8.

Held that the Customs authorities had secured the applicant's conviction in order to obtain documents which they thought must exist in an attempt to compel him to provide the evidence of offences which he had allegedly committed. The special features of customs law could not justify such an infringement of the right of anyone charged with a criminal offence within the autonomous meaning of Article 6 to remain silent and not to contribute to incriminating himself.

The Court did not find it necessary to consider whether the search had been in accordance with law. It did consider that the interference with the applicant's Article 8 rights was in pursuit of the interests of the economic well-being of the country and within Article 8 to that extent. However, although there is a margin of appreciation applicable to Article 8, the exceptions provided for by Article 8.2 are to be interpreted narrowly and the need for them in a given case must be convincingly established. The relevant legislation and practice must afford adequate and effective safeguards against abuse. The powers available to the customs authorities at the material time were very wide and, in the absence of any requirement for a judicial warrant, such protections as existed were too lax and full of loopholes for the interferences in the applicant's right to have been strictly proportionate to the legitimate aim pursued.

(*Note*: On the same day on which it decided *Funke*, the Court applied identical reasoning as regards Article 8 in *Mialhe* v *France* and in *Cremieux* v *France*. These cases are, for that reason, not separately summarised.)

Laskey, Jaggard and Brown v United Kingdom (1997) 24 EHRR 39

In 1987, in the course of routine investigations into other matters, the police came into possession of a number of video films which were made during sado-masochistic encounters involving the applicants and as many as 44 other homosexual men. As a result, the applicants, with several other men, were charged with a series of offences, including assault and wounding, relating to sado-masochistic activities that had taken place over a 10-year period. Although the instances of assault were very numerous, the prosecution limited the counts to a small number of exemplary charges. The acts consisted in the main of maltreatment of the genitalia and ritualistic beatings. There were instances of branding and infliction of injuries which resulted in the flow of blood and which left scarring. These activities were consensual and were conducted in private for no apparent purpose other than the achievement of sexual gratification. The infliction of pain was subject to certain rules including the provision of a code word to be used by any "victim" to stop an "assault", and did not lead to any instances of infection, permanent injury or the need for medical attention. Video cameras were used to record events and the tapes copied and distributed amongst members of the group. The prosecution was largely based on the contents of those videotapes. There was no suggestion that the tapes had been sold or used other than by members of the group.

The applicants pleaded guilty to the assault charges after the trial judge ruled that they could not rely on the consent of the "victims" as an answer to the prosecution case. Prison sentences were imposed. On passing sentence, the trial judge commented: that "the unlawful conduct now before the court would be dealt with equally in the prosecution of heterosexuals or bisexuals if carried out by them. The homosexuality of the defendants is only the background against which the case must be viewed".

The applicants complained that their convictions were the result of an unforeseeable application of a provision of the criminal law which, in any event, amounted to an unlawful and unjustifiable interference with their right to respect for their private life.

It was common ground among those appearing before the Court that the criminal proceedings against the applicants which resulted in their conviction constituted an "interference by a public authority" with the applicants' right to respect for their private life. It was similarly undisputed that the interference had been "in accordance with the law". Furthermore, the Commission and the applicants accepted the Government's assertion that the interference pursued the legitimate aim of the "protection of health or morals", within the meaning of the second paragraph of Article 8.

Held that not every sexual activity carried out behind closed doors necessarily falls within the scope of Article 8. The applicants were involved in consensual sado-masochistic activities for purposes of sexual gratification. There could be no doubt that sexual orientation and activity concern an intimate aspect of private life. However, a considerable number of people were involved in the activities in question which included, *inter alia*, the recruitment of new "members", the provision of several specially equipped "chambers", and the shooting of many videotapes which were distributed among the "members". It might thus be open to question whether the sexual activities of the applicants fell entirely within the notion of "private life" in the particular circumstances of the case. The matter had not been argued.

Assuming, therefore, that the prosecution and conviction of the applicants amounted to an interference with their private life, the question arose whether such an interference was "necessary in a democratic society" within the meaning of the second paragraph of Article 8. According to the Court's established case law, the notion of necessity implies that the interference corresponds to a pressing social need and, in particular, that it is proportionate to the legitimate aim pursued; in determining whether an interference is "necessary in a democratic society", the Court would take into account that a margin of appreciation is left to the national authorities whose decision remains subject to review by the Court for conformity with the requirements of the Convention. The scope of this margin of appreciation is not identical in each case but will vary according to the context. Relevant factors include the nature of the Convention right in issue, its importance for the individual and the nature of the activities concerned. The Court considered that one of the roles which the State was unquestionably entitled to undertake was to seek to regulate, through the operation of the criminal law, activities which involve the infliction of physical harm. This was so whether the activities in question occurred in the course of sexual conduct or otherwise. The determination of the level of harm that should be tolerated by the law in situations where the victim consents was in the first instance a matter for the State concerned since what was at stake was related, on the one hand, to public health considerations and to the general deterrent effect of the criminal law, and, on the other, to the personal autonomy of the individual.

It was evident from the facts established by the national courts that the applicants' sado-masochistic activities involved a significant degree of injury or wounding which could not be characterised as trifling or transient. This, in itself, sufficed to distinguish the present case from those applications which had previously been examined by the Court concerning consensual homo-sexual behaviour in private between adults where no such feature was present. Nor did the Court accept the applicants' submission that no prosecution should have been brought against them since their injuries were not severe and since no medical treatment had been required. In deciding whether or not to prosecute, the State authorities were entitled to have regard not only to the actual seriousness of the harm caused but also to the potential for harm inherent in the acts in question. The charges of assault were numerous and referred to illegal activities which had taken place over more than 10 years. However, only a few charges were selected for inclusion in the prosecution case. In recognition of the fact that the applicants had not appreciated their actions to be criminal, reduced sentences were imposed on appeal. In these circumstances, bearing in mind the degree of organisation involved in the offences, the measures taken against the applicants could not be regarded as disproportionate. There was no violation of Article 8.

McLeod v United Kingdom (1999) 27 EHRR 493

In connection with divorce proceedings, the applicant was ordered by a County Court to deliver to her ex-husband a number of items and furniture from the former matrimonial home, where she lived with her elderly mother. According to the order, if she did not deliver the items by 6 October 1989, she was liable to be committed to prison. On 3 October 1989, Mr McLeod, who mistakenly believed that the applicant had agreed to allow him to collect the property in question, arrived at the former matrimonial home, accompanied by his brother and sister and a solicitor's clerk. Fearing that there would be a breach of the peace because of Ms McLeod's previous unwillingness to comply with orders of the court, her ex-husband's solicitors had arranged for two police officers to be present while the property was being removed. Ms McLeod was not at home when her ex-husband and his party arrived. Her mother allowed them to enter the house. Mr McLeod, his brother and sister and the solicitor's clerk then entered, in circumstances which were subsequently held to have amounted to trespass. They removed his property and placed it in a van.

The police officers also entered the house and checked the items taken against the list that had been attached to the court order. When the applicant returned home, she objected to the removal of the property. One of the police officers intervened and insisted that she allow her former husband to leave with the property. He explained that any continuing dispute should be resolved later by their respective solicitors.

The applicant instituted civil proceedings against the police, amongst others. On 12 November 1992, these proceedings were dismissed by the High Court on the grounds that the police officers had not trespassed on her land or goods, but had only acted in accordance with their duty at common law to prevent any breach of the peace which they reasonably feared would occur. In such circumstances they were entitled to enter and remain on private property without the owner's consent. The High Court's decision was upheld on appeal. The applicant complained to the Commission of a breach of Article 8.

Held that the Convention required full compliance with domestic law and also that the applicable domestic law be formulated with sufficient precision to allow the citizen—if need be with legal advice—to foresee to a reasonable degree the legal consequences of any given action. In this case, it was evident that the concept of "breach of the peace" had been clarified by the English courts to the extent that it was sufficiently established that a breach of the peace was committed only when a person caused harm, or appeared likely to cause harm, to persons or property or acted in a manner the natural consequence of which was to provoke others to violence.

Furthermore, the English courts had recognised that the police had a duty to prevent a breach of the peace occurring and that, in the execution of this duty, they had the power to enter into and remain on private property without the consent of the owner or occupier. This power had been preserved by section 17(6) of the Police and Criminal Evidence Act 1984. The aim of the power enabling police officers to enter private premises to prevent a breach of the peace was clearly a legitimate one for the purposes of Article 8, namely the prevention of disorder or crime.

The Court considered that the police could not be faulted for responding to the solicitors' request for assistance, since there had been a genuine fear that a breach of the peace might occur when Mr McLeod removed his property from the former matrimonial home. However, notwithstanding that the police had been contacted in advance and that the solicitor's clerk had offered to return to his office and collect the court order, the officers had not taken any steps to ascertain whether or not Mr McLeod was entitled to enter his ex-wife's house on the day in question. Sight of the court order would have indicated that it was for Ms McLeod to deliver the property, and that she had three more days in which to do so. Admittedly, the police officers had been informed that Mr McLeod believed an agreement had been reached with his wife whereby he would come and collect the property. None the less, given the circumstances, and particularly the facts that the applicant was not present and her mother lacked knowledge of any agreement, the police should not have taken this agreement for granted. In any case, as soon as it became apparent that Ms McLeod was not at home, the officers should not have entered the house, since it should have been clear to them that there was little or no risk of disorder or crime occurring. On these grounds, the Court found that the officers' entry had been disproportionate to the legitimate aim pursued and that there had been a violation of Article 8 of the Convention.

Lustig-Prean and Beckett v United Kingdom (31417/96; 32377/96)

The applicants had both served in the Royal Navy but had been dismissed on account of their homosexuality. Prior to the discovery of their sexual orientation, both had received highly complimentary reports on their performance. When it came to the attention of the Naval authorities that they might be homosexual, investigations were commenced and both applicants were interviewed. At those interviews they both acknowledged their homosexuality but the interviews continued and the second applicant in particular was asked highly detailed questions about his sexual practices. The applicants complained that the investigations into their homosexuality and their subsequent discharge from the Royal Navy on the sole ground that they were homosexual, in pursuance of the Ministry of Defence's absolute policy against homosexuals in the British armed forces, constituted a violation of their right to respect for their private lives protected by Article 8 of the Convention. The Government accepted that there had been interferences with the applicants' right to respect for their private lives.

Held that such interferences could only be considered justified if the conditions of the second paragraph of Article 8 were satisfied. The parties did not dispute that there had been compliance with the requirement that the interference was authorised by law and the Court found that requirement to be satisfied. As to legitimate aim, the Court observed that the essential justification offered by the Government for the policy and for the consequent investigations and discharges was the maintenance of the morale of service personnel and, consequently, of the fighting power and the operational effectiveness of the armed forces. The Court found no reason to doubt that the policy was designed with a view to ensuring the operational effectiveness of the armed forces or that investigations were, in principle, intended to establish whether the person concerned was a homosexual to whom the policy was applicable. To this extent, therefore, the Court considered that the resulting interferences could be said to pursue the legitimate aims of "the interests of national security" and "the prevention of disorder".

It remained to be determined whether the interferences could be considered "necessary in a democratic society" for those aims. An interference would be considered "necessary in a democratic society" for a legitimate aim if it answered a pressing social need and, in particular, was proportionate to the legitimate aim pursued. Given the matters at issue in the present case, the Court underlined the link between the notion of "necessity" and that of a "democratic society", the hallmarks of the latter including pluralism, tolerance and broadmindedness.

The Court recognised that it is for the national authorities to make the initial assessment of necessity, though the final evaluation as to whether the reasons cited for the interference were relevant and sufficient was for the Court. A margin of appreciation is left open to Contracting States in the context of this assessment, which varies according to the nature of the activities restricted and of the aims pursued by the restrictions. Accordingly, when the relevant restrictions concern a most intimate part of an individual's private life, there must exist particularly serious reasons before such interferences can satisfy the requirements of Article 8.2 of the Convention.

When the core of the national security aim pursued is the operational effectiveness of the armed forces, it was accepted that each State is competent to organise its own system of military discipline and enjoys a certain margin of appreciation in this respect. The Court also considered that it was open to the State to impose restrictions on an individual's right to respect for his private life where there was a real threat to the armed forces' operational effectiveness, as the proper functioning of an army was hardly imaginable without legal rules designed to prevent service personnel from undermining it. However, the national authorities could not rely on such rules to frustrate the exercise by individual members of the armed forces of their right to respect for their private lives, which right applies to service personnel as it does to others within the jurisdiction of the State.

Moreover, assertions as to a risk to operational effectiveness must be substantiated by specific examples. It was common ground that the sole reason for the investigations conducted and for the applicants' discharge was their sexual orientation. The core argument of the Government in support of the policy was that the presence of open or suspected homosexuals in the armed forces would have a substantial and negative effect on morale and, consequently, on the fighting power and operational effectiveness of the armed forces. The Court found that the perceived problems were founded solely upon the negative attitudes of heterosexual personnel towards those of homosexual orientation. To the extent that they represent a predisposed bias on the part of a heterosexual majority against a homosexual minority, these negative attitudes could not, of themselves, be considered by the Court to amount to sufficient justification for the interferences with the applicants' rights any more than similar negative attitudes towards those of a different race, origin or colour.

The Court noted the lack of concrete evidence to substantiate the alleged damage to morale and fighting power that any change in the policy would entail. The Court considered it reasonable to assume that some difficulties could be anticipated as a result of any change in policy but was of the view that it had not been shown that conduct codes and disciplinary rules could not adequately deal with any behavioural issues arising. Accordingly, the Court concluded that convincing and weighty reasons had not been offered by the Government to justify the policy against homosexuals in the armed forces or, therefore, the consequent discharge of the applicants from those forces. In sum, the Court found that neither the investigations conducted into the applicants' sexual orientation, nor their discharge on the grounds of their homosexuality in pursuance of the Ministry of Defence policy, were justified under Article 8.2 of the Convention. Accordingly, there had been a violation of Article 8.

ARTICLES 8 AND 14

Abdulaziz, Cabales and Balkandali v United Kingdom (1985) 7 EHRR 471

The applicants were lawfully and permanently settled in the UK. In accordance with immigration rules in force at the time (which were a product of the transformation of the British Empire into the Commonwealth), their husbands were refused permission to remain with or join them. The applicants complained that they had been the victims of discrimination, *inter alia* on the ground of sex, so that there had been violations of Article 8, alone or in conjunction with Article 14. The Government argued that immigration control was dealt with by Protocol 4 (which the UK had not ratified) and not by Article 8 at all.

Held that Article 8 was applicable because the applicants were the wives who were settled in the UK, not the husbands who sought to immigrate. The applicants were being deprived of, or threatened with the deprivation of, the society of their husbands. Moreover, the Convention and its protocols have to be read as a whole. The fact that an issue is dealt with specifically by one provision does not mean that it is not also within the ambit of another. However, States enjoy a wide margin of appreciation as regards respect for family life and Article 8 does not oblige States to respect the choice of a state of residence by couples who are marrying. The applicants must all have known at the time of marrying of the limitations on their husbands' rights to be in the UK and there was, therefore, no breach of Article 8 taken on its own. Nevertheless, it was easier for a man settled in the UK to get permission for his wife to join him than for a woman to get such permission for her husband. The advancement of equality of the sexes is a major goal in the Member States of the Council of Europe, so very weighty reasons would have to be advanced before a difference in treatment on the ground of sex could be regarded as compatible with the Convention. The Government's argument that male immigrants would have a more significant effect on the labour market than female ones was not convincing. There had been a breach of Article 8 in conjunction with Article 14.

Burghartz v Switzerland (1994) 18 EHRR 101

Swiss nationals chose to use the wife's surname, "Burghartz", the husband putting his own surname before it and calling himself "Schnyder Burghartz". The Swiss authorities registered them both as "Schnyder", refusing to recognise any other formula on the basis that in Swiss law only a wife could put her surname before the family name. Applications to the national courts were unsuccessful. As a result, a large number of official documents, including the husband's certificate of his doctorate in history, did not include the "Burghartz" element. Their application was made jointly. The Court had to consider the Government's preliminary objections that the wife was not a victim and, therefore, lacked standing and that domestic remedies had not been exhausted, in that Articles 8 and 14 ECHR had not been pled in the domestic courts. It had then to consider the substantive issue under those Articles, as to which the Government argued that equality of spouses in choice of surname was governed exclusively by Article 5 of Protocol 7, to which there was Swiss reservation subjecting the international rule to national law and that examining the case under Articles 8 and 14 would be tantamount to ignoring that reservation.

Held that, having regard to the concept of family which prevails in the Convention system, Mrs Burghartz could claim to be a victim, at least indirectly. Since the Swiss Federal Court was obliged to apply legislation and could not suspend laws which conflicted with treaties, the applicants could not be blamed for having based their applications to the national courts on national law alone. The preliminary objections were, therefore, dismissed. Under Article 7 of Protocol 7, Article 5 of that Protocol was to be regarded as an addition to the Convention; it could not, therefore, replace Article 8 or reduce its scope. Article 8 does not contain any explicit provisions on names. However, as a means of personal identification and of linking to a family, a person's name none the less concerns his or her private and family life. The fact that society and the State have an interest in regulating the use of names does not exclude this, since these public law aspects are compatible with private life, conceived of as including, to a certain degree, the right to establish and develop relationships with other human beings, in professional or business contexts as in others. In Mr Burghartz's case the retention of the surname by which he was known in academic circles might affect his career. Article 8, therefore, applied.

The Court reiterated that the advancement of the equality of the sexes is a major goal in the Member States of the Council of Europe and that this means that very weighty reasons would have to be put forward before a difference of treatment on the sole ground of sex could be regarded as compatible with the Convention. The Government relied on the Swiss legislature's concern that family unity should be reflected in a single, joint surname but family unity would be no less reflected if the husband added his own surname to his wife's, adopted as the joint surname. There was no tradition at issue, since married women had only enjoyed the right to add their maiden names to the joint surname since 1984. In any event, the Convention had to be interpreted in the light of present-day conditions, especially the importance of the principle of non-discrimination. Nor was there any distinction to be derived from the choice of one of the spouse's names in preference to the other. It could not be said that it reflected greater deliberateness on the part of the husband than on the part of the wife. The difference of treatment between husbands and wives complained of lacked an objective and reasonable justification and accordingly contravened Article 14 taken together with Article 8.

ARTICLE 9

THE RIGHT TO FREEDOM
OF CONSCIENCE AND RELIGION

1. Everyone has the right to freedom of thought, conscience and religion; this right includes freedom to change his religion or belief and freedom, either alone or in community with others and in public or private, to manifest his religion or belief, in worship, teaching, practice and observance.

2. Freedom to manifest one's religion or beliefs shall be subject only to such limitations as are prescribed by law and are necessary in a democratic society in the interests of public safety, for the protection of public order, health or morals, or for the protection of the rights and freedoms of others.

Kokkinakis v Greece (1993) 17 EHRR 397

The applicant was a Jehovah's Witness who had been arrested more than 60 times for proselytism. He was also interned and imprisoned on several occasions. On 2 March 1986 he and his wife called at the home of Mrs Kyriakaki in Sitia and engaged in a discussion with her. Mrs Kyriakaki's husband, who was the cantor at a local Orthodox church, informed the police, who arrested Mr and Mrs Kokkinakis and took them to the local police station, where they spent the night of 2–3 March 1986. They were then prosecuted under section 4 of Law No. 1363/1938 making proselytism an offence. The court found Mr and Mrs Kokkinakis guilty of proselytism and sentenced each of them to four months' imprisonment. The Court of Appeal quashed Mrs Kokkinakis's conviction and upheld her husband's but reduced his prison sentence to three months.

The applicant complained, *inter alia*, of a breach of Article 9.

Held that, as enshrined in Article 9, freedom of thought, conscience and religion is one of the foundations of a "democratic society" within the meaning of the Convention. It is, in its religious dimension, one of the most vital elements that go to make up the identity of believers and their conception of life, but it is also a precious asset for atheists, agnostics, sceptics and the unconcerned. The pluralism indissociable from a democratic society, which has been dearly won over the centuries, depends on it. While religious freedom is primarily a matter of individual conscience, it also implies, *inter alia*, freedom to "manifest [one's] religion". Bearing witness in words and deeds is bound up with the existence of religious convictions.

According to Article 9, freedom to manifest one's religion is not only exercisable in community with others, "in public" and within the circle of those whose faith one shares, but can also be asserted "alone" and "in private"; furthermore, it includes in principle the right to try to convince one's neighbour, for example through "teaching", failing which, moreover, "freedom to change [one's] religion or belief", enshrined in Article 9, would be likely to remain a dead letter.

The fundamental nature of the rights guaranteed in Article 9.1 is also reflected in the wording of the paragraph providing for limitations on them. Unlike the second paragraphs of Articles 8, 10 and 11 which cover all the rights mentioned in the first paragraphs of those Articles, that of Article 9 refers only to "freedom to manifest one's religion or belief". In so doing, it recognises that in democratic societies, in which several religions coexist within one and the same population, it may be necessary to place restrictions on this freedom in order to reconcile the interests of the various groups and ensure that everyone's beliefs are respected.

The sentence passed on the applicant amounted to an interference with the exercise of his right to "freedom to manifest [his] religion or belief". Such an interference is contrary to Article 9 unless it is "prescribed by law", directed at one or more of the legitimate aims in paragraph 2 and "necessary in a democratic society" for achieving them.

The wording of many statutes is not absolutely precise. The need to avoid excessive rigidity and to keep pace with changing circumstances means that many laws are inevitably couched in terms which, to a greater or lesser extent, are vague. Criminal law provisions on proselytism fall within this category. The interpretation and application of such enactments depend on practice. In this instance there existed a body of settled national case law, which had been published and was accessible and was such as to enable Mr Kokkinakis to regulate his conduct in the matter. The measure complained of was, therefore, "prescribed by law" within the meaning of Article 9.2.

Having regard to the circumstances of the case and the actual terms of the relevant courts' decisions (which emphasised the need to avoid deceitful methods of proselytism aimed at those of low intellect), the Court considered that the impugned measure was in pursuit of a legitimate aim under Article 9, namely the protection of the rights and freedoms of others.

The Court had consistently held that a certain margin of appreciation is to be left to the Contracting States in assessing the existence and extent of the necessity of an interference, but this margin is subject to European supervision, embracing both the legislation and the decisions applying it, even those given by an independent court. The Court's task is to determine whether the measures taken at national level were justified in principle and proportionate. In order to rule on this latter point, the Court had to weigh the requirements of the protection of the rights and liberties of others against the conduct of which the applicant stood accused. In exercising its supervisory jurisdiction, the Court must look at the impugned judicial decisions against the background of the case as a whole.

First, a distinction had to be made between bearing Christian witness and improper proselytism. The former corresponds to true evangelism, which a report drawn up in 1956 under the auspices of the World Council of Churches describes as an essential mission and a responsibility of every Christian and every Church. The latter represents a corruption or deformation of it. It may, according to the same report, take the form of activities offering material or social advantages with a view to gaining new members for a Church or exerting improper pressure on people in distress or in need; it may even entail the use of violence or brainwashing; more generally, it is not compatible with respect for the freedom of thought, conscience and religion of others. Scrutiny of the Greek legislation showed that the relevant criteria adopted by the Greek legislature were reconcilable with the foregoing if and in so far as they were designed only to punish improper proselytism, which the Court did not have to define in the abstract in the present case. The Court noted, however, that in their reasoning the Greek courts established the applicant's liability by merely reproducing the wording of the legislation and did not sufficiently specify in what way the accused had attempted to convince his neighbour by improper means. None of the facts they set out warranted that finding. That being so, it had not been shown that the applicant's conviction was justified in the circumstances of the case by a pressing social need. The contested measure, therefore, did not appear to have been proportionate to the legitimate aim pursued or, consequently, "necessary in a democratic society ... for the protection of the rights and freedoms of others". In conclusion, there had been a breach of Article 9.

Manoussakis and Others v Greece (1997) 23 EHRR 387

The applicants were all Jehovah's Witnesses who lived in Crete. The applicant Manoussakis rented a room for use "for all kinds of meetings, weddings, etc. of Jehovah's Witnesses". The applicants sought the authorisation required to use the room as a place of worship but the authorities were unco-operative. Ultimately, the applicants were prosecuted for, and convicted of, having established and operated a place of worship for religious meetings and ceremonies of followers of a denomination other than the Orthodox Church without authorisation from the recognised ecclesiastical authorities and the Minister of Education and Religious Affairs.

Held that the applicants' conviction for having used the premises in question without the prior authorisation required was an interference with the exercise of their "freedom ... , to manifest [their] religion ... , in worship ... and observance". Such interference breaches Article 9 unless it was "prescribed by law", pursued one or more of the legitimate aims referred to in paragraph 2 and was "necessary in a democratic society" to attain such aim or aims.

Although argument was addressed to the Court about the law under which the interference had taken place, it did not consider it necessary to deal with those arguments, since it was clear on other grounds that there was a breach of Article 9.

According to the Government, the penalty imposed on the applicants served to protect public order and the rights and freedoms of others. It argued that, although the notion of public order had features that were common to the democratic societies in Europe, its substance varied on account of national characteristics. In Greece virtually the entire population was of the Christian Orthodox faith, which was closely associated with important moments in the history of the Greek nation. The Orthodox Church had kept alive the national conscience and Greek patriotism during the periods of foreign occupation. Moreover, various sects sought to manifest their ideas and doctrines using all sorts of "unlawful and dishonest" means. The intervention of the State to regulate this area with a view to protecting those whose rights and freedoms were affected by the activities of socially dangerous sects was indispensable to maintain public order on Greek territory.

The Court recognised that the States are entitled to verify whether a move-ment or association carries on, ostensibly in pursuit of religious aims, activities which are harmful to the population. It recalled that Jehovah's Witnesses came within the definition of "known religion" as provided for under Greek law but nevertheless considered, having regard to the circumstances of the case, that the impugned measure pursued a legitimate aim for the purposes of Article 9.2, namely the protection of public order.

As a matter of case law, the Court had consistently left the Contracting States a certain margin of appreciation in assessing the existence and extent of the necessity of an interference, but this margin is subject to European supervision, embracing both the legislation and the decisions applying it. The Court's task was to determine whether the measures taken at national level were justified in principle and proportionate.

In delimiting the extent of the margin of appreciation in the present case the Court had to have regard to what is at stake, namely the need to secure true religious pluralism, an inherent feature of the notion of a democratic society. Further, considerable weight has to be attached to that need when it comes to determining, pursuant to paragraph 2 of Article 9, whether the restriction was proportionate to the legitimate aim pursued.

The restrictions imposed on the freedom to manifest religion by the provisions of Greek Law called for very strict scrutiny by the Court. The law allowed far-reaching interference by the political, administrative and ecclesiastical authorities with the exercise of religious freedom. The right to freedom of religion as guaranteed under the Convention excludes any discretion on the part of the State to determine whether religious beliefs or the means used to express such beliefs are legitimate. Accordingly, the Court took the view that the authorisation requirement was consistent with Article 9 of the Convention only in so far as it was intended to allow the Minister to verify whether the formal conditions laid down in the legislation were satisfied. It appeared from the evidence and from the numerous other cases cited by the applicants and not contested by the Government that the State had tended to use the possibilities afforded by the above-mentioned provisions to impose rigid, or indeed prohibitive, conditions on practice of religious beliefs by certain non-Orthodox movements, in particular Jehovah's Witnesses.

In the instant case, the applicants were prosecuted and convicted for having operated a place of worship without first obtaining the authorisations required by law. The impugned conviction had such a direct effect on the applicants' freedom of religion that it could not be regarded as proportionate to the legitimate aim pursued, nor, accordingly, as necessary in a democratic society. There had been a violation of Article 9.

ARTICLE 10

THE RIGHT TO FREEDOM OF EXPRESSION

1. Everyone has the right to freedom of expression. This right shall include freedom to hold opinions and to receive and impart information and ideas without interference by public authority and regardless of frontiers. This article shall not prevent States from requiring the licensing of broadcasting, television or cinema enterprises.

2. The exercise of these freedoms, since it carries with it duties and responsibilities, may be subject to such formalities, conditions, restrictions or penalties as are prescribed by law and are necessary in a democratic society, in the interests of national security, territorial integrity or public safety, for the prevention of disorder or crime, for the protection of health or morals, for the protection of the reputation or rights of others, for preventing the disclosure of information received in confidence, or for maintaining the authority and impartiality of the judiciary.

Handyside v United Kingdom (1979–80) 1 EHRR 737

The applicant was the proprietor of a publishing firm which published a book called "The Little Red Schoolbook". The book had first been published in Denmark and then in a wide range of other European countries. After receipt of a number of complaints, the Director of Public Prosecutions asked the Metropolitan Police to undertake inquiries, in the course of which the applicant's premises were searched under warrant and copies of the book were seized. The applicant was thereafter prosecuted and convicted under the Obscene Publications Act 1959. He complained of a violation of Article 10.

Held that (as the Government had conceded) there had been interference by a public authority with the right guaranteed by Article 10. Such interferences entail a violation of Article 10 if they do not fall within one of the exceptions provided for in paragraph 2.

They must, in the first place, have been "prescribed by law" and this they clearly were. The legislation had an aim that was legitimate under Article 10.2, namely the protection of morals in a democratic society. The Court had

173

to investigate whether the protection of morals in a democratic society necessitated the various measures taken against the applicant.

The machinery of protection established by the Convention is subsidiary to the national systems safeguarding human rights. The Convention leaves to each Contracting State, in the first place, the task of securing the rights and liberties it enshrines. These observations applied, notably, to Article 10.2. In particular, it was not possible to find in the domestic law of the various Contracting States a uniform European conception of morals. The view taken by their respective laws of the requirements of morals varies from time to time and from place to place, especially in an era which was characterised by a rapid and far-reaching evolution of opinions on the subject. By reason of their direct and continuous contact with the vital forces of their countries, State authorities are in principle in a better position than the international judge to give an opinion on the exact content of these requirements as well as on the "necessity" of a "restriction" or "penalty" intended to meet them. The Court noted that, whilst the adjective "necessary", within the meaning of Article 10.2, is not synonymous with "indispensable", it does not have the flexibility of such expressions as "admissible", "ordinary", "useful", "reasonable" or desirable". Nevertheless, it was for the national authorities to make the initial assessment of the reality of the pressing social need implied by the notion of "necessity". Consequently, Article 10.2 leaves to the Contracting States a margin of appreciation. This margin is given both to the domestic legislator and to the bodies, judicial amongst others, that are called upon to interpret and apply the laws in force. Nevertheless, Article 10.2 does not give the Contracting States an unlimited power of appreciation. The Court, which is responsible for ensuring the observance of those States' engagements, is empowered to give the final ruling on whether a "restriction" or "penalty" is reconcilable with freedom of expression as protected by Article 10. The domestic margin of appreciation thus goes hand in hand with a European supervision. Such supervision concerns both the aim of the measure challenged and its "necessity"; it covers not only the basic legislation but also the decision applying it, even one given by an independent court.

The Court's supervisory functions oblige it to pay the utmost attention to the principles characterising a "democratic society". Freedom of expression constitutes one of the essential foundations of such a society, one of the basic conditions for its progress and for the development of every man. Subject to paragraph 2 of Article 10, it is applicable not only to "information" or "ideas" that are favourably received or regarded as inoffensive or as a matter of indifference, but also to those that offend, shock or disturb the State or any sector of the population. Such are the demands of that pluralism, tolerance and broadmindedness without which there is no "democratic society". This means, amongst other things, that every "formality", "condition", "restriction" or "penalty" imposed in this sphere must be proportionate to the legitimate aim pursued. From another standpoint, whoever exercises his freedom of expression undertakes "duties and responsibilities" the scope of which depends on his situation and the technical means he uses. The Court could not overlook such a person's "duties" and "responsibilities" when it inquired whether "restrictions" or "penalties" were conducive to the "protection of morals" which made them "necessary" in a "democratic society".

The Court went on to examine the facts of the case in detail and held that the action taken in relation to a publication aimed at adolescents which included material that young people at a critical stage of their development could have interpreted as an encouragement to indulge in precocious activities harmful for them or even to commit certain criminal offences could properly be regarded as having been in pursuit of the protection of morals and as necessary (and proportionate) to that aim. There was no breach of Article 10.

Barthold v Federal Republic of Germany (1985) 7 EHRR 383

The applicant was a veterinary surgeon practising in Hamburg-Fuhlsbüttel. He was a member of the Hamburg Veterinary Surgeons' Council, whose task, among other things, was to ensure that its members complied with their professional obligations. These obligations were laid down principally in the Rules of Professional Conduct of Hamburg Veterinary Surgeons. The applicant provided, and campaigned for the wider provision of, a round-the-clock veterinary emergency service. In August 1978, there appeared in the daily newspaper *Hamburger Abendblatt* an article entitled "Veterinary surgeons hard to reach after 8 pm—why 'Shalen' managed to survive the night after all". The article recounted the difficulties experienced by the owners of a cat called "Shalen" in getting emergency treatment for the animal overnight until the applicant came to the rescue. It was accompanied by a photograph of the applicant and a larger photograph of the cat.

A number of Dr Barthold's fellow practitioners instigated proceedings against him for breach of the Rules of Professional Conduct. The proceedings were dealt with on the basis that the applicant's involvement in the article had been a species of unfair competition and in the end he was made the subject of an injunction which forbade him

"to report in the press (except in professional journals), giving his full name, a photograph of himself and an indication of his occupation as director of the Fuhlsbüttel veterinary clinic, that at least on working days between 8 pm and 8 am, animal lovers in Hamburg would get sore fingers from trying to telephone veterinary surgeons ready to help them, in conjunction with (a) the statement that only veterinary clinics were on voluntary emergency duty round the clock, and/or (b) the statement that in his practice the telephone rang between two and 12 times between 8 pm and 8 am, though not all these calls were emergency cases and advice over the telephone would sometimes be sufficient, and/or (c) the description of a case in which the owner of an animal had tried in vain one ordinary weekday between 7.30 pm and 10 pm to find a veterinary surgeon to treat his cat, until finally he was lucky enough to contact Dr Barthold, who acted when it was more than 'high time', and/or to contribute to such reports by giving journalists information".

For each and every breach of the injunction, he was liable to a maximum fine of 500,000 DM or non-criminal imprisonment (Ordnungshaft) of up to six months, the precise penalty to be fixed by the court.

The matter went ultimately to the Hanseatic Court of Appeal, which took the view that the intention of enhancing the applicant's own competitiveness to the detriment of his competitors was to be presumed in the case of this type of publication, and that the presumption was not rebutted in the circumstances. It mattered little that he may additionally or even primarily have been pursuing other objectives, as there was an act done for the purposes of commercial competition as long as the intent to stimulate such competition had not been entirely overridden by other motives. The applicant complained of a breach of Article 10.

Held that Article 10 specifies that freedom of expression "shall include freedom to hold opinions and to ... impart information and ideas". The restrictions imposed in the present case related to the inclusion, in any statement of Dr Barthold's views as to the need for a night veterinary service in Hamburg, of certain factual data and assertions regarding, in particular, his person and the running of his clinic. All these various components overlapped to make up a whole, the gist of which was the expression of "opinions" and the imparting of "information" on a topic of general interest. It was not possible to dissociate from this whole those elements which went more to manner of presentation than to substance and which, so the German courts held, had a publicity-like effect. This was especially so since the publication prompting the restriction was an article written by a journalist and not a commercial advertisement. The Court accordingly found that Article 10 was applicable, without needing to inquire in the present case whether or not advertising as such comes within the scope of the guarantee under this provision.

There had clearly been an "interference by public authority" with the exercise of the applicant's freedom of expression. This interference would not be compatible with Article 10 unless it satisfied the conditions laid down in paragraph 2, a clause calling for a narrow interpretation. Thus, the interference must be "prescribed by law", have an aim or aims that is or are legitimate under Article 10.2 and be "necessary in a democratic society" for the aforesaid aim or aims.

As to whether the interference was "prescribed by law", according to the Court's case law on this point, the interference must have some basis in domestic law, which itself must be adequately accessible and be formulated with sufficient precision to enable the individual to regulate his conduct, if need be with appropriate advice. The legal basis of the interference under consideration was provided by two legislative provisions and one of the Rules of Professional Conduct promulgated by the Veterinary Surgeons' Council but applied, nevertheless, by the appeal court. That Rule was to be regarded as a "law" within the meaning of Article 10.2 of the Convention. The competence of the Veterinary Surgeons' Council in the sphere of professional conduct derived from the independent rule-making power that the veterinary profession—in company with other liberal professions—traditionally enjoyed, by parliamentary delegation, in the Federal Republic of Germany and was a competence exercised by the Council under the control of the State, which in particular satisfied itself as to observance of national legislation, and the Council was obliged to submit its rules of professional conduct to the Land Government for approval. The "accessibility" of the relevant texts had not been the subject of any dispute.

On the other hand, the applicant argued that the injunctions complained of were not foreseeable, either subjectively or objectively. In his submission, the relevant legislation did not fix the limits of freedom of expression with sufficient clarity to indicate in advance to each member of the veterinary profession the dividing line between what was permitted and what was not. The legislation did indeed employ somewhat imprecise wording, notably the expression "honest practices". It thereby conferred a broad discretion on the courts. The Court had, however, in other cases had the occasion to recognise the impossibility of attaining absolute precision in the framing of laws. Such considerations are especially cogent in the sphere of competition, this being a subject where the relevant factors are in constant evolution in line with developments in the market and in means of communication. Accordingly, the injunctions complained of were "prescribed by law".

The Government argued that the interference had a legitimate purpose in that it served to protect human "health" as well as the "rights" of the applicant's fellow veterinary surgeons and of clients of veterinary surgeons, that is to say, "others"; and that the interference was also aimed at the protection of "morals". The Court noted that, according to the reasons given in the judgment, the final injunction was issued in order to prevent the applicant from acquiring a commercial advantage over professional colleagues prepared to conduct themselves in compliance with the rule of professional conduct that requires veterinary surgeons to refrain from advertising. The Hanseatic Court of Appeal grounded its decision on the protection of the "rights of others" and there was no cause for believing that it was pursuing other objectives alien to the Convention. The judgment thus had an aim that was, in itself, legitimate. There was no need to inquire whether that judgment was capable of being justified under Article 10.2 on other grounds as well.

The Government argued that the restriction imposed was one that was "necessary in a democratic society". Their arguments were that the statements that the applicant was restrained, by the judgment of 24 January 1980, from repeating denigrated his fellow veterinary surgeons and were in part erroneous; by reason of the form they took and the type of publication in which they appeared, these statements went beyond objective criticism and amounted to advertising incompatible with the Rules of Professional Conduct; that although Dr Barthold was not himself the author of the article in the

Hamburger Abendblatt, the Hanseatic Court of Appeal was not mistaken to hold him responsible. In addition, the Government maintained, the prohibition complained of was consistent with the principle of proportionality. Being circumscribed within narrow limits, it did not bar Dr Barthold from expressing an opinion on the issue of a night veterinary service in Hamburg. Nor did the penalties that the applicant risked incurring if he were to repeat the prohibited statements fall foul of the principle of proportionality, since they amounted to no more than an "abstract threat" that the domestic courts would have to implement in the event of wrongful conduct in the light of the particular circumstances obtaining at that time. Finally, in the submission of the Government, in the field of the repression of unfair competition the Contracting States enjoyed a wide margin of appreciation and the legal traditions of the Contracting States had to be respected by the Convention institutions.

The Court recalled that the adjective "necessary", within the meaning of Article 10.2, is not synonymous with "indispensable", neither does it have the flexibility of such expressions as "admissible", "ordinary", "useful", "reasonable" or "desirable"; rather, it implies a "pressing social need". The Contracting States enjoy a power of appreciation in this respect, but that power of appreciation goes hand in hand with a European supervision which is more or less extensive depending upon the circumstances; it is for the Court to make the final determination as to whether the interference in issue corresponds to such a need, whether it is "proportionate to the legitimate aim pursued" and whether the reasons given by the national authorities to justify it are "relevant and sufficient".

The article in the *Hamburger Abendblatt* pursued a specific object, that is to say, informing the public about the situation obtaining in Hamburg, at a time when, according to the two practitioners interviewed, the enactment of new legislation on veterinary surgeons was under consideration. It had not been disputed that the problem discussed in the article was a genuine one.

Freedom of expression holds a prominent place in a democratic society. Freedom of expression constitutes one of the essential foundations of a democratic society and one of the basic conditions for its progress and for the development of every man and woman. The necessity for restricting that freedom for one of the purposes listed in Article 10.2 must be convincingly established. When considered from this viewpoint, the interference complained of went further than the requirements of the legitimate aim pursued. It was true that the applicant retained the right to express his opinion on the problem of a night service for veterinary surgeons in Hamburg and even, in so doing, to divulge his name, have a photograph of himself published and disclose that he was the director of the Fuhlsbüttel veterinary clinic. He was, however, directed not to supplement his opinion, when accompanied by such indications, with certain factual examples drawn from his own experience and illustrating the difficulties encountered by animal owners in obtaining the assistance of a veterinary surgeon during the night. It might well be that these illustrations had the effect of giving publicity to Dr Barthold's own clinic, thereby providing a source of complaint for his fellow veterinary surgeons, but in the particular circumstances this effect proved to be altogether secondary having regard to the principal content of the article and to the nature of the issue being put to the public at large. The injunction did not achieve a fair balance between the two interests at stake.

According to the Hanseatic Court of Appeal, there remained an intent to act for the purposes of commercial competition, within the meaning of the legislation, as long as that intent has not been entirely overriden by other motives. A criterion as strict as this in approaching the matter of advertising and publicity in the liberal professions is not consonant with freedom of expression. Its application risks discouraging members of the liberal professions from contributing to public debate on topics affecting the life of the community if ever there is the slightest likelihood of their utterances being treated as entailing, to some degree, an advertising effect. By the same token, application of a criterion such as this is liable to hamper the press in the performance of its task of purveyor of information and public watchdog. The injunctions complained of were, therefore, not proportionate to the legitimate aim pursued and, accordingly, were not "necessary in a democratic society" "for the protection of the rights of others", with the result that they gave rise to a violation of Article 10 of the Convention.

Open Door and Dublin Well Woman v Ireland (1992) 15 EHRR 244

The case originated in two applications against Ireland lodged with the Commission. The first was brought by Open Door Counselling Ltd, a company incorporated in Ireland; the second by another Irish company, Dublin Well Woman Centre Ltd, and one citizen of the United States of America, Ms Bonnie Maher, and three Irish citizens, Ms Ann Downes, Mrs X and Ms Maeve Geraghty. The two companies were engaged, *inter alia*, in counselling pregnant women in Dublin and in other parts of Ireland. Bonnie Maher and Ann Downes worked as trained counsellors for Dublin Well Woman. Mrs X and Maeve Geraghty joined in the Dublin Well Woman application as women of child-bearing age. The applicants complained of an injunction imposed by the Irish courts on Open Door and Dublin Well Woman to restrain them from providing certain information to pregnant women concerning abortion facilities outside the jurisdiction of Ireland by way of non-directive counselling.

The injunction had been commenced as a private action brought by the Society for the Protection of Unborn Children (Ireland) Ltd ("SPUC") and converted into a relator action brought at the suit of the Attorney General. The action sought a declaration that the activities of the applicant companies in counselling pregnant women within the jurisdiction of the court to travel abroad to obtain an abortion were unlawful having regard to that provision of the Irish Constitution which protected the right to life of the unborn and an order restraining the defendants from such counselling or assistance. No evidence was adduced at the hearing of the action which proceeded on the basis of certain agreed facts, which included the information that abortion or termination of pregnancy might be one of the options discussed within counselling, that if a pregnant woman wanted to consider the abortion option further, arrangements would be made by the applicant to refer her to a medical clinic in Great Britain and that, in certain circumstances, the applicant might arrange for the travel of such pregnant women.

The High Court granted the injunction. In due course, the Supreme Court unanimously rejected the applicants' appeal but varied the terms of the order as follows: ". . . that the defendants and each of them, their servants or agents be perpetually restrained from assisting pregnant women within the jurisdiction to travel abroad to obtain abortions by referral to a clinic, by the making for them of travel arrangements, or by informing them of the identity and location of and the method of communication with a specified clinic or clinics or otherwise".

Subsequently, SPUC applied successfully to the High Court for a declaration that the dissemination in certain student publications of information concerning the identity and location of abortion clinics outside the jurisdiction was unlawful and for an injunction restraining its distribution.

Held that, because Ms Maher and Ms Downes were subject to the restraint of the Supreme Court injunction, they could properly claim to have suffered an interference with their Article 10 right and, therefore, to be "victims" of an interference with their rights. As regards Mrs X and Ms Geraghty, the Convention entitled individuals to contend that a law violated their rights by itself, in the absence of an individual measure of implementation, if they ran the risk of being directly affected by it. The injunction restrained the corporate applicants and their servants and agents from providing certain information to pregnant women. Although it had not been asserted that Mrs X and Ms Geraghty were pregnant, it was not disputed that they belonged to a class of women of child-bearing age which might be adversely affected by the restrictions imposed by the injunction. They were not seeking to challenge *in abstracto* the compatibility of Irish law with the Convention since they ran a risk of being directly prejudiced by the measure complained of. They could thus claim to be "victims" within the meaning of the Convention.

The Government accepted that the injunction interfered with the freedom of the corporate applicants to impart information. Having regard to the scope of the injunction which also restrained the "servants or agents" of the corporate applicants from assisting "pregnant women", there could be no doubt that there was also an interference with the rights of the applicant counsellors to impart information and with the rights of Mrs X and Ms Geraghty to receive information in the event of being pregnant.

To determine whether such an interference entails a violation of Article 10 the Court had to examine whether or not it was justified under Article 10.2 by reason of being a restriction "prescribed by law" which was necessary in a democratic society on one or other of the grounds specified in Article 10.2.

Open Door and Dublin Well Woman submitted that the law was not formulated with sufficient precision to have enabled them to foresee that the non-directive counselling in which they were involved would be restrained by the courts. This question had to be approached by considering not merely the wording of the legislation in isolation but also the protection given under Irish law to the rights of the unborn in statute law and in case law. It was clear from Irish case law that infringement of constitutional rights by private individuals as well as by the State might be actionable. Furthermore, the constitutional obligation that the State defend and vindicate personal rights "by its laws" had been interpreted by the courts as not being confined merely to "laws" which have been enacted by the Irish Parliament but as also comprehending judge-made "law". Taking into consideration the high threshold of protection of the unborn provided under Irish law generally and the manner in which the courts had interpreted their role as the guarantors of constitutional rights, the possibility that action might be taken against the corporate applicants must have been, with appropriate legal advice, reasonably foreseeable. The restriction was accordingly "prescribed by law".

The Government submitted that the relevant provisions of Irish law were intended for the protection of the rights of others—in this instance the unborn, for the protection of morals and, where appropriate, for the prevention of crime. The Court could not accept that the restrictions at issue pursued the aim of the prevention of crime since neither the provision of the information in question nor the obtaining of an abortion outside the jurisdiction involved any criminal offence. However, it was evident that the protection afforded under Irish law to the right to life of the unborn is based on profound moral values concerning the nature of life which were reflected in the stance of the majority of the Irish people against abortion as expressed in a recent referendum. The restriction thus pursued the legitimate aim of the protection of morals of which the protection in Ireland of the right to life of the unborn was one aspect.

The Government submitted that the Court's approach to the assessment of the "necessity" of the restraint should be guided by the fact that the protection of the rights of the unborn in Ireland could be derived from, *inter alia*, Article 2 of the Convention which, they argued, also protected unborn life. The "proportionality" test was inadequate where the rights of the unborn were at issue. The right to life could not, like other rights, be measured according to a graduated scale. It was either respected or it was not. Accordingly, the traditional approach of weighing competing rights and interests in the balance was inappropriate where the destruction of unborn life was concerned. Since life was a primary value which was antecedent to, and a prerequisite for, the enjoyment of every other right, its protection might involve the infringement of other rights such as freedom of expression in a manner which might not be acceptable in the defence of rights of a lesser nature. The view that abortion was morally wrong was the deeply held view of the majority of the people in Ireland and it was not the proper function of the Court to seek to impose a different viewpoint. The Court observed that in the present case it was not called upon to examine whether a right to abortion is guaranteed under the Convention or whether the fetus is encompassed by the right to life as contained in Article 2. The applicants had not claimed that the Convention contains a right to abortion as such, their complaint being limited to that part of the injunction which restricted their freedom to impart and receive information concerning abortion abroad. Thus, the only issue to be addressed was whether the restrictions on the freedom to impart and receive information contained in the relevant part of the injunction were necessary in a democratic society for the legitimate aim of the protection of morals. It followed from this approach that the Government's argument based on Article 2 of the Convention did not fall to be examined in the present case.

The Court acknowledged that the national authorities enjoy a wide margin of appreciation in matters of morals, particularly in an area such as the present which touched on matters of belief concerning the nature of human life. It was not possible to find in the legal and social orders of the Contracting States a uniform European conception of morals, and the State authorities are, in principle, in a better position than the international judge to give an opinion on the exact content of the requirements of morals as well as on the "necessity" of a "restriction" or "penalty" intended to meet them. However, this power of appreciation is not unlimited. It is for the Court, in this field also, to supervise whether a restriction is compatible with the Convention. As regards the application of the "proportionality" test, the logical consequence of the Government's argument was that measures taken by the national authorities to protect the right to life of the unborn or to uphold the constitutional guarantee on the subject would be automatically justified under the Convention where infringement of a right of a lesser stature was alleged. It is, in principle, open to the national authorities to take such action as they consider necessary to respect the rule of law or to give effect to constitutional rights. However, they must do so in a manner which is compatible with their obligations under the Convention and subject to review by the Convention institutions. To accept the Government's pleading on this point would amount to an abdication of the Court's responsibility under Article 19 "to ensure the observance of the engagements undertaken by the High Contracting Parties . . .". Accordingly, the Court had to examine the question of "necessity" in the light of the principles developed in its case law. It had to determine whether there existed a pressing social need for the measures in question and, in particular, whether the restriction complained of was "proportionate to the legitimate aim pursued". In this context, it was appropriate to recall that freedom of expression is also applicable to "information" or "ideas" that offend, shock or disturb the State or any sector of the population. Such are the demands of that pluralism, tolerance and broadmindedness without which there is no "democratic society".

The Court was struck by the absolute nature of the Supreme Court injunction which imposed a "perpetual" restraint on the provision of information to pregnant women concerning abortion facilities abroad, regardless of age or state of health or their reasons for seeking counselling on the termination of pregnancy. On that ground alone the restriction appeared overbroad and disproportionate. Moreover, this assessment was confirmed by other factors. The corporate applicants were engaged in the counselling of pregnant women in the course of which counsellors neither advocated nor encouraged abortion, but confined themselves to an explanation of the available options. The decision as to whether or not to act on the information so provided was that of the woman concerned. There could be little doubt that following such counselling there were women who decided against a termination of pregnancy. Accordingly, the link between the provision of information and the destruction of unborn life was not as definite as the Government had contended.

Furthermore, the information that was provided by the relevant applicants concerning abortion facilities abroad was not made available to the public at large. Information concerning abortion facilities abroad could be obtained from other sources in Ireland such as magazines and telephone directories or by persons with contacts in Great Britain. Accordingly, information that the injunction sought to restrict was already available elsewhere although in a manner which was not supervised by qualified personnel and thus less protective of women's health. Furthermore, the injunction appeared to have been largely ineffective in protecting the right to life of the unborn since it did not prevent large numbers of Irish women from continuing to obtain abortions in Great Britain.

In addition, the available evidence suggested that the injunction had created a risk to the health of those women who were seeking abortions at a later stage in their pregnancy, due to lack of proper counselling, and who were not availing themselves of customary medical supervision after the abortion had taken place. Moreover, the injunction may have had more adverse effects on women who were not sufficiently resourceful or had not the necessary level of education to have access to alternative sources of information. The Court concluded that the restraint imposed on the applicants from receiving or imparting information was disproportionate to the aims pursued. Accordingly, there had been a breach of Article 10.

Casado Coca v Spain (1994) 18 EHRR 1

The applicant was a lawyer in Barcelona who had been disciplined by the Barcelona Bar Council for breach of a (subsequently relaxed) prohibition on professional advertising. He applied unsuccessfully to the courts. He then applied to the Commission on the basis that his right of freedom of expression in Article 10 had been breached. The Government argued that Article 10 did not extend to advertising and that the Barcelona Bar Council was not a public authority within the meaning of Article 10.

Held that Article 10 guarantees freedom of expression to everyone. No distinction is made in it according to whether the type of aim is profit making or not and a difference in treatment in this sphere might fall foul of Article 14. Article 10 does not apply solely to certain types of information or ideas or forms of expression, in particular those of a political nature; it also encompasses artistic expression and information of a commercial nature. Article 10, therefore, applied.

The Bar Council was a public-law corporation. An appeal against its decisions lay to the courts which had upheld those decisions. The interference with the applicant's right of freedom of expression was, therefore, by a public authority and contravened Article 10 unless it was prescribed by law, had an aim which was legitimate under Article 10.2 and was necessary in a democratic society.

The prohibition was founded on the Statute of the Spanish Bar and the Spanish courts had proceeded on the basis of existing case law. It was, therefore, prescribed by law. The Court did not have any reason to doubt that the rules were designed to protect the public whilst ensuring respect for members of the Bar and the restrictions on advertising were traditionally justified by reference to special features of the profession such as exclusive rights of audience and immunity from process in respect of oral presentation of cases in court.

As to the necessity of the restrictions in a democratic society, States parties to the Convention have a certain margin of appreciation in assessing the necessity of an interference in the complex and fluctuating area of unfair competition. The same applies to advertising. The rules regulating lawyers vary with culture from country to country. Because of their direct, continuous contact with their members, the Bar authorities and the country's courts are in a better position than an international court to determine how, at a given time, the right balance can be struck between the various interests involved. At the material time—1982/83—the relevant authorities' reaction could not be considered unreasonable and disproportionate to the aim pursued. No breach of Article 10 had been made out.

Fressoz and Roire v France (29183/95)

September 1989 was a period of industrial unrest within the Peugeot motor company. The workforce's demands included pay rises, which the management, led by the company chairman and managing director Mr Jacques Calvet, refused to award. On 27 September 1989, *Le Canard enchaîné* published an article by Mr Roire under the headline: "Calvet turbo-charges his salary." In the article, the applicant made use of Mr Calvet's tax returns to show that he had received very substantial recent salary increases.

The applicants were subsequently charged with handling copies of notices of assessment to tax obtained through a breach of professional confidence, unlawful removal of deeds or documents and theft. At first instance, they were acquitted on the ground that there was insufficient evidence to show who had handled the tax returns but the Court of Appeal reversed the judgment and found the applicants guilty. Mr Fressoz and Mr Roire applied to the Commission on 3 August 1995. They asserted that their conviction had infringed Article 10 of the Convention.

Held that freedom of expression constitutes one of the essential foundations of a democratic society. Subject to paragraph 2 of Article 10, it is applicable not only to "information" or "ideas" that are favourably received or regarded as inoffensive or as a matter of indifference, but also to those that offend, shock or disturb. Such are the demands of pluralism, tolerance and broad-mindedness without which there is no "democratic society". The press plays an essential role in a democratic society. Although it must not overstep certain bounds, in particular in respect of the reputation and rights of others and the need to prevent the disclosure of confidential information, its duty is nevertheless to impart—in a manner consistent with its obligations and responsibilities—information and ideas on all matters of public interest. In addition, journalistic freedom also covers possible recourse to a degree of exaggeration, or even provocation. As a matter of general principle, the "necessity" for any restriction on freedom of expression must be convincingly established. It is in the first place for the national authorities to assess whether there is a "pressing social need" for the restriction and, in making their assessment, they enjoy a certain margin of appreciation. In cases, such as the present one, concerning the press, the national margin of appreciation is circumscribed by the interest of democratic society in ensuring and maintaining a free press. Similarly, that interest will weigh heavily in the balance in determining, as must be done under paragraph 2 of Article 10, whether the restriction was proportionate to the legitimate aim pursued. The Court's task in exercising its supervisory function was not to take the place of the national authorities but rather to review under Article 10 the decisions they have taken pursuant to their power of appreciation. In so doing, the Court must look at the "interference" complained of in the light of the case as a whole and determine whether the reasons adduced by the national authorities to justify it were relevant and sufficient.

The Court was unconvinced by the Government's argument that the information was not a matter of general interest. The article was published during an industrial dispute—widely reported in the press—at one of the major French car manufacturers. The workers were seeking a pay rise which the management were refusing. The article showed that the company chairman had received large pay increases during the period under consideration while at the same time opposing his employees' claims for a rise. By making such a comparison against that background, the article contributed to a public debate on a matter of general interest. It was not intended to damage Mr Calvet's reputation but to contribute to the more general debate on a topic that interested the public.

Not only did the press have the task of imparting information and ideas on matters of public interest: the public also had a right to receive them. Admittedly, people exercising freedom of expression, including journalists, undertake "duties and responsibilities" the scope of which depends on their situation and the technical means they use. While recognising the vital role played by the press in a democratic society, the Court stressed that journalists could not, in principle, be released from their duty to obey the ordinary criminal law on the basis that Article 10 affords them protection. Indeed, paragraph 2 of Article 10 defines the boundaries of the exercise of freedom of expression.

It fell to be decided whether, in the particular circumstances of the case, the interest in the public's being informed outweighed the "duties and responsibilities" the applicants had as a result of the suspect origin of the documents that were sent to them. The Court had, in particular, to determine whether the objective of protecting fiscal confidentiality, which in itself was legitimate, constituted a relevant and sufficient justification for the interference.

In that connection, it had to be noted that although the applicants' conviction was based solely on the reproduction in *Le Canard enchaîné* of documents in the possession of the tax authorities that were held to have been communicated to Mr Fressoz and Mr Roire in breach of professional confidence, it inevitably concerned the disclosure of information; but it was information which, in French law, was already available to the public. Accordingly, there was no overriding requirement for the information to be protected as confidential.

If, as the Government accepted, the information about Mr Calvet's annual income was lawful and its disclosure permitted, the applicants' conviction merely for having published the documents in which that information was contained, namely the tax assessments, could not be justified under Article 10. In essence, that Article leaves it for journalists to decide whether or not it is necessary to reproduce such documents to ensure credibility. It protects journalists' rights to divulge information on issues of general interest provided that they are acting in good faith and on an accurate factual basis and provide "reliable and precise" information in accordance with the ethics of journalism. In sum, there was not, in the Court's view, a reasonable relationship of proportionality between the legitimate aim pursued by the journalists' conviction and the means deployed to achieve that aim, given the interest a democratic society has in ensuring and preserving freedom of the press. There had, therefore, been a violation of Article 10 of the Convention.

Ahmed and Others v United Kingdom (65/1997/849/1065)

In 1990, following the report of a Committee of Inquiry, the Secretary of State for the Environment, pursuant to section 1(5) of the Local Government and Housing Act 1989, made Regulations to restrict the political activities of local government officers in "politically restricted posts". The applicants all held such posts and had all been politically active before the Regulations came into effect. They sought unsuccessfully to have the Regulations judicially reviewed. They applied to the Commission, claiming that their right of freedom of expression had been breached since the Regulations interfered with normal political activities.

Held that the interferences which resulted from the application of the Regulations to the applicants pursued the legitimate aim of protecting the rights of others, council members and the electorate alike, to effective political democracy at the local level. The intention behind the Regulations was to underpin the long tradition of political neutrality which local government officers owed to elected council members and to ensure that the effectiveness of local political democracy was not diminished through the corrosion of the neutrality of certain categories of officers characterised by the sensitivity of their functions. The Court recalled the basic principles which had been laid down in its case law concerning the conditions which must be satisfied before a restriction on freedom of expression can be said to be "necessary in a democratic society". In applying these principles to the instant case, the Court noted that the Regulations had been adopted in response to the identification by the Committee of a pressing social need for action in this area. It observed that the Committee had found that there were specific instances of abuse of power by certain local government officers and that there was increased potential for more widespread abuse in the light of the trend towards confrontational politics in local government affairs. In the Court's view, the adoption of the Regulations could be considered a valid response by the legislature to addressing that need and one which was within the respondent State's margin of appreciation in this area.

As to whether the aim of the Regulations was achieved with minimum impairment of the applicants' rights under Article 10, the Court noted that the restrictions only applied to carefully defined categories of senior officers distinguished by the nature of the activities which they performed and in respect of which political impartiality was a paramount consideration. Furthermore, the Regulations were not intended to silence all comment on political matters, whether controversial or not. The Regulations only sought to preclude comment of a partisan nature which judged reasonably could be considered as espousing or opposing a party political view. As with speech and writing of a partisan nature, the restrictions on the activities of officers by reason of their membership of political parties were applied only to those types of activity which, on account of their visibility, would be likely to link a politically restricted post-holder in the eyes of the public or council members with a particular party political line. There was no restriction on the applicants' rights to join political parties.

In assessing the necessity of the restrictions, the Court also found it significant that the current Government since coming to office had conducted a review of the Regulations which were introduced when they were in opposition and that review showed that the maintenance in force of the restrictions continued to be justified. The Court found, accordingly, that there had been no violation of Article 10 by reason of the existence of the legislation and its impact on the applicants' rights under that Article in the circumstances of this case.

ARTICLE 11

THE RIGHT TO FREEDOM OF ASSEMBLY

1. Everyone has the right to freedom of peaceful assembly and to freedom of association with others, including the right to form and to join trade unions for the protection of his interests.

2. No restrictions shall be placed on the exercise of these rights other than such as are prescribed by law and are necessary in a democratic society in the interests of national security or public safety, for the prevention of disorder or crime, for the protection of health or morals or for the protection of the rights and freedoms of others. This article shall not prevent the imposition of lawful restrictions on the exercise of these rights by members of the armed forces, of the police or of the administration of the State.

Plattform "Arzte Fur Das Leben" v Austria (1991) 13 EHRR 204

Plattform "Arzte fur das Leben" was an association of doctors who were campaigning against abortion and seeking to bring about reform of the Austrian legislation on the subject. In 1980 and 1982 it held two demonstrations which were disrupted by counter-demonstrators despite the presence of a large contingent of police. The applicant association had decided to hold a religious service at Stadl-Paura Church (Upper Austria) on 28 December 1980, after which there was to be a march to the surgery of a doctor who carried out abortions. As required by law, it gave notice to the police authority for the district. The police made no objection and gave the participants permission to use the public highway. The police did, however, have to ban two other planned demonstrations, which were subsequently announced by supporters of abortion, as these demonstrations were to be held at the same time and in the same place as the Plattform demonstration. As the organisers feared that incidents might none the less occur, they sought—shortly before the beginning of the march—to change their plans, in consultation with the local authorities. They gave up the idea of demonstrating outside the doctor's surgery and decided instead to march to an altar erected on a hillside quite a distance away from the church and hold a religious ceremony there. The police representatives pointed out to them that the main body of the

189

police officers had already been deployed along the route originally planned and that because of the lie of the land the new route was not suited to crowd control. They did not refuse to provide protection but stated that—irrespective of the route chosen or to be chosen—it would be impossible to prevent counter-demonstrators from throwing eggs and disrupting both the march and the religious service. During the mass, a large number of counter-demonstrators, who had not given the notice required assembled outside the church and were not dispersed by the police. They disrupted the march to the hillside by mingling with the marchers and shouting down their recitation of the rosary. The same thing happened at the service celebrated in the open air: some 500 people attempted to interrupt it using loudspeakers and threw eggs and clumps of grass at the congregation. At the end of the ceremony, when tempers had risen to the point where physical violence nearly broke out, special riot-control units—which had until then been standing by without intervening—formed a cordon between the opposing groups, and this enabled the procession to return to the church. The applicant association subsequently lodged a complaint alleging that the local police had failed to provide sufficient protection for the demonstration. The authorities considered that the behaviour of the police had been irreproachable and decided not to take any disciplinary measures against them. The Association's appeal to the Constitutional Court was unsuccessful. Attempts to prosecute counter-demonstrators were discontinued by the public prosecutor but one person caught in the act of throwing eggs was fined 1,000 Sch under the Administrative Proceedings Acts.

Permission was obtained for a second demonstration against abortion to be held in the cathedral square in Salzburg on 1 May 1982. An anniversary meeting was due to be held in the square by the Socialist Party on the same day, but it had to be cancelled because notice of it had been given after the applicant association had given notice of its own meeting. The demonstration began at 2.15 pm and ended with an hour of prayers inside the cathedral. At about 1.30 pm some 350 people angrily shouting their opposition had passed through the three archways which provide access to the square and gathered outside the cathedral. A hundred policemen formed a cordon around the Plattform demonstrators to protect them from direct attack. Other trouble was caused by sympathisers of an extreme right-wing party, the NDP, who voiced their support for Plattform. The police asked the association's chairman to order these people to disperse, but without success. In order to prevent the religious ceremony being disrupted, the police cleared the square. No proceedings were taken after these incidents. The applicants complained that they had not had sufficient police protection during the demonstrations and that there had been a violation of Articles 9, 10 and 11 of the Convention. It also relied on Article 13, claiming that the Austrian legal system did not provide an "effective remedy before a national authority" to ensure the effective exercise of the rights in question. The Commission declared inadmissible, as being manifestly ill-founded, the complaints under Articles 9, 10 and 11; on the other hand, it declared admissible the complaint under

Article 13. Although it declared the complaint under Article 11 inadmissible as being manifestly ill-founded, the Commission considered it arguable for the purposes of Article 13. The Government argued that it was contradictory to declare one and the same complaint to be manifestly ill-founded under a substantive provision and yet arguable under Article 13.

Held that Article 13 secures an effective remedy before a national "authority" to anyone claiming on arguable grounds to be the victim of a violation of his rights and freedoms as protected in the Convention; any other interpretation would render it meaningless. In order to ascertain whether Article 13 was applicable in the instant case, it was sufficient that the Court should determine, in the light of the facts of the case and the nature of the legal issue or issues raised, whether the claim that the requirements of Article 11 had not been complied with was arguable notwithstanding that the Commission dismissed it as manifestly ill-founded. The latter's decision on admissibility might provide the Court with useful pointers as to the arguability of the relevant claim. The Court did not have to develop a general theory of the positive obligations which may flow from the Convention, but before ruling on the arguability of the applicant association's claim it had to give an interpretation of Article 11.

A demonstration may annoy or give offence to persons opposed to the ideas or claims that it is seeking to promote. The participants must, however, be able to hold the demonstration without having to fear that they will be subjected to physical violence by their opponents; such a fear would be liable to deter associations or other groups supporting common ideas or interests from openly expressing their opinions on highly controversial issues affecting the community. In a democracy the right to counter-demonstrate cannot extend to inhibiting the exercise of the right to demonstrate. Genuine, effective freedom of peaceful assembly cannot, therefore, be reduced to a mere duty on the part of the State not to interfere: a purely negative conception would not be compatible with the object and purpose of Article 11. Like Article 8, Article 11 sometimes requires positive measures to be taken, even in the sphere of relations between individuals, if need be.

While it is the duty of Contracting States to take reasonable and appropriate measures to enable lawful demonstrations to proceed peacefully, they cannot guarantee this absolutely and they have a wide discretion in the choice of the means to be used. In this area the obligation they enter into under Article 11 of the Convention is an obligation as to measures to be taken and not as to results to be achieved. The Court did not have to assess the expediency or effectiveness of the tactics adopted by the police but only to determine whether there was an arguable claim that the appropriate authorities failed to take the necessary measures.

As regards the incidents at Stadl-Paura on 28 December 1980, it had to be noted that the two demonstrations planned by supporters of abortion, which were due to be held at the same time and place as Plattform's demonstration, had been prohibited. Furthermore, a large number of uniformed and plain-clothes policemen had been deployed along the route originally planned, and the police representatives did not refuse the applicant association their protection even after it decided to change the route despite their objections. Lastly, no damage was done nor were there any serious clashes; the counter-demonstrators chanted slogans, waved banners and threw eggs or clumps of grass, which did not prevent the procession and the open-air religious service from proceeding to their conclusion; special riot-control units placed them-selves between the opposing groups when tempers had risen to the point where violence threatened to break out.

For the 1982 demonstration in Salzburg the organisers had chosen the date of 1 May, the day of the traditional Socialist march which had to be cancelled— as regards the cathedral square—because the applicant association had given notice of its demonstration earlier. Furthermore, 100 policemen were sent to the scene to separate the participants from their opponents and avert the danger of direct attacks; they cleared the square so as to prevent any dis-turbance of the religious service.

It thus clearly appears that the Austrian authorities did not fail to take reasonable and appropriate measures. No arguable claim that Article 11 was violated had thus been made out. Article 13, therefore, did not apply in the instant case.

ARTICLE 12

THE RIGHT TO MARRY

Men and women of marriageable age have the right to marry and to found a family, according to the national laws governing the exercise of this right.

Rees v United Kingdom (1986) 9 EHRR 56

The applicant had been born a girl and registered as such. However, from a tender age the child started to exhibit masculine behaviour and was ambiguous in appearance. In 1970, after learning that the transsexual state was a medically recognised condition, she sought treatment. She was prescribed methyl testosterone (a hormonal treatment) and started to develop secondary male characteristics. In September 1971, the applicant (referred to in the masculine from this point in the judgment on) changed his name to a male one and began to live as a male. After the change of name, the applicant requested and received a new passport containing his new names. The prefix "Mr" was, however, at that time denied to him.

The applicant underwent surgical treatment for physical sexual conversion by the removal of feminine external characteristics. The costs of the medical treatment, including the surgical procedures, were borne by the National Health Service.

The applicant made several unsuccessful efforts from 1973 onwards to persuade Members of Parliament to introduce a Private Member's Bill to resolve the problems of transsexuals. Representations were also made by him, and by a number of Members of Parliament on his behalf, to the Registrar General to secure the alteration of his birth certificate to show his sex as male, but to no avail.

On the basis that the UK was not fully recognising his sex change, the applicant complained of breaches of Articles 8 and 12.

Held that, although the essential object of Article 8 is to protect the individual against arbitrary interference by the public authorities, there may, in addition, be positive obligations inherent in an effective respect for private life, albeit subject to the State's margin of appreciation. In the present case it was the existence and scope of such "positive" obligations which had to be determined. The mere refusal to alter the register of births or to issue birth certificates whose contents and nature differed from those of the birth register could not be considered as interferences.

The notion of "respect" is not clear-cut, especially as far as those positive obligations are concerned: having regard to the diversity of the practices followed and the situations obtaining in the Contracting States, the notion's requirements will vary considerably from case to case. Several States had, through legislation or by means of legal interpretation or by administrative practice, given transsexuals the option of changing their personal status to fit their newly-gained identity. They had, however, made this option subject to conditions of varying strictness and retained a number of express reservations. In other States, such an option did not—or did not yet—exist. It would be true to say, therefore, that there was little common ground between the Contracting States in this area and that, generally speaking, the law appeared to be in a transitional stage. Accordingly, this was an area in which the Contracting Parties enjoy a wide margin of appreciation.

In determining whether or not a positive obligation exists, regard must be had to the fair balance that has to be struck between the general interest of the community and the interests of the individual, the search for which balance is inherent in the whole of the Convention. In striking this balance the aims mentioned in the second paragraph of Article 8 may be of a certain relevance, although this provision refers in terms only to "interferences" with the right protected by the first paragraph—in other words is concerned with the negative obligations flowing therefrom.

Transsexualism was not a new condition, but its particular features had been identified and examined only fairly recently. The developments that had taken place in consequence of these studies had been largely promoted by experts in the medical and scientific fields who had drawn attention to the considerable problems experienced by the individuals concerned and found it possible to alleviate them by means of medical and surgical treatment. The term "transsexual" was usually applied to those who, whilst belonging physically to one sex, felt convinced that they belonged to the other; they often sought to achieve a more integrated, unambiguous identity by undergoing medical treatment and surgical operations to adapt their physical characteristics to their psychological nature. Transsexuals who had been operated upon thus formed a fairly well-defined and identifiable group.

In the UK no uniform, general decision had been adopted either by the legislature or by the courts as to the civil status of post-operative transsexuals. Moreover, there was no integrated system of civil status registration, but only separate registers for births, marriages, deaths and adoption. These recorded the relevant events in the manner they occurred without, except in special circumstances, mentioning changes (of name, address, etc.) which in other States were registered. However, transsexuals, like anyone else in the UK, were free to change their first names and surnames at will. Similarly, they could be issued with official documents bearing their chosen first names and surnames and indicating, if their sex is mentioned at all, their preferred sex by the relevant prefix. This freedom gave them a considerable advantage in comparison with States where all official documents had to conform with the records held by the registry office.

Conversely, the drawback—emphasised by the applicant—was that, as the country's legal system made no provision for legally valid civil-status certificates, such persons had on occasion to establish their identity by means of a birth certificate which was either an authenticated copy of, or an extract from, the birth register. The nature of this register is that the certificates mentioned the biological sex which the individuals had at the time of their birth. The production of such a birth certificate was not a strict legal requirement, but might on occasion be required in practice for some purposes.

It was also clear that the UK did not recognise the applicant as a man for all social purposes. He would be regarded as a woman, *inter alia*, as far as marriage, pension rights and certain employments were concerned. The existence of the unamended birth certificate might also prevent him from entering into certain types of private agreements as a man.

The Court considered that to require the UK to follow the example of other Contracting States was from one perspective tantamount to asking that it should adopt a system in principle the same as theirs for determining and recording civil status. Albeit with delay and some misgivings on the part of the authorities, the UK had endeavoured to meet the applicant's demands to the fullest extent that its system allowed. The alleged lack of respect, therefore, seemed to come down to a refusal to establish a type of documentation showing, and constituting proof of, current civil status. The introduction of such a system had not hitherto been considered necessary in the UK. It would have important administrative consequences and would impose new duties on the rest of the population. The governing authorities in the UK were fully entitled, in the exercise of their margin of appreciation, to take account of the requirements of the situation pertaining there in determining what measures to adopt. While the requirement of striking a fair balance might possibly, in the interests of persons in the applicant's situation, call for incidental adjustments to the existing system, it could not give rise to any direct obligation on the UK to alter the very basis thereof. Accordingly, there was no breach of Article 8 in the circumstances of the present case.

In the Court's opinion, the right to marry guaranteed by Article 12 refers to the traditional marriage between persons of opposite biological sex. This appears also from the wording of the Article which makes it clear that Article 12 is mainly concerned to protect marriage as the basis of the family. Furthermore, Article 12 lays down that the exercise of this right shall be subject to the national laws of the Contracting States. The limitations thereby introduced must not restrict or reduce the right in such a way or to such an extent that the very essence of the right is impaired. However, the legal impediment in the UK on the marriage of persons who were not of the opposite biological sex could not be said to have an effect of this kind.

There was, accordingly, no violation in the instant case of Article 12 of the Convention.

PROTOCOL 1 : ARTICLE 1

THE RIGHT TO PEACEFUL ENJOYMENT OF POSSESSIONS

Every natural or legal person is entitled to the peaceful enjoyment of his possessions. No one shall be deprived of his possessions except in the public interest and subject to the conditions provided for by law and by the general principles of international law.

The preceding provisions shall not, however, in any way impair the right of a State to enforce such laws as it deems necessary to control the use of property in accordance with the general interest or to secure the payment of taxes or other contributions or penalties.

AGOSI v United Kingdom (1987) 9 EHRR 1

The applicants were a company which dealt in gold and silver coins. Between August 1974 and May 1975, they bought from a person resident in the UK a large quantity of pre-1947 British coinage which had a high content of silver. Unknown to them, the coins had been illegally exported from the UK. On 2 August 1975, after normal business hours, the person from whom they had bought the coins visited them, with another man, and asked to make an immediate purchase of 1,500 Krugerrands, worth about £120,000. The sale was agreed and the coins were loaded into a car bearing UK number plates. Payment was accepted in the form of an unguaranteed cheque drawn on an English bank. The cheque bore no sign of having been cleared for exchange control purposes. On 11 August, the bank notified the applicants that the cheque had been dishonoured. The contract of sale contained a provision according to which ownership of the coins remained with the applicants until full payment had been received. Meanwhile, the buyers had attempted to smuggle the gold coins by car into the UK. The coins were discovered and seized by the customs authorities in Dover. The buyers were prosecuted for fraudulent evasion of a prohibition on importation and ultimately convicted. Meanwhile, the applicants, who co-operated with Customs and Excise throughout the criminal investigation, asked for the return of the coins on the basis that they were their rightful owners and had been the innocent victims of fraud. The Commissioners of Customs and Excise inquired whether it was contended by the applicants that they had a valid claim that the coins were not liable to forfeiture. The Commissioners stated that, if so, they would be required to institute condemnation proceedings before the High Court in order to have the coins forfeited. When, at the close of the prosecution of the buyers, the Commissioners of Customs and Excise did not return the coins, the applicants issued proceedings in the High Court in an attempt to recover them. They were unsuccessful both there and in the Court of Appeal. They complained to the Commission that the forfeiture of the coins constituted a breach of Article 6.2 of the Convention and of Article 1 of Protocol 1.

Held that Article 1 of Protocol 1 in substance guarantees the right of property. It comprises "three distinct rules": the first rule, set out in the first sentence of the first paragraph, is of a general nature and enunciates the principle of the peaceful enjoyment of property; the second rule, contained in the second sentence of the first paragraph, covers deprivation of possessions and subjects it to certain conditions; the third rule, stated in the second paragraph, recognises that the Contracting States are entitled, amongst other things, to control the use of property in accordance with the general interest. However, the three rules are not 'distinct' in the sense of being unconnected: the second and third rules are concerned with particular instances of interference with the right to peaceful enjoyment of property and should, therefore, be construed in the light of the general principle enunciated in the first rule. It was not disputed that the forfeiture of the smuggled Krugerrands amounted to an interference with the applicant company's right to peaceful enjoyment of their possessions. The prohibition on the importation of gold coins into the UK clearly constituted a control of the use of property. The seizure and forfeiture of the Krugerrands were measures taken for the enforcement of that prohibition. The forfeiture of the coins did involve a deprivation of property, but in the circumstances the deprivation formed a constituent element of the procedure for the control of the use in the UK of gold coins such as Krugerrands. It was, therefore, the second paragraph of Article 1 of Protocol 1 which applied. That paragraph recognises the right of a State "to enforce such laws as it deems necessary to control the use of property . . . in accordance with the general interest". Undoubtedly, the prohibition on the importation of Krugerrands into the UK was in itself compatible with the terms of this provision. Nevertheless, as the second paragraph is to be construed in the light of the general principle enunciated in the opening sentence of Article 1 there must, in respect of enforcement of this prohibition, also exist a reasonable relationship of proportionality between the means employed and the aim sought to be realised; in other words, the Court had to determine whether a fair balance had been struck between the demands of the general interest in this respect and the interest of the individual or individuals concerned. In determining whether a fair balance existed, the Court recognised that the State enjoys a wide margin of appreciation with regard both to choosing the means of enforcement and to ascertaining whether the consequences of enforcement are justified in the general interest for the purpose of achieving the object of the law in question. Under the general principles of law recognised in all Contracting States, smuggled goods may, as a rule, be the object of confiscation. Although there was a trend in the practice of the Contracting States that the behaviour of the owner of the goods and in particular the use of due care on his part should be taken into account in deciding whether or not to restore smuggled goods, different standards were applied and no common practice could be said to exist. For forfeiture to be justified under the terms of the second paragraph of Article 1 of Protocol 1 it is enough that the explicit requirements of the paragraph are met and that the State has struck a fair balance between the interests of the State and those of the individual. The striking of a fair balance depends on many factors and the behaviour of the owner of the property, including the degree of fault or care which he has displayed, is one element of the entirety of circumstances which should be taken into account. Taking a comprehensive view of the applicable procedures, they were such as to enable, amongst other things, reasonable account to be taken of the degree of fault or care of the applicant company or, at least, of the relationship between the company's conduct and the breach of the law which undoubtedly occurred; and also whether the procedures in question afforded the applicant company a reasonable opportunity of putting its case to the responsible authorities. In particular, there was available the remedy of judicial review of the Commissioners' decisions. That afforded an opportunity of testing whether the decision taken was one which a public authority properly directing itself on the relevant law and acting reasonably could not have reached and had, in similar circumstances in the past, proved to be an effective remedy. The Court considered that in the circumstances the scope of judicial review under English law is sufficient to satisfy the requirements of the second paragraph of Article 1 of Protocol 1.

As to the argument that the condemnation proceedings amounted to a determination of a criminal charge, within the meaning of Article 6, the fact that measures consequential upon an act for which third parties were prosecuted affected in an adverse manner the property rights of the applicants could not of itself lead to the conclusion that, during the course of the procedures complained of, any "criminal charge", for the purposes of Article 6 could be considered as having been brought against the applicant company. Accordingly, there was no breach, either of Article 1 of Protocol 1 or of Article 6.

Pine Valley Developments Ltd and Others v Ireland (1992) 14 EHRR 319

The first and second applicants, Pine Valley and Healy Holdings, had as their principal business the purchase and development of land. The first of these companies, which was a wholly-owned subsidiary of the second, was struck off the register of companies on 26 October 1990 and dissolved on 6 November 1990, for failure to file annual returns for more than eight years. Since 1981

Healy Holdings too had filed no annual returns; on 14 October and 29 November 1985 a receiver to this company was appointed by two secured creditors. The third applicant, Mr Daniel Healy, was the managing director of Healy Holdings and its sole beneficial shareholder; on 19 July 1990, by order of an English court, he was adjudged bankrupt. In November 1978 Pine Valley had agreed to purchase, for IR £550,000, 21½ acres of land at Clondalkin, County Dublin. It did so in reliance on an outline planning permission for industrial warehouse and office development on the site. This permission, which was recorded in the official planning register, had been granted in March 1977 by the Minister for Local Government to the then owner on his appeal against the refusal, in April 1976, by the planning authority of full planning permission. One of the grounds for that refusal was that the site was in an area zoned for the further development of agriculture so as to preserve a green belt. In September 1980, the planning authority refused the detailed planning approval for which Pine Valley had applied in reliance on the outline permission. Pine Valley thereupon successfully sought a conditional order of mandamus, directing the council to grant such approval. In July 1981, Pine Valley sold the land to Healy Holdings for IR £550,000. In February 1982, on appeal by Dublin County Council against the High Court's decision, the Supreme Court held that the grant of outline planning permission had been *ultra vires* and was, therefore, a nullity. As a result of this decision the land could not be developed and its value was, therefore, substantially reduced. In June 1988 it was sold in the open market by the receiver of Healy Holdings for IR £50,000. With a view to retrospectively validating planning permissions and approvals the validity of which came into question as a result of the Supreme Court's decision, the Local Government (Planning and Development) Act 1982 was enacted; but it contained an exception in relation to cases which were the subject of judicial procedure so that, while it assisted others, it did not assist the applicants. The applicants complained that, as a result of the Supreme Court's decision holding the outline planning permission to be invalid, coupled with the respondent State's alleged failure to validate that permission retrospectively or its failure to provide compensation for the reduction in value of their property, they had been victims of a breach of Article 1 of Protocol 1 to the Convention and of Article 14 taken with Article 1 of Protocol 1.

Held that Pine Valley and Healy Holdings were no more than vehicles through which Mr Healy proposed to implement the development for which outline planning permission had been granted. On this ground alone it would be artificial to draw distinctions between the three applicants as regards their entitlement to claim to be "victims" of a violation. More specifically, with respect to Pine Valley, neither its sale of the land nor its later dissolution altered the fact that it was for a certain period of time, as one of those vehicles, the owner of the property to which the planning permission attached. In the Court's view, this sufficed to permit a claim of violation to be made on its behalf. And, whilst the financial status of Healy Holdings and Mr Healy might be of importance or have effects on the domestic level, it was of no relevance as far as entitlement to claim to be a victim of a violation is concerned. Insolvency cannot remove the right which Article 25 confers.

Bearing in mind that the Supreme Court had held that the outline planning permission granted to Mr Thornton was a nullity *ab initio*, a first question that arose was whether the applicants ever enjoyed a right to develop the land in question which could have been the subject of an interference. This question had to be answered in the affirmative. When Pine Valley purchased the site, it did so in reliance on the permission which had been duly recorded in a public register kept for the purpose and which it was perfectly entitled to assume was valid. That permission amounted to a favourable decision as to the principle of the proposed development, which could not be reopened by the planning authority. In these circumstances it would be unduly formalistic to hold that the Supreme Court's decision did not constitute an interference. Until it was rendered, the applicants had at least a legitimate expectation of being able to carry out their proposed development and this has to be regarded, for the purposes of Article 1 of Protocol 1 as a component part of the property in question. Pine Valley had parted with ownership of the land, without retaining any right thereover that was protected by Article 1 of Protocol 1. That provision, whether taken alone or in conjunction with Article 14 of the Convention, therefore, did not apply to this applicant. The Court thus concluded that there was an interference with the right of Healy Holdings and Mr Healy to the peaceful enjoyment of their possessions.

The applicants contended that the interference in question, by annulling the outline planning permission, constituted a "deprivation" of possessions, within the meaning of the second sentence of the first paragraph of Article 1 of Protocol 1. The Commission, on the other hand, saw it as a "control of the use of property", within the meaning of the second paragraph of that provision. There was no formal expropriation of the property in question and neither could it be said that there was a *de facto* deprivation. The impugned measure was basically designed to ensure that the land was used in conformity with the relevant planning laws and title remained vested in Healy Holdings, whose powers to take decisions concerning the property were unaffected. Again, the land was not left without any meaningful alternative use, for it could have been farmed or leased. Finally, although the value of the site was substantially reduced, it was not rendered worthless. Accordingly, the interference must be considered as a control of the use of property falling within the scope of the second paragraph of Article 1. The applicants did not dispute that the interference was in conformity with planning legislation and, like that legislation, was designed to protect the environment. This, in the Court's view, was clearly a legitimate aim "in accordance with the general interest" for the purposes of the second paragraph of Article 1. But the applicants maintained that, in the absence of compensation or retrospective validation of their outline planning permission, the interference complained of could not be described as proportionate to the aim pursued. However, the applicants were engaged on a commercial venture which, by its very nature, involved an element of risk and they were aware not only of the zoning plan but also of the opposition of the local authority to any departure from it. That being so, the Court did not consider that the annulment of the permission without any remedial action being taken in their favour could be regarded as a disproportionate measure. The Court thus concluded that there had been no violation of Article 1 of Protocol 1 taken on its own. However, the applicants also alleged that since the remedial action taken by the legislature in the shape of section 6 of the 1982 Act benefited all the holders of permissions in the relevant category other than themselves, they had been victims of discrimination contrary to Article 14 of the Convention, taken in conjunction with Article 1 of Protocol 1. The Government did not advance any justification for the difference of treatment between the applicants and the other holders of permissions in the same category as theirs. The Court, therefore, found that there had been a violation of Article 14 of the Convention, taken together with Article 1 of Protocol 1 as regards Healy Holdings and Mr Healy.

Raimondo v Italy (1994) 18 EHRR 237

The applicant was prosecuted, and ultimately acquitted, on charges relating to his alleged membership of a mafia-type organisation. In connection with the prosecution, the District Court had, on 13 May 1985, ordered preventive seizure of ten plots of land, six buildings and six vehicles. On 16 October 1985, it ordered the confiscation of some of those assets on the ground that it had not been proved that they had been lawfully acquired. The applicant was placed under special police supervision, which entailed a prohibition on leaving his home between 9 pm and 7 am. Following his acquittal on 30 January 1986, the Court of Appeal on 4 July 1986 annulled the special supervision measure and ordered the return of the confiscated property. There was, however, delay of over four years in the return of some of the property. The applicant complained that the confiscation had breached Article 1 of Protocol 1 in itself and in that the property had not been adequately supervised and had suffered damage, that the supervision had breached Article 2 of Protocol 4 and that the length of the proceedings in relation to his appeal in relation to the confiscation and supervision had breached Article 6.

Held that the seizure ordered on 13 May was clearly a provisional measure intended to ensure that property which appears to be the fruit of unlawful activities carried out to the detriment of the community can subsequently be confiscated if necessary. The measure as such was, therefore, justified by the general interest and, in view of the extremely dangerous economic power of an 'organisation' like the Mafia, it cannot be said that taking it at this stage of the proceedings was disproportionate to the aim pursued. The confiscation pursued an aim that was in the general interest, namely it sought to ensure that the use of the property in question did not procure for the applicant, or the criminal organisation to which he was suspected of belonging, advantages to the detriment of the community. The Court is fully aware of the difficulties encountered by the Italian State in the fight against the Mafia. As a result of its unlawful activities, in particular drug-trafficking, and its international connections, this 'organisation' has an enormous turnover that is subsequently invested, *inter alia*, in the real property sector. Confiscation, which is designed to block these movements of suspect capital, is an effective and necessary weapon in the combat against this cancer. It, therefore, appears proportionate to the aim pursued. The preventive effect of confiscation justifies its immediate application notwithstanding any appeal. With regard to the confiscation, the state did not overstep its margin of appreciation. As to damage, that is an inevitable consequence of any seizure or confiscation. It was not clear that the damage sustained exceeded that which was inevitable. However, the Court found it hard to see why there had been such a long delay in returning property to the applicant. That delay was neither provided for by law nor necessary and in that respect there was a breach of Article 1 of Protocol 1. The supervision order did not amount to a deprivation of liberty for the purposes of Article 5.1 and fell to be dealt with under Article 2 of Protocol 4. In view of the threat posed by the Mafia to democratic society, the measure was necessary for the maintenance of public order and the prevention of crime. It was also proportionate to the aim pursued. However, a delay in drafting the grounds for the decision to lift that supervision, once it had been taken, could not be understood and did constitute a violation. Article 6 did not apply to proceedings concerning the supervision, because they did not involve the determination of a criminal charge. Since Article 6 does apply to any action whose subject-matter is pecuniary in nature, it did apply to the proceedings in relation to the confiscation; but since those proceedings had to go before two domestic courts their total length was not unreasonable.

Holy Monasteries v Greece (1995) 20 EHRR 1

The applicant monasteries, which were founded between the ninth and thirteenth centuries, accumulated a considerable amount of property, in particular through donations made before the creation of the Greek State in 1829, but a large part of this property was expropriated during the early years of the State's existence. The monasteries themselves also gave away whole tracts of land to the State or to individuals who had none. During the Byzantine and Ottoman empires the monasteries and religious institutions in general were almost the only institutions discharging important social, cultural and educational functions; even in the nineteenth century after the creation of the modern Greek State, they still discharged some of these functions. The State never challenged their ownership, and the monasteries always relied on adverse possession as a subsidiary means of establishing it, particularly in cases where Byzantine or Ottoman title deeds were lacking or had been destroyed. Apart from property thus amassed over the centuries, the monasteries acquired numerous plots of land and buildings more recently, either as gifts or legacies or through purchase.

Act 1700/1987 changed the rules on the management and representation of monastery property and provided that within six months of its publication the State would become the owner of all monastery property unless the monasteries proved title established either by a duly registered deed or by a statutory provision or by a final court decision against the State. In this connection, it should be noted that only real-property transactions concluded since 1856 have had to be registered and the Civil Code has required legacies and inheritances to be registered only since 1946. Except in the Dodecanese, Greece does not have any official land survey.

Held that Article 1, which guarantees in substance the right of property, comprises three distinct rules. The first, which is expressed in the first sentence of the first paragraph and is of a general nature, lays down the principle of peaceful enjoyment of property. The second rule, in the second sentence of the same paragraph, covers deprivation of possessions and subjects it to certain conditions. The third, contained in the second paragraph, recognises that the Contracting States are entitled, amongst other things, to control the use of property in accordance with the general interest. The second and third rules, which are concerned with particular instances of interference with the right to peaceful enjoyment of property, are to be construed in the light of the general principle laid down in the first rule.

The Court considered that by creating a presumption of State ownership, Greek law shifted the burden of proof so that it now fell on the applicant monasteries, which could only assert their ownership of the land in issue if it derived from a duly registered title deed, from a statutory provision or from a final court decision against the State. The law thus deprived them of the possibility of relying, in order to adduce proof to the contrary, on all the means of acquiring property provided for in Greek law and by which the applicant monasteries possibly accumulated their property, including adverse possession and even a final court decision against a private individual.

The Court noted that the applicant monasteries, which were primordial constituent parts of the Greek Church and were established long before the creation of the Greek State, accumulated substantial immoveable property over the centuries. Undoubtedly, title deeds acquired during the Byzantine and Ottoman empires had been lost or destroyed. In respect of such land occupied for so long, even if without any legal title, the period of possession required in order that adverse possession might be relied upon both against the State and against third parties had certainly been completed by the time Act 1700/1987 came into force. On this point the Court attached particular importance to the acquisition of property by adverse possession because there was no land survey in Greece and it was impossible to have title deeds registered before 1856 and legacies and inheritances registered before 1946. The State, deemed to be the owner of such agricultural and forest property, was automatically given the use and the possession of it.

That was not merely a procedural rule relating to the burden of proof but a substantive provision whose effect is to transfer full ownership of the land in question to the State. The law gave the applicant monasteries a period of two months in which to hand over the land in issue to the head of the appropriate agricultural or forestry department, failing which the latter was empowered to make an administrative eviction order. That being so, and notwithstanding the fact that the provision had not yet been enforced, there had been an interference with the applicant monasteries' right to the peaceful enjoyment of their possessions which amounted to a "deprivation" of possessions within the meaning of the second sentence of the first paragraph of Article 1. The Court had, therefore, to determine whether this deprivation of possessions pursued a legitimate aim "in the public interest", within the meaning of the second rule under Article 1.

The Court noted that the explanatory memorandum to the Bill, submitted to Parliament, set out the reasons for the impugned measure: to end illegal sales of the relevant land, encroachments on it and the abandonment or uncontrolled development of such land. The optional nature of the transfer of the use of the land to farmers or agricultural co-operatives (section 2(1) of the Act) and the inclusion of public bodies among the beneficiaries of such transfers might inspire some doubt as to the reasons for the measures, but they could not suffice to deprive the overall objective of Act 1700/1987 of its legitimacy as being "in the public interest".

An interference with peaceful enjoyment of possessions must strike a "fair balance" between the demands of the general interests of the community and the requirements of the protection of the individual's fundamental rights. The concern to achieve this balance is reflected in the structure of Article 1 as a whole, including, therefore, the second sentence, which is to be read in the light of the general principle enunciated in the first sentence. In particular, there must be a reasonable relationship of proportionality between the means employed and the aim sought to be realised by any measure depriving a person of his possessions. Compensation terms under the relevant legislation are material to the assessment whether the contested measure respects the requisite fair balance and, notably, whether it does not impose a disproportionate burden on the applicants.

In this connection, the taking of property without payment of an amount reasonably related to its value will normally constitute a disproportionate interference and a total lack of compensation can be considered justifiable under Article 1 only in exceptional circumstances. Article 1 does not, however, guarantee a right to full compensation in all circumstances, since legitimate objectives of "public interest" may call for less than reimbursement of the full market value.

In 1952 the Greek legislature took measures to expropriate a large portion of monastery agricultural property. In 1952, as in 1987, the monasteries no longer discharged the same social, educational and cultural functions they had assumed before the Greek State was established. The legislature nevertheless provided for compensation of one-third of the real value of the expropriated land. However, there was no similar provision in the new legislation. The five per cent provided for in return for the grant to farmers of a right to use the land in issue would be paid, after the transfer of ownership to the State, to the private law entity to be established under the Act for the needs of the national education service. The power to grant land to monasteries which do not have sufficient immoveable property, "solely for the purposes of cultivation by the monks themselves" and the budgetary appropriation provided for in section 10, could not be regarded as payment of compensation. By thus imposing a considerable burden on the applicant monasteries deprived of their property, the Act did not preserve a fair balance between the various interests in question as required by Article 1 of Protocol 1. There was, therefore, a breach of that Article.

Article 6.1 embodies the "right to a court", of which the right of access, that is the right to institute proceedings before courts in civil matters, constitutes one aspect. Article 6.1 may thus be relied on by anyone who considers that an interference with the exercise of one of his civil rights is unlawful and complains that he has not had the possibility of submitting that claim to a tribunal meeting the requirements of Article 6.1. The right of property is without doubt a "civil right".

Section 1(1) of Act 1700/1987 made the applicants entirely dependent on the Greek Church for the defence of such of their property as is exempt from the transfer of ownership effected by the Act. By depriving them of any further possibility of bringing before the appropriate courts any complaint they might make against the Greek State, third parties or the Greek Church itself in relation to their rights of property, or even of intervening in such proceedings, section 1(1) impairs the very essence of their "right to a court". There was, therefore, a breach of Article 6.1.

Air Canada v United Kingdom (1995) 20 EHRR 150

On a number of occasions between 1983 and 1987 incidents of drug-smuggling gave rise to concern over the adequacy of the applicant company's security procedures at Heathrow Airport, London. Customs and Excise wrote expressing concern about this and the applicants promised to improve their security. On 15 December 1986 Customs and Excise wrote to all airline operators at Heathrow and Gatwick warning them that consideration would be given to the seizure and forfeiture of aircraft where drug-smuggling occurred. On 26 April 1987 a Tristar aircraft owned and operated by the applicants and worth over £60 million, landed at Heathrow where it discharged a container which was found to contain 331 kgs of cannabis resin valued at about £800,000. The documentation for the container was incomplete and false. On 1 May 1987, at a time when passengers were waiting to board the aircraft, Customs officers seized it as liable to forfeiture. On the same day the Commissioners of Customs and Excise delivered the aircraft back to the applicant company on payment of a penalty of £50,000. No reasons were given to the applicants at the time for the decision either to seize the aircraft or to levy the penalty. It was only during the course of proceedings before the European Commission of Human Rights that the Government offered the earlier security problems as an explanation for the actions of the Commissioners. On 20 May 1987 the applicant company gave notice of a claim disputing that the aircraft was liable to forfeiture. The Commissioners, therefore, brought condemnation proceedings before the High Court in London to confirm, *inter alia*, that the aircraft was liable to forfeiture at the time of seizure. In that Court, the applicant was successful but the Court of Appeal overruled the decision of the High Court. Leave to appeal to the House of Lords was refused. The applicant complained to the Commission that the seizure of its aircraft and its subsequent return on conditions violated its right to peaceful enjoyment of its possessions as guaranteed by Article 1 of Protocol No. 1 and that the proceedings did not comply with the requirements of Article 6.1. The Government contended that this was not a case involving a deprivation of property since no transfer of ownership of the applicant's aircraft had taken place. The seizure and demand for payment were to be seen as part of the system for the control of the use of an aircraft which had been employed for the import of prohibited drugs.

Held that the Government's analysis was correct. The seizure of the aircraft amounted to a temporary restriction on its use and did not involve a transfer of ownership, and the decision of the Court of Appeal to condemn the property as forfeited did not actually have the effect of depriving the applicant of ownership since the sum required for the release of the aircraft had been paid. It was clear from the scheme of the legislation that the release of the aircraft subject to the payment of a sum of money was, in effect, a measure taken in furtherance of a policy of seeking to prevent carriers from bringing, *inter alia*, prohibited drugs into the UK. As such, it amounted to a control of the use of property. It was, therefore, the second paragraph of Article 1 of Protocol 1 which was applicable in the present case. It, therefore, had to be decided whether the interference with the applicant's property rights was in conformity with the State's right under the second paragraph of Article 1 of Protocol No. 1 "to enforce such laws as it deems necessary to control the use of property in accordance with the general interest". That paragraph must be construed in the light of the principle laid down in the Article's first sentence, so that it must achieve a "fair balance" between the demands of the general interest of the community and the requirements of the protection of the individual's fundamental rights. There must be a reasonable relationship of proportionality between the means employed and the aim pursued. It was clear from the decision of the Court of Appeal that both the seizure of the aircraft and the requirement of payment, in the absence of any finding of fault or negligence on the part of the applicant, were in conformity with the relevant legislation. While the width of the powers of forfeiture conferred on the Commissioners of Customs and Excise was striking, the seizure of the applicant's aircraft and its release subject to payment were undoubtedly exceptional measures which were resorted to in order to bring about an improvement in the company's security procedures. The incident was the latest in a long series of alleged security lapses which had been brought to the applicants' attention. There could be no doubt that the measures taken conformed to the general interest in combating international drug-trafficking. The Court noted that it would have been open to the applicants to have instituted judicial review proceedings to challenge the failure of the Commissioners to provide reasons for the seizure of the aircraft or to contend that the acts of the Commissioners constituted an abuse of their authority. The Court recalled that on a previous occasion (*AGOSI* v *United Kingdom*) it had decided that the scope of judicial review under English law was sufficient to satisfy the requirements of the second paragraph of Article 1 of Protocol No. 1. Finally, taking into account the large quantity of cannabis that was found and the value of the aircraft that had been seized, the Court did not consider the requirement to pay £50,000 to be disproportionate to the aim pursued, namely the prevention of the importation of prohibited drugs into the UK.

The case did not involve the determination of a criminal charge but did involve the applicant's civil rights. As regards the seizure, the relevant provisions of UK law required the Commissioners to take proceedings for forfeiture once the seizure of the aircraft had been challenged. Such proceedings were in fact brought and so the requirement of access to court inherent in Article 6.1 was met. Furthermore, it had been open to the applicant to bring judicial review proceedings contesting the decision of the Commissioners to require payment as a condition for the return of the aircraft. Had such proceedings been brought, the applicant could have sought to contest the factual grounds on which the exercise of discretion by the Commissioners was based. Accordingly, there had been no violation of either Article 1 of Protocol 1 or of Article 6.

Pressos Compania Naviera S.A. and Others v Belgium (1995) 21 EHRR 301

The applicants were shipowners, mutual shipping insurance associations and, in one case, an insolvency administrator whose ships were involved in casualties in Belgian or Netherlands territorial waters prior to 17 September 1988, whilst pilots were on board. In Belgium the piloting of sea-going vessels was a public service organised by the State in the interests of shipping. In practice, pilot services are provided either directly by the State itself, for maritime and river navigation, or by private companies acting under licence, such as the Brabo company, which had a monopoly of pilot services within the port of Antwerp. Historically, liability in negligence did not attach to the employer of a pilot in respect of any incident while the master was on board the vessel, upon the basis that the pilot was the agent of the master. In December 1983, however, the Court of Cassation departed from this rule and the applicants took the opportunity to commence proceedings in respect of the casualties in which their ship had been involved. By an Act of 30 August 1988, the legislature reversed that decision with retrospective effect for a period of 30 years from the date on which the Act entered into effect. The applicants complained of a breach of Article 1 of Protocol 1.

Held that in order to determine whether in this instance there was a "possession", the Court could have regard to the domestic law in force at the time of the alleged interference, as there was nothing to suggest that that law ran counter to the object and purpose of Article 1 of Protocol 1. The rules in question were rules of tort, under which claims for compensation come into existence as soon as the damage occurs. A claim of this nature constituted an asset and, therefore, amounted to "a possession" within the meaning of the first sentence of Article 1. This provision was accordingly applicable.

On the basis of the judgments of the Court of Cassation, the applicants could argue that they had a legitimate expectation that their claims deriving from the accidents in question would be determined in accordance with the general law of tort. According to the Court's case law, Article 1, which guarantees in substance the right of property, comprises three distinct rules. The first, which is expressed in the first sentence of the first paragraph and is of a general nature, lays down the principle of peaceful enjoyment of property. The second rule, in the second sentence of the same paragraph, covers deprivation of possessions and subjects it to certain conditions. The third, contained in the second paragraph, recognises that the Contracting States are entitled, amongst other things, to control the use of property in accordance with the general interest. The second and third rules, which are concerned with particular instances of interference with the right to peaceful enjoyment of property, are to be construed in the light of the general principle laid down in the first rule. The 1988 Act exempted the State and other organisers of pilot services from their liability for negligent acts for which they could have been answerable. It resulted in an interference with the exercise of rights deriving from claims for damages which could have been asserted in domestic law up to that point and, accordingly, with the right that everyone, including each of the applicants, has to the peaceful enjoyment of his or her possessions. In so far as that Act concerns the accidents that occurred before 17 September 1988, the only ones in issue in the present proceedings, that interference amounted to a deprivation of property within the meaning of the second sentence of the first paragraph of Article 1. The Court had then to consider whether that interference was "in the public interest" and whether it satisfied the requirements of proportionality. In order to justify the impugned interference, the Government put forward three different "major considerations linked to the general interest". These were the need to protect the State's financial interests, the need to re-establish legal certainty in the field of tort and the need to bring the relevant Belgian legislation into line with that of neighbouring countries and notably that of The Netherlands. The Court recalled that the national authorities enjoy a certain margin of appreciation in determining what is "in the public interest", because under the Convention system it is for them to make the initial assessment both of the existence of a problem of public concern warranting measures of deprivation of property and of the remedial action to be taken. Furthermore, the notion of "public interest" is necessarily extensive. In particular, the decision to enact laws expropriating property will commonly involve consideration of political, economic and social issues on which opinion in a democratic society may reasonably differ widely. The Court, finding it natural that the margin of appreciation available to the legislature in implementing social and economic policies should be a wide one, will respect the legislature's judgment as to what is "in the public interest" unless that judgment be manifestly without reasonable foundation which was clearly not the case in this instance.

An interference with the peaceful enjoyment of possessions must strike a "fair balance" between the demands of the general interest of the community and the requirements of the protection of the individual's fundamental rights. The concern to achieve this balance is reflected in the structure of Article 1 as a whole, including, therefore, the second sentence, which is to be read in the light of the general principle enunciated in the first sentence. In particular, there must be a reasonable relationship of proportionality between the means employed and the aim sought to be realised by any measure depriving a person of his possessions.

Compensation terms under the relevant legislation are material to the assessment whether the contested measure respects the requisite fair balance and, notably, whether it imposes a disproportionate burden on the applicants. In this connection, the taking of property without payment of an amount reasonably related to its value will normally constitute a disproportionate interference and a total lack of compensation can be considered justifiable under Article 1 only in exceptional circumstances. In the present case the 1988 Act quite simply extinguished, with retrospective effect going back 30 years and without compensation, claims for very high damages that the victims of the pilot accidents could have pursued against the Belgian State or against the private companies concerned, and in some cases even in pro- ceedings that were already pending. The Government invoked the financial implications, which were both enormous and unforeseeable, of the Court of Cassation's judgment of 15 December 1983. The financial considerations cited by the Government and their concern to bring Belgian law into line with the law of neighbouring countries could warrant prospective legislation in this area to derogate from the general law of tort. Such considerations could not justify legislating with retrospective effect with the aim and consequence of depriving the applicants of their claims for compensation. Such a fundamental interference with the applicants' rights is inconsistent with preserving a fair balance between the interests at stake. It followed that in so far as the 1988 Act concerned events prior to 17 September 1988, the date of its publication and its entry into force, it breached Article 1 of Protocol 1.

PROTOCOL 1 : ARTICLE 2

THE RIGHT TO EDUCATION

No person shall be denied the right to education. In the exercise of any functions which it assumes in relation to education and to teaching, the State shall respect the right of parents to ensure such education and teaching in conformity with their own religious and philosophical convictions.

Case Relating to Certain Aspects of the Laws on the Use of Languages in Education in Belgium (Preliminary Objection) — Belgian Linguistic Case (No. 2) (1979–80) 1 EHRR 252

The applicants were French-speaking Belgians, who lived in districts considered by law as Dutch-speaking but where significant parts of the population in fact spoke French. They wished their children to be educated in French and complained that the Belgian State did not make any, or any adequate, provision for French language education so that their children either had to be educated locally in Dutch or travel a significant distance to reach French-speaking schools. They also complained that certificates of secondary education required homologation—that is, validation—before the holders could enter certain professions and that such homologation was dependent on conformity with linguistic legislation (the purpose being to ensure that those practising such professions could speak the language of the area in which they practised).

Held that, although Article 2 of the First Protocol is expressed negatively, it does enshrine a positive right. It does not require States to establish systems of education; they already had them. Rather, it guarantees to persons subject to the jurisdiction of the Contracting Parties the right, in principle, to avail themselves of the means of instruction existing at a given time. It does not specify the language in which education is to be given, but the right to education would be meaningless if it did not imply, in favour of its beneficiaries, the right to be educated in the national language, or in one of the national languages, as the case may be. The first sentence of Article 2 of the Protocol consequently guarantees, in the first place, a right of access to educational establishments existing at a given time. It is further necessary that, *inter alia*, the individual who is the beneficiary should have the possibility of drawing profit from the education received, that is to say, the right to obtain official recognition of the studies which he has completed. The second sentence does not require of States that they should, in the sphere of education or teaching, respect parents' linguistic preferences but only their religious and philosophical convictions. To interpret the terms "religious" and "philosophical" as covering linguistic preferences would amount to a distortion of their ordinary and usual meaning and to read into the Convention something which is not there. As to Article 14, it is as though it forms an integral part of each of the Articles laying down rights and freedoms. Whilst it does not forbid every difference in treatment in the exercise of the rights and freedoms recognised, the principle of equality of treatment is violated if the distinction has no objective and reasonable justification. The existence of such a justification must be assessed in relation to the aim and effects of the measure under consideration, regard being had to the principles which normally prevail in democratic societies. A difference of treatment in the exercise of a right laid down in the Convention must not only pursue a legitimate aim: Article 14 is likewise violated when it is clearly established that there is no reasonable relationship of proportionality between the means employed and the aim sought to be realised. In attempting to find out, in a given case, whether or not there has been an arbitrary distinction, the Court cannot disregard those legal and factual features which characterise the life of the society in the State which, as a Contracting Party, has to answer for the measure in dispute. In so doing, it cannot assume the role of the competent national authorities, for it would thereby lose sight of the subsidiary nature of the international machinery of collective enforcement established by the Convention. The national authorities remain free to choose the measures which they consider appropriate in those matters which are governed by the Convention. Review by the Court concerns only the conformity of those measures with the requirements of the Convention. Reading Article 2 of the First Protocol and Article 14 together, their object is to secure the right to education without discrimination on the ground, for instance, of language, but to interpret them as conferring a right to obtain education in the language of one's own choice would lead to absurd results, for it would be open to anyone to claim any language of instruction in any of the territories of the Contracting Parties.

In dealing with the particular facts of the case, the Court decided that the Government's refusal to establish or subsidise schooling in French within the Dutch unilingual region was not incompatible with the Convention. There was a right of access to education in one of the national languages and any disruption to family life as a result of children travelling to school was their parents' choice. The provision of education only in the language of the large majority in each of the unilingual regions was not arbitrary. Arrangements for areas which were traditionally Dutch-speaking but which had a particularly high proportion of French speakers, whereby education could be provided in French, but must be accompanied by an in-depth study of Dutch, was not discriminatory in a traditionally Dutch-speaking area, though to the extent that children in such areas on the outskirts of Brussels were prevented, solely on the basis of the residence of their parents, from having access to French-speaking schools, there was a breach of Article 2 of the First Protocol. The refusal to homologate certificates of secondary schooling not in conformity with the language requirements in education, whilst it might theoretically breach Article 14, had not affected any of the applicants or their children and did not, therefore, constitute any breach in this case.

PROTOCOL 1 : ARTICLE 3

THE RIGHT TO FREE ELECTIONS

The High Contracting Parties undertake to hold free elections at reasonable intervals by secret ballot, under conditions which will ensure the free expression of the opinion of the people in the choice of the legislature.

Gitonas v Greece (1998) 26 EHRR 691

The Greek Constitution provides that salaried civil servants and others, including members of staff of public law entities, may not stand for election as members of Parliament in any constituency where they have performed their duties for more than three months during the three years preceding the election. The applicants had all been elected as members of Parliament but their elections were all annulled by the Supreme Court on the ground that they had been within the constitutional prohibition. They complained that these annulments breached Article 3 of Protocol 1 in that they infringed the right of the electorate freely to choose its representatives and their own right to be elected.

Held that the rights conferred by Article 3 of Protocol 1 are not absolute. States have a wide margin of appreciation in setting conditions for election. The Court must satisfy itself that the conditions set do not curtail the rights to such an extent as to impair their very essence and deprive them of their effectiveness; that they are imposed in pursuit of a legitimate aim; and that the means employed are not disproportionate. The disqualification to which Greek public servants are subjected serves a dual purpose that is essential for the proper functioning and upholding of democratic regimes, namely ensuring that candidates of different political persuasions enjoy equal means of influence (since holders of public office may on occasion have an unfair advantage over other candidates) and protecting the electorate from pressure from such officials who, because of their position, are called upon to take many decisions and enjoy substantial prestige in the eyes of the ordinary citizen, whose choice of candidate might be influenced. It is primarily for the national authorities, and in particular the courts, to construe and apply national law. The Supreme Court had analysed the posts held by the applicants and on reasonable grounds it considered it necessary to annul their election. There was nothing to suggest that the annulments were contrary to Greek legislation, arbitrary or disproportionate or thwarted the free expression of the opinion of the people in the choice of the legislature. There was no breach of the Convention.